RUTHERFORD B. HAYES

STATESMAN OF REUNION

AMERICAN POLITICAL LEADERS
EDITED BY ALLAN NEVINS

RUTHERFORD B. HAYES
By H. J. Eckenrode

In preparation
THOMAS B. REED
By William A. Robinson

PRESIDENT RUTHERFORD B. HAYES

Rutherford B. Hayes

Statesman of Reunion

By

H. J. ECKENRODE

Author of Jefferson Davis, President of the South, *etc.*

Assisted by Pocahontas Wilson Wight

DODD, MEAD & COMPANY

New York   *1930*

PRINTED IN THE UNITED STATES OF AMERICA
BY THE VAIL-BALLOU PRESS, INC., BINGHAMTON, N. Y.

To

WILLIAM E. CARSON,

*Chairman of the Virginia Commission
on Conservation and Development,*

A PUBLIC SERVANT WHOSE SOLE THOUGHT
IS THE PUBLIC GOOD.

PREFACE

The need of a rewriting of later American history in the light of our fast-growing knowledge has long been evident, and Mr. Bowers's notable work, *The Tragic Era,* is one of numerous indications that the task is now well under way. The greatest problems that the United States has been called to face are the adaptation of a simple agricultural republic to a most complicated industrial development, and the fitting of institutions originated by one race to other and alien breeds of men. These problems have not been solved, but some of the earliest and most dangerous crises in their solution have been safely passed, and we may well hope for the future. Few men have made a greater contribution toward the final solution of these problems than did Rutherford B. Hayes, who is ungratefully forgotten today and to the revival of whose memory this work is dedicated.

The book is greatly indebted to Pocahontas Wilson Wight, who did much of the research work, visited Ohio in search of material, and wrote several of the chapters dealing with Hayes's personal life. For the political portion of the book—the chapters on the campaign of 1876 and the administration of Hayes—I am solely responsible. These chapters embody views of American history matured by years of study and unpartizan reflection. Thanks are due Colonel Webb C. Hayes, son of the President, who opened the invaluable collection of Hayes Papers at Fremont, Ohio, to our research and who lent us pictures that could not otherwise have been obtained. I am also grateful for the most helpful editorial assistance of Professor Allan Nevins, whose suggestions were invaluable.

H. J. Eckenrode

CONTENTS

ILLUSTRATIONS

RUTHERFORD B. HAYES

STATESMAN OF REUNION

PROPAGANDA in one age becomes history in the next. This is peculiarly true of American history, which has been so coated with the passions and prejudices of the past that it is now being really written for the first time. It is the misfortune of historical characters who do not fit the spirit of the age in which they live to be forgotten, no matter how significant they may appear to succeeding generations. Thus Rutherford B. Hayes, nineteenth President of the United States, is little known to the American public for the reason that he represented the principle of peace in an age of war and worked for conciliation in an atmosphere surcharged with hate. But for this very reason he should be remembered in our time, when peace is recognized as the greatest achievement of the human spirit.

Hayes was no borderer, no dweller in a land of compromise. His was an isolated spirit, a far-reaching vision. A product of the Western Reserve of Ohio, he was born in the small town of Delaware on October 4, 1822. He was a posthumous child, for his father had been dead for some months when he first saw the light of day. In the absence of the natural head of the house, Sardis Birchard, the young brother of Mrs. Hayes, comforted the mother and looked out for the welfare of her brood.

Ohio, in the twenties, was a raw Middle Western community, just a stage beyond the pioneer period. Rutherford B. Hayes, however, belonged to the new generation that was pouring into the Middle West from all the North and South and making it the most characteristically American part of the United States. Consequently, Hayes was not born in a cabin, like Lincoln, but in a brick house—indeed, in the first brick house in Delaware,

Ohio. The fact that he was born in a brick house to some extent colored his whole existence. Unlike the first Republican Presidents—all humble enough—Hayes had something of the flavor of aristocracy.

His father, Rutherford Hayes, had perhaps worn himself out in the effort to get ahead in a country where life was hard. The family would probably have known want if it had not been for Sardis Birchard. On the rugged character and strong sense of this younger brother of Sophie Hayes the family fortunes rested. Birchard devoted himself to those fortunes, for he never married and reared a family of his own. He occupied the place of father to the future President, and no father could have been more faithful to his charge. Indeed, he shaped the career of Rutherford B. Hayes, largely paying for his education, assisting him in his profession, putting him on his feet, and guiding him in every emergency that called for an elder's advice.

Like nearly all children of destiny, Hayes was sickly; healthy youngsters seldom have other than commonplace aspirations. His first fragile years were colored by the personality of his elder sister, Fanny, who piloted him about the garden and barnyard and mothered him after the fashion of sisters of weak brothers. Hayes loved her more than anyone else in the world; the loss of her in later years was the most poignant grief he ever felt. Together they explored such fairylands of literature as were available in Ohio a century ago. They tried Shakespeare and, perhaps, found him tough, but reveled in *The Lady of the Lake,* then the best-loved poem of the language. The two children, ambitious, undertook to dramatize it. Fanny Hayes, rather a splendid creature, longed to be a boy and go to college, but she could not overcome the crushing handicaps of a girl a century ago. Clever and literary, she was also an adept at outdoor sports. But all she could do was to marry and bear children, and die of childbearing. The pale

little boy she sheltered under her wings—the presidency was
for him. So much for sex.

Hayes was never very close to his mother. Sophie Hayes
was a thorough Puritan, but Rutherford B. Hayes, in spite of
certain puritanical traits—in spite even of the strict prohibitionist views which he held in manhood—was not a Puritan.
He was no introspective brooder but a cheerful, sociable spirit.
Naturally, then, his mother's excessive religiosity and morality
bored and antagonized him. She was a Calvinist of the most
rugged type. He never had definite religious beliefs of any
kind. That humorless mother of his would have made a
preacher of him, if she could have had her way, but he would
have none of it. Yet he was fond of her if not of her spirit.
Once she returned home on a five-day trip on horseback
through water and mud after an absence of six weeks spent in
nursing her brother; and the children ran to her and clung to
her skirts with a welcome that must have gladdened her,
serious-minded woman that she was, acutely sensible of her
responsibilities before God.

The Hayes family had come to Connecticut from Scotland
in 1680. Thence they had passed on into Vermont, where they
settled. Innkeepers and blacksmiths they were, strong, solid
men of the best New England sort. Rutherford Hayes, father
of the President, was put in a store because he was not considered sufficiently robust for hard work. In 1813 he married
Sophie Birchard, of Wilmington, Vermont. Her ancestors had
come to Norwich, Connecticut, in 1635.

In 1817 Hayes was smitten with the western fever and set out
for Ohio in a covered wagon, with his wife, two infants, boy
brother-in-law, Sardis Birchard, and an orphan girl relative.
Forty days they wandered in the wilderness before arriving at
the Canaan of Delaware, Ohio. Hayes found Ohio farm life
too rough for his family and settled in town. He went into the

business of distilling whiskey and rose to prominence as a man of honesty and a leading church member. Whiskey, be it remembered, was considered a necessity then, and perhaps it was. Sundry people of those days had no other real sport than drinking whiskey. A fine man, Hayes, but not tough enough for Ohio then, so he died young.

Sophie Hayes was New Englander through and through, as was Rutherford Hayes, physically. The Birchards were part Huguenot, part Vermont Yankee, a notable fusion of stocks. Rutherford Hayes was wont to trace with pride his Scotch ancestry, but the majority of his forefathers were English on both lines.

Hayes marked, as the chief source of what talent and character there was in the family, his grandmother, Chloe Smith Hayes, whom the ungallant Sardis Birchard dubbed the homeliest woman he had ever seen. There was also a Meade connection, though probably not with George Gordon Meade.

The family had a narrow living, and yet a living not won by work; this distinguished the Hayeses from most of their toiling neighbors. Several times a year Sophie Hayes went on horseback to the Whetstone farm, ten miles from Delaware, the rent of which supplied the main support. Her son usually accompanied her and must have had engraved on his mind the rural scenes of that distant day, now so largely passed away—the fragrant smell of sugar making, the crunching of apples in the cider press, the nutting in the crisp autumn, the red-speckled cherry trees in spring. The tenants indulged the children with Easter eggs filled with maple sugar, with pet birds, squirrels, and rabbits.

The children went to the district school, just opened, for popular education was then new. A skinny, wiry Yankee, with black hair, black eyes and sallow complexion, dealt out skimpy portions of knowledge to shivering children of assorted ages.

This schoolmaster made strapping fellows twice his size "dance about like a parched pea" under the influence of the hickory, and even cast a jackknife so as just to miss a small whisperer near Ruddy Hayes. Thus the boy's first draft of the Pierian spring was not appetizing. He went to other schools, where he dabbled in Latin and similar vexations.

But for the heir apparent of the first brick house in Delaware, the ward of the prospering Sardis Birchard, something more than an Ohio education was needed. Perhaps Sophie Hayes had visions; Uncle Sardis certainly had. These Middle Westerners from New England looked back to Boston with nostalgia, veneration. At twelve years of age Rutherford Hayes made his first venture into the world, going all the way to Vermont and New Hampshire to visit relatives. At fourteen he went to Norwalk Seminary, the Methodist school of Jonah Chaplin. A year later he was put in the private academy of Isaac Webb at Middletown, Connecticut. Webb was a Yale man who dispensed culture to twenty select young gentlemen at the rate of two hundred and fifty dollars a session, a high price in those days. His seductive catalogue declared that his school rested "on thorough study, faithful instruction, and steady discipline. Habits, principles, feelings, and tastes are to be assiduously cultivated; truth, justice, honor, and religion to be regarded as the cardinal points of character." The Hayes family surrendered to such assurances and Rutherford set out for Middletown in the autumn of 1837.

It was a momentous year for Rutherford Hayes. He passed from the virile rawness of Ohio to the sedateness of New England, older then than now; the New England of such Yankee farmers as had fought at Bunker Hill, of large barns, of stone-fenced fields, of prim women, of pumpkin pies; the New England of history and legend, now unhappily gone forever.

Most of all was Ruddy Hayes impressed by the New England Thanksgiving, that strange festival which has become incorporated in American life. In those days it was a season for gastronomic feats, and the habitual economy of New England was cast to the winds. "Our dessert alone," wrote the awed Hayes, "I think would cost fifty dollars."

At first he missed the freedom of Ohio and found his spirits weighed upon by New England. Later he grew fonder of Connecticut. "There are divers things in this blue country that I like better than Ohio," he confessed; but he rather objected to the excessive churchgoing. "The priest prays thirty minutes; everything else in proportion." They called Congregational ministers "priests" in those days.

The time came for the principal to write a letter to Mother and Uncle Sardis at home. "Rutherford," he penned, "has applied himself industriously to his studies and has maintained a consistent and correct deportment. He is well informed, has good manners and is respected and esteemed by his companions. He is strictly economical and regular in his habits and has established a very favorable character among us." A dreadful letter to write about any live American boy and no doubt a slander on Rutherford Hayes, who was never wanting in spirit, but the kind of colorless, negative, innocuous "character" the parent of those days desired of his young; a schoolmaster's professional letter to clients who paid up and were desired to return their offspring to his shop.

Now came the first crisis in the life of Rutherford B. Hayes, the decision that shaped his whole career. Was he to go to college—since Uncle Sardis had decided that he *was* to go—in New England or in Ohio? Was he to absorb culture at the head fount or in one of the derived rills? He was in New England, enthusiastic about Yale, which he always considered the best American college. Beyond doubt he wanted to go to Yale, dreamed of Yale. But he needed another year of preparatory

HOUSE OF CAPTAIN EZEKIEL HAYES AT BRANFORD, CONNECTICUT

school for that; it meant delay and long absence from home and larger expense. There were colleges in Ohio; at least there were institutions called colleges. Sophie Hayes wanted him nearer her; perhaps Uncle Sardis thought it would be best for an Ohioan to grow up in Ohio. The matter seems, however, to have been left to Rutherford, who decided in favor of Kenyon College, at Gambier, Ohio, probably to spare Uncle Sardis too much expense.

Hayes went home in the autumn of 1838; he spent his sixteenth birthday on board a steamer on Lake Erie. He landed at Sandusky and went thence to Delaware, where he was rapturously welcomed by the family after a year's absence.

On the last day of October, 1838, he set out for Gambier, arriving there the next day. He passed the entrance examination without trouble; it was a mere formality to a boy who had prepared for Yale; a college which was not as yet much more than a high school presented no difficulty.

Hayes had time for outdoor sports, and he needed outdoor sports, for he was still not hardy, though stronger than in his first years. He had the inherited courage of the pioneer stock. Breaking through ice one skating day, he felt no panic but remained calm until his companions rescued him. He was indeed of the soldier breed, as he was to show nearly twenty-five years later. In the Christmas holidays he walked home to Delaware, a distance of forty miles. Venturing to walk back to college, he was come upon by a snow storm and had to plow for miles through the drifts. Already he was developing the vice (according to Henry Ford) of economy. He noted gleefully that he had spent only seventy-five cents in the whole holiday season. What an admission for an American boy!

Kenyon College in that age upheld the torch of culture in the Middle West under somewhat adverse circumstances. Few people respected culture more (theoretically) than the frontiersmen, and few people practiced it less. Indeed, there was little room for the arts and graces. Natural selection worked unhampered by old customs and ancient institutions. There life was hard, narrow, dull, unimaginative, and strenuous, though hopeful. Life was hard in Ohio but it was by no means so hard as the struggles of the New England farmers with an infertile soil; there was abundant opportunity for growth, for wealth, for power. Perhaps he did not clearly realize what he did, but Rutherford Hayes decided wisely when he cast in his lot with the Middle West rather than with New England. He chose the land of opportunity.

Kenyon College was quaint and childish, as small colleges were in those days. The petty discipline rather annoyed the freedom-loving Hayes, but he did not actually rebel. Others did rebel and Hayes sympathized with them. He even thought of leaving Kenyon and going to Hudson College, but did not. He stayed on at Kenyon and finally came to like it fairly well, though he always appreciated its limitations. He was never quite reconciled to the loss of Yale.

College life in those distant days was deliciously simple. Hayes' small allowance went for the following items:

Wood	$ 2.00
Society expenses	9.00
Sugar and my expense coming back	1.00
Tuition in oratory	1.50
Paper, stationery, etc.	1.00
Postage on paper and letters	1.00
Portfolio	1.25
Gallon of oil	1.00
Algebra	1.50
Slate	.25
Mended shoes	1.00
Supper at Cake Shop	.25
Total	$20.75

Left in treasury, $4.25. Plus $40.00 equals $44.25.

Of the $44.25 which I now have, I must pay $2.00 for washing, $34.75 for board, and $2.00 which I owe to Mr. Jones in Mount Vernon. My debts are in all $38.75. So you see my expenses this season, buying furniture and all, will be 'most $100. This included traveling expenses, etc.

It should be noted that college students in those days used slates, a useful custom. But the supper in the cake shop! Twenty-five cents wasted on riotous living! Very agreeably different the students of those days from some of the pampered, money-wasting undergraduates of our age.

Kenyon College was a little wearing on Hayes because it was so dreadfully precise, matter-of-fact, unimaginative. Of literary culture in the broad sense it had none, yet a better school for the times was not to be found. If Hayes had fulfilled his dream and gone to Yale, he would probably have become a literary man, almost certainly something of a scholar and a dreamer, for in the beginning he had imagination—a good deal of imagination. He had dramatized *The Lady of the Lake* and no doubt would have written stories if he had been encouraged. However, it was not the business of Kenyon College to turn out *litterateurs* and æsthetes, but lawyers, business men and politicians. How dreadful and yet how efficient its discipline was may be seen when one considers that among its graduates were Edwin M. Stanton, David Davis, Henry Winter Davis and Salmon P. Chase. They were the products of semi-frontier life, cold, keen, able men, of the sort who were destined to strike down the South and erect on its ruins the political power of the Middle West. Kenyon College was admirably adapted to a materialistic age tempered a little by fanaticism.

It is hardly too much to say that Kenyon College made Hayes what he became. It made him what he was not before, a Middle Westerner, for in the beginning he was a New England. He grew to be a typical Middle Westerner, with the long, untrimmed beard, ill-fitting clothes, father-of-a-family look of the average Middle Westerner of that period. Kenyon College lessened his tendency to real thinking, smothered his imagination, and blunted his humor, the qualities sometimes so fatal to success in life. Kenyon College gave him a superficial culture, such as he found useful in the discussions of literary societies. It gave him the practical outlook on life, the bread-and-butter vision, the eye for the main chance that survival in the Middle West before the Civil War demanded. It hardened him, though it never made his genial nature hard. Hayes took some steps toward the presidency of the United States at Kenyon, but he also lost much that he would have gained at Yale. Perhaps he always felt this. His whimsical humor lessened, but never entirely left him. A Fourth-of-July dinner he described as follows:

The first course there was beef, veal, pig, bacon, mutton, chickens, turkeys, peas, beans, new 'taters, new turnips, plum pudding, bread, butter, water, and other articles too numerous to mention.

Second course: twenty-nine kinds of cake more or less as the case may be.

Third course: lemonade to drink toasts in and ice cream.

Of steel pens, then just coming into general use, he wrote to his sister:

I am astonished at your cruelty in preferring quills to steel pens, for in using a steel pen you are assisting thousands of poor souls to gain their bread, viz., ironmongers, miners, blacksmiths, etc., who gain their living by making steel pens.

Hayes was a good student but never entirely absorbed in

BIRTHPLACE OF RUTHERFORD B. HAYES AT DELAWARE, OHIO

college work. He was restless, speculative, peering ahead into the future. He confessed that the desire for fame was his ruling passion, and in those early days he dreamed of military fame. Why he never thought of going to West Point it is difficult to say; perhaps he felt that he lacked the influence. At moments ugly reality shook these war fancies. On one Fourth of July he saw a man dying who had cut his own throat, and, for the rest of that day, he had no more taste for glory. But the next day, boylike, the desire came back to him. It stayed with him, suppressed but not eliminated, for years. The Mexican War revived it, and Hayes almost went to the war. Unfortunately, he did not; if he had learned soldiering then, he might have played an important part in the Civil War. When 1861 came, he was too old to learn much.

Next to war Hayes dreamed of politics, as every American boy did in those days; it was before the time of Big Business, and millionaires were few and far between. Politics was the consuming vision of the ambitious American; the Legislature, the House of Representatives, the Senate, the presidency—that way the dream ran. Hayes was at Kenyon at the time of the ever-memorable "Tippecanoe and Tyler" election of 1840, the first whirlwind campaign in American history. Observant, he believed that the Whigs at last had a chance to win. He was an ardent Whig; it was the family party, and when Harrison was found to have been elected, he exclaimed: "I never was more elated in my life. . . . Glorious!" It was indeed a victory full of promise to an Ohio lad, for the first Ohioan had been elected to the White House. Hayes could not have imagined that he would be the second.

His last year in college found him still discontentedly striving for further attainments. It was the autumn of 1841; and he was a senior, trying, to make up his mind what he would do, and, at the same time, feverishly reading in many fields.

He tackled mathematics with renewed ardor under the delusion, popular then, that mathematics is especially useful as a mental training. Philosophy appealed to him, and he was quite convinced that Beattie (Dr. Johnson's friend) had refuted David Hume's reasoning as to the non-existence of matter. Hayes was never a recluse and, socially acceptable, he became a member of the Phi Zeta Club, an ancestor of the Greek-letter fraternity. Even in that remote age, the age of men reared in pioneer cabins on corn bread and bear meat, snobbishness asserted its ubiquitous self, and many of the poorer clad, less self-confident students were excluded from the sacred circle. What is the use of trying to establish social democracy? The aged are democratic, but what can they do against the eternal aristocracy of youth?

Not that Rutherford Hayes was snobbish; he was too broadminded and tolerant for that. He did not conceal his small economies, even mended his own clothes. He was gay and fond of society but had not associated much with women. He thought himself, rather unjustly, to be shy and awkward. Certainly he could not have been so long, for one of his chief outer merits during his whole life was a pleasant and easy address.

By nature Rutherford B. Hayes was anything but fanatical. At this time he drank wine and jested about it with his vigilant mother. He wrote to her that the temperance movement was gaining such headway at Gambier that he dared not be seen drinking in public more than once a day. Perhaps she took this in earnest and mourned over him. In January, 1842, he had another laugh at the mother, who feared that a slight cough he had might lead to something serious. Hayes wrote her that the doctors held out hopes that his life might be prolonged for several years "if I will only stop drinking, regulate my diet, keep out of the cold, and entirely refrain from laughing."

He was the usual boylike bundle of contradictions. He was reading Paley's *Natural Theology* in intense earnest and yet, at the same time, was thinking of the figure he cut in the world. He wrote that he had had his peaked-toed shoes blacked and was wearing his new brindle-colored trousers. He wore his sorrel overcoat every day. His cowhide boots were yellow, his old trousers were shy of buttons. He was evidently longing for a new, more fashionable outfit.

In his last term Hayes participated, apparently out of mischief, in a class mutiny; the seniors refused to attend chemistry examination. Doubtless he was glad to get out of writing a paper on chemistry, for he loathed science and voted chemistry a particular bore. Except for this one departure from the path of virtue his conduct had been most exemplary, as the faculty wrote his mother.

In 1842, when Hayes was twenty years old, there came his commencement week at Kenyon. There were parties with "silly ladies and weak lemonade." Hayes, with all of his later proclivities toward prohibition, never seems to have acquired a taste for soft drinks. Uncle Sardis and his mother came up dutifully to Gambier to see their boy graduate, properly proud of him, for in those days he was handsome enough, before age had marred him and fashion or laziness planted on his chin one of the luxuriant beards that ornamented faces in the middle and third quarters of the nineteenth century. Hayes enjoyed the whirl of the commencement but woke up to find himself "the same old Rud."

He left college a well-educated man for the time and place. He had read a bit of Latin and dabbled in a dozen subjects. He knew nothing well and had not acquired a very real appreciation of literature. He read heavy books dutifully but again and again turned for relief to novels—"trash," as he called them. He had come into contact with students from a wide range of the Middle West and his natural self-confidence had been strengthened. His mind, if not much cultured, was well burnished, ready for the practical tasks of life.

In 1841 he had written: "What shall I do after leaving college?" but already he had pretty well decided. The ambitious American boy of that day did not look to business as he does now; he would be a lawyer and emulate Patrick Henry. He dreamed of hypnotizing juries with the florid eloquence of the mid-century, of which Webster and Prentiss were the acknowledged masters. If he could not have fame in war— and no wars loomed on the horizon—there was the forum. Fame was still Hayes's lodestar.

By the time he left Kenyon it was fully decided that Hayes should be a lawyer. But at first he had no thought of attending law school, for in those days most embryo lawyers read in law offices, just as embryo surgeons waited on doctors; a professional education was regarded as a somewhat superfluous luxury.

Ten profitless months at Columbus followed for Hayes. He read law in the office of one Sparrow. He plunged into the dismal rubbish of Blackstone but, still true to his ambition to gain culture, studied German in his leisure. Of all his acquirements this turned out to be one of the most profitable, because it enabled him to exchange greetings with Germans in Cincinnati and thereby win votes. The winter of 1842–1843 passed. The following summer it was decided that Ruddy should attend Harvard Law School. Probably Uncle Sardis, so anxious to give his nephew the best, was responsible for this.

August, 1843, found Hayes at Cambridge. To his surprise, the commencement exercises were no better than at Kenyon, but Webster and John Quincy Adams were there. Hayes plunged into law at once; Story and Greenleaf were his teachers. It was the golden age at Harvard, the golden age of New

England. Jared Sparks gave lectures on history, which Hayes sometimes attended. Longfellow aroused his enthusiasm. George Bancroft and Choate were in the offing. It was a stimulating time, and manhood came to Rutherford B. Hayes then —at least the age of twenty-one. "A man in years," he lamented; "a boy in knowledge and wisdom."

Hayes put most of his time on law and German, for he still clung to German and perhaps dreamed of reading *Faust* in the original. He rather palpitated when the moment came for his first appearance in moot court. His success was not flattering, but he had too much self-esteem to be discouraged. He was not a good speaker then, as speakers go, but continued practice in the end made him effective. He was studying oratorical effects, and wrote in his diary of some of the great New Englanders he heard. "Senator Choate is a strong man. His style of speaking is that of an impulsive, ardent, able, practised lawyer of the O'Connell stamp. Daniel Webster has been called 'the godlike,' in derision. But if any man born of woman deserves the epithet, it is Daniel Webster. The majesty of pure intellect shines forth in him." [1]

He was still bent on acquiring as much culture as was possible in the chief American temple. He visited the theatre for the first time in his somewhat puritanical life and without being moved saw Macready play Hamlet. He read Cicero and dabbled in Aristotle; he found time for social intercourse. He made a bet with a fellow student that the fellow student would fall in love in the year 1843. He was at the happy age in which men make wagers about romance.

Hayes's mental life was active. Law studies were not light, but he found time to dabble in Latin, Greek, German, French, literature, philosophy—made himself indeed a somewhat respectable mental furnishing of patches of literatures and cul-

[1] C. R. Williams, *The Life of Rutherford Birchard Hayes*, I, 35.

tures. He knew that his attainments were fragmentary, unsatisfactory. He realized that he read too much in too many subjects.
"The result is," he groaned, "that I am now as dull and stupid
as an ass." Imagination was being destroyed to make way for a
hodgepodge of foreign grammars and vocabularies. It is a
common mistake. Perhaps Hayes was getting too deep for a
mind that was good but not profound. He wrestled sorely with
Locke's *Essay on Human Understanding,* a tedious introduc-
tion to modern philosophy.

Contact at Harvard with many men from many schools did
Hayes good. The provincialism of the Middle West wore off
and he became a man of the world. Characteristically enough,
he observed that of all the men in the Harvard Law School the
Yale graduates were the best. In spite of his own self-esteem he
saw what he lacked, that he was still somewhat unpolished.
"Must try to acquire greater mildness and affability of manners," he mournfully jotted down. His cardinal sin he discovered was "boyish conduct," as if youth were an offense!

Athletics were then only in the dawn. Football was (happily)
little known; but some primitive ancestor of baseball existed on
the Harvard campus, and Hayes, who was physically active
if not strong, played ball and hurt his fingers, unprotected by
gloves. He concluded that ball-playing was a poor pursuit for
a student who had reached the advanced age of twenty-one.
They took twenty-one seriously in that era, when a large
proportion of men married at that age and some of them even
succeeded in raising beards.

At Harvard, Rutherford Hayes was very busy and rather
happy. He did nothing startling but he gained a much wider
outlook on life, an outlook that he always kept. His already
faint religious faith was still further weakened by the spiritual
ferment then going on in Harvard. Then to deny the literal
truth and the immediate inspiration of the Scriptures required

audacity, and the liberals of those distant days imagined that they were enlightening the world, doing good. At least they shook the simple faith of many a farmer boy from the still believing rural districts.

Hayes on the whole had a healthy and hopeful outlook on life. The world was not out of joint with him. He was somewhat surprised to hear that embittered statesman, John Quincy Adams, pour out the vials of denunciation on slavery. To the Middle West of the forties the slaveholding South was by no means the Gehenna it seemed after years of propaganda. Hayes thought Adams unreasonable and unfair, and called him "a deluded old man." Perhaps he had some subconscious inkling that the old man was making a war for him to fight. Probably not. He was not of the age or temperament that finds grievance everywhere.

Law studies were vague in those days when few lawyers graduated with parchments. At the end of his third semester, in February, 1845, Rutherford Hayes found that he had had enough. He was getting on toward twenty-three and it was high time to be doing his work in the world.

He returned to Ohio, to Columbus. A month later, March 10, 1845, he was admitted to the bar, a mere formality then. He hung out his shingle in the village then known as Lower Sandusky, but later renamed for that somewhat shabby hero, Frémont. Sardis Birchard was in business there, and Uncle Sardis was a satisfying sheet anchor for a young lawyer. He might wait but he would not starve.

LAW was a slow business in the Roaring Forties; the youthful attorney did not expect to be given a case of importance for years. Few people trusted their affairs to fledglings. On the other hand, by the inconsistency of human nature, raw doctors, just beginning their life-and-death business, were often called in to handle dangerous illness. So true it is that people value their property more than their lives.

The inevitable period of probation, passed by most novices in attempting to grow imposing beards, gave Rutherford Hayes another opportunity for self-improvement. He still plugged away at German, reading a chapter each day in a German New Testament, probably in lieu of performing the same exercise in English. Essentially orderly in his mental processes, he parceled out the day, tackling heavy books such as Bacon's *Novum Organum* in the morning—Bacon for breakfast—and relaxing in the evening with poetry and fiction. Later on he took up geology and read French. He was always feeding his mind, but he nibbled at too many foods, dabbled in varied fields. Still it had become a strong, flexible mind, adapted to its environment.

Although he had little religious faith left—Harvard had seen to that—Hayes attended church regularly, having that somewhat pathetic New England yearning for spiritual form even if denied the substance. Hayes's mother was a Presbyterian of the gloomiest dye, viewing the greater portion of mankind as indubitably damned; but Hayes himself attended the Episcopal church, probably because of associations formed at Kenyon College. After his marriage he went with his wife to the Methodist church for the remainder of his life, but never joined any communion. Again and again he tells us he had no belief, but in this respect he possibly wronged himself. He had none of the certainty that men felt in that age regarding religion, but he had the religious temperament. Moreover, he had the worldly-wise attitude toward religion, and this somewhat influenced his acts. In the forties a man who did not go to church was likely to be branded an "infidel," a social and business stigma of the worst sort. Hayes sometimes dubbed himself an infidel but he would have been astounded if others had called him by that detested name.

The prospects seemed promising to Hayes as he began practice in March, 1845. Expenses were light, for he was ever thrifty. He shared a room with his cousin, John R. Pease, an eccentric person of whom he was fond. His talent for invention was illustrated by his improvisation of a shower bath, a rare novelty in 1845, when the American people "washed" on Saturday night in the ordinary tubs that were used on Monday for clothes. By June, Hayes had settled down to life in Lower Sandusky, "contented as a clam," he said.

To get some of the business he yearned for, Hayes went into partnership with Ralph D. Buckland, whom he characterized as a good lawyer, a Whig politician, and a rather ill-tempered individual. This partnership lasted as long as Hayes remained in Fremont and, like most law partnerships, was not advantageous.

Hayes read much but was anything but a recluse. He was of a rather gay nature, a good talker, fond of men and fonder of women. The society of Lower Sandusky, in which he freely mingled, was wholesome if somewhat naïve. Dancing was not much in vogue, though there were great balls on occasions. Sleigh riding was the chief winter diversion. Hayes had his full share of the fun. He assured his mother, whom he so loved to tease, that if he supposed it would interest her he would try to describe the eating, kissing, playing button and blind hood, screaming, giggling, singing and other elegant diversions of these sleigh rides.

Petting parties are not new, but the Middle West mothers of those days did not have the saintly resignation of modern matrons. Hayes delighted in tormenting his solemn mother, an earnest believer in total abstinence with descriptions of the drinking parties in which he indulged in Lower Sandusky. Sophie Hayes winced a little, though she knew perfectly well that it was merely teasing, for Rutherford was the best of sons.

Hayes had settled in Lower Sandusky for the sole but sufficient reason that Uncle Sardis lived there, and Uncle Sardis was his financial support as well as his familiar friend. Besides, Lower Sandusky seemed to be as promising as any other small town in Ohio. But Hayes was energetic and ambitious and, after enduring Lower Sandusky for a year or two, began to realize that he would never succeed there, never become anything but a small-town attorney. He had no practice and no promise of any, and, moreover, the place was wearing on him. His taste of urban life at Harvard had unfitted him for a frontier town. In 1847 he exclaimed, exasperated, "This lively (?) village has been dirtier than usual this spring." He had grown tired of "rowdy sleigh rides." To kiss squealing girls under the frosty stars no longer thrilled him. Worst of all, he was bothered by a sore throat that was not helped at all by the ungenial climate of Lake Erie.

The throat furnished him with an excuse. He must go to a softer clime, and where else in Ohio was it to be found? Cincinnati! It was almost a Southern city and, what is more, it was a city. Yes, Cincinnati was the one city of the West in those days; it was the next best thing to Boston. It was the Chicago of that age, a bustling place of pigpens and slaughter

RUTHERFORD B. HAYES, 1845
Student at the Harvard Law School, from a Daguerreotype

houses, factories and river steamers; and, rich for the times, was determined to acquire culture. It was on Cincinnati that Rutherford Hayes fixed his hopes.

There was an interlude that put the city out of his mind for a time. With 1846 came war with Mexico, and Hayes, like most Middle Westerners, greeted it with enthusiasm. Only later did many Middle Westerners, following Corwin, discover that the war was a gross attack on the rights of a weaker nation and a diabolical device for the spread of slavery. At first the Ohio boys volunteered by thousands and demonstrated their valor on many fields.

War! Instantly the old dream of military glory flamed up in Hayes's mind. The doctors had advised him to seek a warmer climate for a time and cure the throat, and Mexico was indubitably a warmer climate. He might heal the throat and win glory at the same time; consequently he determined to volunteer if the doctors sanctioned it. Off to Cincinnati, where several medicine men peered and punched and advised. The doctors did not think that Mexico would benefit him; they declared that military service might be bad for a weak throat. Reluctantly, Hayes abandoned the vision of the tented field. It was an unfortunate decision. He was young and adaptable; he had the soldier temperament, courage, and an excellent constitution. A year in Mexico would have made a soldier of him and probably a leading figure in the Civil War. It was not to be.

Lower Sandusky was on Hayes's nerves; he must get away for a time. If not Mexico, what? He pondered. If not Mexico —Vermont! He would go once more to New England, see relatives, revive his soul by the vistas of the Holy Land. Those expatriated Yankees of the forties and fifties did not look forward toward Oregon and California as much as they looked back to Boston.

Late in July, Hayes made his way to Troy and thence to the east. He chatted with kinsfolk at Brattleboro and Northampton, and found Springfield to be a "splendid town," which illustrates his enthusiasm for New England. He fished for a week in Long Island Sound, a glorious experience for an inlander; viewed Newport, then just rising to glory; wended his way to the White Mountains. He spent a night in a hut on Mount Washington, in order to see the famous sunrise, refreshing himself with pork pie and brandy. Abstinent as he later became, he did not then refuse comfort on a cold morning on a mountain top. He looked in on Boston, New Haven, almost all New England.

Hayes returned to Lower Sandusky much invigorated, but by this time the place so wore on him that he escaped to Columbus for the Christmas holidays. However, he returned home in time to take part in several gorgeous balls. Cincinnati was back in his mind, and he felt that he had to make a final decision before long. But to leave Uncle Sardis and to tackle Cincinnati without income or friends was a serious adventure. Hayes pondered it for months and years. In July, 1848, he wrote:

I want to spend another fortnight in Cincinnati to satisfy myself whether an attorney of my years and calibre would be likely to get business enough to pay office rent in that growing village.

At least if he were not to go at once to Cincinnati he was to have a change. For years Hayes had fretted at his narrow environment and longed for a great experience. This came in 1848, when the sore throat demanded a sojourn in a softer zone.

Hayes had had a Texan classmate at Kenyon College, Guy M. Bryan, of whom he always remained fond despite the separation of the Civil War. Bryan had invited Hayes to visit him with Uncle Sardis, and at length the invitation was accepted. Rutherford started out on November 21, 1848, when it was getting cold in northern Ohio but while summer still reigned on the Brazos.

His itinerary is not without interest, as it demonstrates the difficulties involved in journeying from the Middle West to Texas in those distant days. Hayes went by railroad from Lower Sandusky to Mansfield, thence by stage to Mount Vernon, then by stage to Columbus, where he remained a week. He went by stage to Springfield and from Springfield to Cincinnati by railway. On December 13, he left Cincinnati by a Mississippi River steamer. The next day he reached Louisville and passed Cairo on December 16. On December 17, the steamboat stopped at Memphis. On December 21, New Orleans was reached. On December 23, Hayes sailed for Galveston, where he arrived on December 26.

The voyage down the Mississippi River was the most enjoyable experience Hayes had ever had. It was the grand tour of those days, the one journey in America that was made in comfort. Hayes was steeped in the romance of the thing. The genial warmth; the wide river; the bayous; the vast cabin; the strange characters; the picturesque gamblers and their pistol-flourishing; the plantations, so exotic to a Middle Westerner; New Orleans, that dirty, adorable place which, almost alone in the America of those days, provided an atmosphere of romance.

Hayes liked the vast reaches of the cotton plantations and sugar fields. The neat slave villages of white cabins, the old Louisiana towns pleased him. It was all new and wonderful to the young Ohioan, who sometimes quite forgot that the trail of the serpent was over the whole smiling Southern landscape.

Hayes was in Texas when that now rather tame state was at its best. He reached his friend Bryan's plantation just as the year 1848 was expiring. Wild it was but not quite so wild as Hayes had anticipated; there were no Indians lurking about on the hunt for scalps, to his disappointment. He was still young enough to dream adventure dreams. But the morning after his arrival one of the negroes about the place killed two deer and brought them in for breakfast, and that was better.

The semi-tropical landscape charmed the Ohioan. He wrote:

I see a garden filled with the richest shrubbery, roses blooming and birds singing as if it were the first of June instead of January.

His greatest surprise was to find the Texans civilized, even cultivated. He had expected to encounter frontiersmen clad in buckskin and bristling with bowie knives. He found none of this. For days he roamed over the prairie and along the gulf shore, hunting and fishing. "Deer, cattle, cranes, wild geese, brant, ducks, plover, prairie hens, and the Lord knows what else, often in sight at the same time!" he exclaimed.

The life of the planter, free and independent, made a great appeal to him. "We here find the pleasures of fashionable life without its tyranny," he declared. Yet seduced as he was by the rich plenty of the land, the climate, the tropical beauty, Hayes felt that his conscience should protest. He felt that no Northern-bred man could ever quite forget his sentiments on the subject of slavery, though he admitted that he had witnessed none of its horrors. The negroes seemed to him to be well looked after. His sympathies were for the plantation ladies, burdened with many cares. He said of his hostess:

Mrs. Perry, instead of having the care of one family, is the nurse, physician, and spiritual adviser of a whole settlement of careless slaves. She feels it her duty to see to their comfort when sick or hurt, and among so many there is always some little brat with a scalded foot or a hand half cut off, and "Missus" must always see to it or there is sure to be a whining time of it in the whole camp. Besides, to have anything done requires all time. It may be I am mistaken, but I don't think Job was ever "tried" by a gang of genuine "Sambos"!

The sojourn on the plantation was followed by an extended tour of the settled regions of Texas. This was probably the happiest experience of Hayes's life. He was in excellent health and good spirits, keyed up to the enjoyment of new scenes. "Last night saw the prairie on fire," he wrote. "Grand!" A norther came, and the party was weather bound at a place where there was "good eating, good sleeping, and fun a-plenty." Austin was then a mere village; the public buildings were cabins, the hotel a row of cabins presided over by a Texas ranger. Hayes visited the Alamo, the memory of which was then green, but he was perhaps more impressed by the Mexican girls dancing the fandango than by the scene of Davy Crockett's last fight.

The great Gold Rush to California had begun, but Hayes was not drawn into that glorious adventure. It is hard to understand why he did not go to the Pacific slope when he was so far advanced on the way as Texas. "There is neither romance nor glory in digging for gold," he concluded. Glory! He had not yet quite lost the old dream of military fame.

Late in March, Hayes and Uncle Sardis left Galveston for New Orleans and proceeded thence up the Mississippi and Ohio Rivers, landing at Cincinnati on April 6, 1849. It had been a fine frolic and had done Rutherford Hayes a world of good.

He had now finally decided to remove to Cincinnati, and wound up his partnership with Buckland preparatory to departure. He was, however, stayed by a new and unforeseen circumstance: the cholera epidemic was paralyzing Cincinnati and everything in that city was at a standstill. For some years cholera, or rather the fear of cholera, continued to plague Ohio. It is characteristic of Hayes' serene temperament that these panics never touched him; on the trip to Texas he had heard much of cholera but had seen no cases and had concluded that it was nothing to worry about.

Hayes went about Ohio in the summer of 1849, spending the autumn in settling his affairs in Lower Sandusky, or Fremont, as the place had been renamed recently, partly through his agency, for he admired the rather flamboyant Pathfinder of the West. On November 10, 1849, he said farewell to Fremont and went to Columbus. He was delayed there by an attack of the quinsy, for the throat had begun to bother him again with the first cool weather. In Columbus he dosed himself vigorously with cod liver oil, in the virtue of which he had much faith. At all events, whether the cure was due to the oil or to faith, he was soon well again, writing on December 16:

My health was never better than now. I have no fears on that score. If I can only get into business within a reasonable time, I shall not be much troubled about colds or sore throat.

He arrived in Cincinnati on December 31, 1849. It was a brave venture, this attacking a city without means. Hayes had so little money that two or three days at a hotel gave him concern. As soon as possible he secured a boarding place, at the corner of Fourth and Vine Streets, in the home of a "very excellent widow lady."

On January 8, 1850, Hayes bade defiance to fate by hanging out his shingle. He shared his office with another young lawyer, John W. Herron, though not as a partner. They slept in the office, and Hayes estimated his expenses, excluding clothes, at thirty dollars a month, which was indeed moderate, even in 1850.

His office was in the Law Building, a typical office structure of that remote period. Below, it harbored an express office, an auction store and a telegraph office; above, were eighteen lawyers, three or four architects, and several "loafers," as Hayes called them. The average rent was ten dollars a month. Hayes's office was the best in the building. One corner was partitioned off for a bedroom and contained two husk mattresses on bunks, a washstand and a bureau.

The routine of the establishment was simple. At five o'clock a drunken Irishman came to make the fire and sweep out; at seven the newsboy brought the paper. Then the two young attorneys would rise, wash their faces and read the news. While Hayes went to breakfast, three blocks away, the Irishman and his wife made the beds, brought water and cleaned up.

After breakfast Hayes read law until noon, when one of the two men went to the post office for the mail. Attending to this consumed the time until one o'clock, when they went to dinner. Hayes returned to his office, leaving it finally at four o'clock to make a round of calls. Five-thirty found him sweating in a gymnasium. About half his evenings were spent in the office; the other half were divided between visits to women and lectures. Hayes attended an Episcopal church on Sunday. Once a week came the great event, the meeting of the literary club, where there were "debates, conversations, essays, and oysters." This club, founded in 1848, included among its early members Alphonso Taft, father of President Taft, Stanley Matthews, and A. R. Spofford, later librarian of Congress.[1]

Now that he had taken the plunge, Hayes regretted that he had not done so long before. "Oh, the waste of those five precious years at Lower Sandusky!" he groaned. "Shall I ever

[1] Mrs. W. H. Taft, *Recollections of Full Years*, 2.

recover what I have lost?" He hoped to regain by study all that he had "lost in the last three or four unfortunate years spent or wasted at the North." He still burned to distinguish himself at the bar, but it is significant that he had largely abandoned German and philosophy and had taken to solacing himself with light literature. For style in court pleading he declared that he would read Webster and Burke—and Byron and Bulwer! For some time past, indeed, he had been a great novel reader, finding his chief diversion in Bulwer, Scott and Dickens. It is characteristic of his correct literary taste that he pronounced *David Copperfield* to be Dickens's best book.

Hayes faced an uphill climb and knew it, but he was not much daunted. In February, 1850, he received his first fee in Cincinnati, a retainer of five dollars in a case from which he hoped to make as much as twenty-five dollars. The excessive exploitation of clients by lawyers is modern; fees were small in the good old days. In March Hayes made his maiden speech at the literary club, pronouncing it "ratherish good, considering."

Cincinnati had brought him nearer to the being he loved most, Fanny. She came to see him on the first train of cars that ran through from Columbus to Cincinnati. It was her first visit to "the city of Pigs," as Hayes gracefully put it. To him it was a delightful novelty that he was only six or eight hours from the beloved sister. Alas! he was not to see a great deal more of her. In July, 1850, visiting her, he wrote:

This morning my sister gave birth to a daughter. I last evening played backgammon with her. I thought Fanny never looked so handsome as then. No portrait flatters her as she then appeared.

It was the fifth baby, and her physical powers were becoming exhausted by child-bearing, the most fatal of all indulgences.

Not long afterward her small son Willie died, and this grief weighed on her. Hayes was much affected himself, for he was a man of tender sensibilities and his sister's perhaps unusual sorrow distressed him. Fanny was never quite herself again. In July, 1856, she collapsed after giving birth to twins who did not live. Rutherford had time to reach her, and she died quietly enough, almost with relief.

This was a blow from which the future President did not entirely recover. Years later, in the plenitude of power, he spoke of the lost sister with tears, and showed tenderness for her children. Cut off from his mother by her stern, humorless view of life, Hayes found in the clever, responsive, affectionate Fanny the best comradeship of his life.

Hayes's way of living was simple, as it had to be. Small as his expenses were he did not earn them, and he could hardly have maintained himself in Cincinnati but for Uncle Sardis, that true friend in every crisis. Did the Burnet House open with "a grand soiree" to which Hayes longed to go? He did not go, because the admission was ten dollars and he had no eagles to spend on vanities. Betting on a foot race, he notes that he lost a dime. Careful Yankee, counting the pennies, he would never come to want.

His beloved diversion was the literary club. On one occasion he hastened home from Columbus that he might not miss an anniversary meeting, with the original poems, toasts, and inevitable "oysters." In this society he found his pleasantest contacts and his warmest friends.

Apart from this, he had the best opportunities for cultivation that the America of that day afforded, for everyone who crossed the Alleghenies into "the West" came to Cincinnati. It was the goal of every actor, lecturer, sensational preacher, writer, swindler, burglar, and every other artist of the forties and the fifties.

Ralph Waldo Emerson came his benignant way to Cincinnati and stayed there for some days. Hayes, much excited by an event so important to New Englanders from everywhere, listened eagerly to Emerson and met him at the literary club, which Emerson deigned to honor. The great man talked for three or four hours without stopping, and the club members gaped, drinking in culture. Hayes was impressed but he remarked, acutely enough, that Emerson was rather a keen observer of life than a profound thinker. Hayes's own powers of close observation are attested by his description of the lecturer:

Mr. Emerson is above the middle height, a tolerable figure, but rather awkward; dresses in the plainly genteel style—black surtout and pants, black satin vest and cravat, common shoes. His head is not large, forehead low and narrow, hair cut short—a brown color, eyes a greyish blue, a rather large nose with deep lines from the nostrils on either side arching around the mouth . . . Talks, as he speaks, freely, and in a somewhat quaint way. [1]

He saw Charlotte Cushman play Meg Merrilies and was awed by that tremendous performance. He listened with no great approval to that "notorious Christian infidel," Theodore Parker. Henry Ward Beecher's deep voice charmed him, though he thought Beecher's matter to be commonplace. Edward Everett delighted him. Agassiz interested him deeply. He liked Jenny Lind but groaned at her prices.

Hayes was broadening, learning the world, testing his own powers, but he was not prospering. Despondent, he believed that his lack of progress was due to his own want of self-assertion, for he was essentially a quiet, unassuming young man, cordial and pleasant but not showy. He was a clear speaker but he was not the lurid orator such as that age delighted in.

Desperately, he sought to make himself what he was not.

[1] C. R. Williams, *The Life of Rutherford Birchard Hayes,* I, 61.

He hung out a new sign, "larger, showier, and more richly gilt than any other on the front." He longed to find some road to success. He wrote:

I am not naturally a quack—yet I have a proper appreciation of the advantages and superiority of this character over mere unpretending merit. And so, for thrift's sake, I mean deliberately and decidedly "to cut" in future all my old ideas on this head. I don't think modesty "pays."

But how to advertise? How to bring one's self to the notice of a bustling city crammed with lawyers, good, bad and indifferent? Hayes saw that he must have some other avenue to renown than his profession, some other means of making himself known to his fellow citizens. Rather deliberately, he took up the cause of temperance as a spiritual relief and as a means of advertisement.

He was a New Englander without faith in religion and yet with the religious imagination. A substitute was needed, which Hayes at length found in the cause of reform. It should be observed that he was not exactly a prohibitionist, and never quite became one. The organization he joined, The Sons of Temperance, aimed rather at doing away with the abuse of drinking than of drinking itself, and Hayes continued to take a little wine until he entered the White House, years later. He soon gained confidence and became an effective pleader for righteousness. It must have increased his reputation for virtue and respectability, always so valuable to a lawyer, as well as aided his oratory. He also joined the Odd Fellows and won a certain fame by delivering addresses at lodge meetings. Anything for business!

And yet, with all this, his progress was dishearteningly slow. His mind was keen, his industry great, but business did not flow his way. In March, 1851, Hayes pronounced on his position:

My prospects here are in some points of view not dark, and in others not so bright as I would desire. I have made friends and with these acquired some position—some reputation—and yet I have next to no practice at all. It is only by practice that I shall ever become a lawyer. To do it by mere study is plainly not in me or my capacity.

In this year 1851, he went to Virginia to investigate coal and iron lands. He made an investment at a ridiculous price— about twenty cents an acre—and in the end realized a considerable profit. In the same year he busied himself in getting engaged to Lucy Webb, but he did not marry then and could never have married if his prospects had not suddenly taken a turn for the better.

Hayes was no orator, no silver-tongued court pleader such as earned the dollars in the fifties. He was essentially a technical lawyer, a strategist, a dealer in subtleties. As such it cannot be said that he did much service to the country by his legal career, for the profession in America is cursed by technicalities to a degree that is almost scandalous. It was in appeals of criminal cases on technical points that Hayes won his reputation and standing.

In January, 1852, he was appointed, by the court, counsel for a criminal. The accused was convicted, but Hayes made a good impression by his defense. It followed that he was appointed counsel for one Nancy Farrer, a poisoner who no one doubted would swing, because she was unquestionably guilty and richly deserved hanging. It was the turning point in the career of Rutherford B. Hayes. If he had failed, he would have never been anything more than a lawyer in small practice. But he succeeded to a remarkable degree.

Like a wise lawyer he reflected regretfully, "The poor girl is homely," knowing well that an American jury never convicts a handsome woman. His client was repellent, half animal,

LUCY WARE WEBB (AFTERWARDS MRS. R. B. HAYES)
At the age of sixteen, from a Daguerreotype

better dead, but she wore the golden face of opportunity for Hayes.

He argued the case at Columbus and the hopeless defendant was convicted. This made no difference to Hayes; he moved for a new trial and argued the case so skillfully that he got it. What is more, he was allowed half of a fee of a hundred and fifty dollars, much the most money he had ever made, an augury of the future. The bill of exceptions he filed covered sixty pages of foolscap and must have occupied him for several weeks, but he thought himself munificently recompensed by seventy-five dollars. Soon afterward he got up another bill of exceptions and argued the motion for a new trial in the case of James Summons, a notorious murderer. Thus Rutherford B. Hayes occupies a noticeable place in the legal history of America as one of those innovators who succeeded in establishing the custom of setting aside verdicts on the ground of almost imperceptible and wholly immaterial flaws.

His reputation as a technical lawyer was bringing him practice—so much so that at the end of 1852 he ventured on the heroic step of getting married. Even then this would have been perfectly impossible but for Uncle Sardis, who desired him to get married, insisted on his getting married, and paid the bills.

Hayes gained the case of Summons, saving a wholly undeserving criminal. It was still worse with Nancy Farrer. She was a servant, a degenerate who poisoned the members of families she worked for, out of sheer viciousness. Earth has no place for such as her; it is the truest mercy to banish these human brutes from life. Hayes raised the plea of insanity and had the state (or the hysterical portion of it) sobbing over the woes of the unhappy murderess in danger of expiating her crimes on the gallows. She was not insane—merely of a low-grade intelligence—and her sanity had never been in doubt until Hayes perceived the opportunity of saving her by question-

ing it. Hayes was also a good business lawyer. He had an eye
for investments, and his investments saved him in later life
when he found politics unremunerative and burdensome. For
a time they were not paying investments, but in the end they
made him independent.

Hayes was rapidly on the upgrade now, and at the close of
1853 he entered a new law partnership. In September, 1854,
he removed into his own house, which had cost him, including
improvements, five thousand five hundred dollars. Uncle
Sardis had lent him four thousand dollars of the amount, but
still the house was his own. As we have said, he had now married and was the proud possessor of a family and a home.

He was prospering and the old dreams that once had
haunted him were dimming. He was becoming contented with
possessing a wife and children and a home. In January, 1855, he
wrote:

Two things are now ascertained. . . . One is, that I have
neither health nor capacity to be a first-rate figure in my profession; the other, that I appear to have enough of both to
acquire a reasonable success—enough for happiness. With this
I am content.

His dreams had failed just as Fate was about to open the
way to him to destiny. About this time the Republican party,
strong from birth, came into being, and Hayes joined as one of
its charter members. This was his supreme move on the chess-
board of life, but it was quite inevitable. Being one of the elect,
he could not have done otherwise.

Uncle Sardis Birchard had always been a fervent Whig, and
Rutherford Hayes had inherited his uncle's politics. He had
been interested in public affairs from childhood. The campaign
of 1852 had awakened his keenest interest. Winfield Scott,
"Old Fuss and Feathers," had visited Cincinnati in the pre-

election season and had been enthusiastically hailed by the Whigs of that city. Hayes thought that Scott measured up to presidential size, which he certainly did physically, being the most imposing-looking man in America. When the Whigs won in the Cincinnati local election of 1848 Hayes briefly exulted, but quickly changed his tune when he found that the state of Ohio had gone Democratic. The wish was never father to the thought with Hayes, who only too surely foresaw the election of Pierce in November. Scott was overwhelmed, and in the hour of that debacle the Whig Party really ended its checkered career.

After a year or two the great struggle over the repeal of the Missouri Compromise, cleverly misrepresented as an effort of the Slavery Power to enchain the free North, brought into being the Republican party, which took over the receivership of the Whig party.

Hayes had no difficulty whatever in becoming a Republican, since the Republican party in the North was strongly Whiggish, though it was also recruited from Democrats won over by the fervent anti-slavery propaganda put out by the New York *Tribune* and other newspapers. Not that Hayes felt the slightest indignation on the subject of slavery. Propaganda made little impression on his cool, analytical mind; and he was too familiar with the Southern institution to discover in it the crimes with which sensationalists all over the world were stirring public opinion. *Uncle Tom's Cabin*, which pictured the slaves as being morally and spiritually superior to the slaveholders, could never have converted Hayes; he does not even appear to have read it.

However, slavery was the burning question of the hour. No matter how sane, no matter how little given to nerves people might be, they could not get away from it. Longfellow, Lowell, Whittier turned to it; when that sunny soul, Washington Irving, and that great imagination, Hawthorne, failed to join the movement, they were almost looked on as traitors. No man can escape the agitation of his age.

When the Republican party nominated Frémont as its first presidential candidate in 1856 Hayes was enthusiastic, though rather as an old Whig than as a new Republican. Yet he was beginning to feel the slavery excitement, attuning himself to it as much as was in his essentially unfanatical nature to do. Clear-minded always, he anticipated Frémont's defeat in November. The country at large, preferring peace to war and union to sectional feuds, turned to the Democratic nominee, James Buchanan. Hayes desponded a little. "I feel seriously the probable defeat of the cause of freedom in the approaching presidential election," he wrote. "Cause of freedom"! He, too, had caught the fever of the day. However, he had found reason for hope in the fact that all was not lost. He added:

After all, the good cause has made a great progress. Anti-slavery sentiment has been created and the people have been educated to a large extent. . . . But further work is to be done and my sense of duty determines me to keep on in the path I have chosen—not to dabble in politics at the expense of duty to my family and to the neglect of my profession, but to do what I can consistently with other duties to aid in forming a public opinion on this subject which will "mitigate and finally eradicate the evil."

Still he was not quite enthusiastic enough. He felt the need of working himself up, and added:

I must study the subject, and am now beginning with Clark-son's "History of the Abolition of the Slave Trade." . . . The election of day after tomorrow is the first pitched battle. However fares the cause, I am enlisted for the war.

This poetic prophesy was much truer than Hayes had the

slightest inkling of. It was indeed a war that began in 1856 with the nomination of Frémont by a purely sectional party on a largely sectional platform. Secession was invited, if not exactly thrust upon the South.

Hayes fancied that he would be doing an unwise thing to neglect his profession to dabble in politics. So far from true was this, that dabbling in politics was the wisest thing he ever did; it made him a national figure. Men who flow with the current must succeed. In business they go, unconsciously enough, with the trend. In speculation they side with the market. In politics they move on the crest of some public wave to place and power. To live in Ohio in 1857 was to be the spoiled child of Fortune. Rutherford Hayes, if he used his opportunities, could hardly escape a high destiny.

The district Republican convention met at Cincinnati in September, 1857, and Hayes's name was brought forward for Congress but was withdrawn at his own request. Already, he was sufficiently a power to be mentioned for important office. The excitement, the bonfires, the torchlight parades of that election were thoroughly enjoyed by Hayes. Politics are not what they used to be; a political parade in our time is a tame performance—unless staged by the Ku Klux Klan—for the street lights pale the flares, and street cars and automobiles ruin everything. But in that age a torchlight parade was an impressive ceremonial. Through the muddy streets, lighted only by oil lamps or gas jets, the paraders marched behind a brass band, carrying torches that turned the dusk into ruddy day. When it is further remembered that most of the paraders and many of the spectators were drunk, that brickbats flew at the least provocation and that real battles sometimes developed, it will be seen that a political parade in 1857–1860 was a spectacle indeed.

Hayes was an eminently practical lawyer and no idealist in

political practices, however idealistic his political views may have been. He wrote of one of his associates of 1857:

Lew Lee, our Republican "rounder" in the Fourteenth Ward, was blown up last night in consequence of the grossest carelessness. Anybody else would have died outright. He is the fellow who was shot all to pieces in '56 and who a year ago was stabbed through the lungs, stomach, bowels, and throat and was on his feet in four weeks. He was in our office yesterday afternoon looking fresh and hearty. The papers say he will die but he won't.

One would like to know something of the subsequent history of this early Republican martyr, this suffering devotee of the anti-slavery crusade.

Being on the right side, that is, the side bound to win, Hayes soon had a sufficient reward. In return for his party services, which were so far rather slight, late in 1858 he was appointed city solicitor of Cincinnati at a salary of thirty-five hundred dollars. As this sum equals ten thousand dollars today, it cannot be said that Rutherford Hayes had sacrificed heavily for the good cause.

He was prospering, partly because he was what he was out of genuine conviction and partly because he was always nimble and fell on his feet. Rutherford Hayes was not given to making sacrifices for principle, though he had principle. He was entirely too sane, too cool-headed, too unemotional to be a martyr. He saw no use in martyrdom. With him the majority was always right; he had no taste for gallant, hopeless minority fights. Was the eradication of the upas tree of slavery the motif of the Republican party, he would be for uprooting slavery. Was something else the issue, he would be for it. He usually sided with his party, no matter for what it stood. He preferred his party to be sane, but he preferred his party to sanity if the party willed to be insane. He was the type of politician that seldom turns against party. But it must also be said, and it is no little thing to say, that he was the kind of politician who seeks to use party power for good. For Rutherford B. Hayes had a kind heart, an upright attitude, the desire to benefit his country. He let few matters come before practical politics, but for that very reason he was able to accomplish important things.

The wages of sin is death; so is the wages of virtue. The wages of moral mediocrity is life. Criminal and saint alike go to the scaffold; the average man is safe. Criminal and saint alike are ineffective; he who compromises accomplishes. Rutherford B. Hayes, whose cool brain knew not the meaning of fanaticism, talked against slavery because it was natural and expedient to do so, and later in Congress he voted for the excesses of his party because to vote against them meant political ruin; yet when, as the result of such compliances, power came to him, he wielded that power for the public welfare. And in so doing he served the country better than the rigid moralists who make no trades with conscience.

RUTHERFORD B. HAYES has not appeared in the eyes of history as large of stature as he really was, because he was a normal man, and we instinctively believe that normality is mediocrity. Nearly all the other figures of the age were abnormal: Lincoln, emotional in youth to the point of hysteria; Grant, total failure dramatically turned into heroic success—and a drinker; Andrew Johnson, also heroic and also a drinker; Thaddeus Stevens, incarnation of hate, a fury rather than a man; Blaine, popular idol ruined by a genius for making enemies; Greeley, the eccentric; Conkling, with his "turkey-gobbler strut." What a stage of Dickensian characters it was! And Hayes the only normal one. Hence almost the only one not famous.

Hayes was a normal boy before he evolved into a normal man. Morally, he was better than the average, thanks to an old-fashioned Presbyterian mother. He was so much better than the average that vicious amours seem to have played no part in his life.

It may be argued that he was abnormal here, but this is not the fact. America produces two types of normal men: the normal loose man and the normal good man. Hayes was of this latter category.

He was physically delicate as a boy, but without a trace of neurosis; in fact, his nervous system all through life was singularly stable. It was for this reason, to be exact, that he was never accused of genius. However, in youth Hayes was worried because several of his relatives had gone insane. He need not have done so. Few saner men—few men more wholly endued with the quality of saneness—have ever lived.

Hayes was never a solitary, a boy of moods. He had no seasons of exaltation followed by depression. He never found his own company to be more agreeable than that of others. All his life he liked society and shone in it in a modest way—not sparkling, not brilliant, but pleasing, satisfying. He had a gift of friendship and most of those he loved in youth he loved in age.

Hayes liked women and was liked by them. There was nothing unusual in the attraction he exerted over them. He did not wear long hair and pose; he was not a football hero or an aviator; he was not a dance partner. He was not even rough in his manners toward women. In fact, he had none of the usual reasons for being successful with women; he was simply a fine, clean, good-looking lad with a healthy, somewhat humorous outlook on life.

Hayes was fifteen before women began to interest him greatly. At that age he scribbled to a boy friend, "Tell me how A. Pickett flourishes with the girls. Tell him I flourish like a green bay tree." At that age his voice had a slippery gamut from soprano to bass and his members were loose-jointed after the manner of the young of cows and human beings. But that dismal period was soon over, and Rutherford Hayes became a tall, personable young fellow, trim and handsome in a dark, rather aquiline way. Indeed, there was race, breeding in his look as a boy, which he succeeded in getting rid of before he became a successful politician. When he was President he was the most representative middle-class public man in the country.

Hayes was even better liked by femininity as he passed from boyhood into manhood. At twenty-two he confided to Fanny: "Between you and me, a little squad of girls have spent a great deal of time and pains in trying to get acquainted with me—calling to see a young married woman at our house and deputizing her to call me in, but I have been so ungallant that they now despair of accomplishing their object." In order to escape their attentions, he told a fib that he was engaged to a girl in Columbus.

Yet Rutherford Hayes would have been easy prey for the experienced husband hunter, for he wished to get married, not as moderns do, with a sufficient income and with all the comforts of home, including automobile, radio and frigidaire; but, as they married in the forties and the fifties—gallantly, defying fate, carrying off the adventure by sangfroid and courage. At twenty-one he risked a twenty-five-dollar bet that he would be married at twenty-five. However, a year before the time was up he was still bemoaning his single state and resolving to delay no longer. "But," he added regretfully, "I have had no loves as yet." He wrote Fanny that the thought that was "uppermost in the medley of ideas that are rolling about under my hair is that before a year rolls around I'll get me a wifey, or at least a sweetheart, if I can find one who agrees with me that I am one of the sunniest fellows in the world."

As the mistletoe season crowned the year, Hayes rioted in day dreams, a haze of warm imagination, a pernicious habit he lamented he could not shake himself free from. The dreams failed to center on any definite object. He pondered every pretty girl he met but could make no decision. Not that he was able, financially, to get married. He was not; he hardly made enough to support himself, let alone a wife and ten or twelve children, the normal family of the fifties. But young men in those days married and trusted in God, and usually did not starve. Hayes would have done the same thing, but he could not do so, he felt, until he had fallen in love, and he had not, so far, fallen in love.

Love was a serious matter in 1850. A man went through a

love conversion that was much like a religious conversion. There was a formula for the process, and love was incomplete if the formula was not fulfilled in all details.

A man was restless, sleepless, appetiteless. He would not know what ailed him; his family would suggest consumption. A whirl of sex emotions would fill his mind, perhaps several women, antagonistic, dragging him in different ways. Then he would see the light! Doubt would disappear; one woman would stand out—the one! He would know, by some sudden, sky-lifting wave of emotion, some experience not to be denied, that this was *the* woman. *He was in love.* Never again could the experience come; never, unless the woman were safely dead and, then, not so utterly as at first.

Such an experience Rutherford Hayes waited for, groped among his emotions to seize upon. He felt that he must have the conviction of love before he could properly become engaged and be married.

Sophie Hayes had chosen for him—Lucy Ware Webb. She added, by way of afterthought, that perhaps the girl was too young. "Youth," Rutherford sententiously returned, "is a defect that she is fast getting over and may be entirely rid of before I shall want her." As for Sister Fanny's objection to Lucy's freckles, Rutherford replied that they were only skin deep.

There was a girl whom Hayes always referred to as F. He wrote in his diary for February 1, 1847 that he had had an understanding with "noble-hearted F." and that circumstances have put an end to "a' that." This marks the definite trend of his thoughts toward Lucy Webb. In October of the same year he is taken up with these thoughts. He wrote:

I wish I had a wife to take charge of my correspondence with friends and relatives. Women of education and sense can always write good letters, but men are generally unable to fish up enough entertaining matters to fill half a sheet. By and by, I hope you and Mother Lamb will see to it that Lucy Webb is properly instructed in this particular. I am not a-going to take a wife on recommendation unless her sponsors will fulfill to the utmost what they assume.

In the last days of 1849, at Columbus, Hayes was making love, though not sincerely, to Miss H. He felt sure that "that flirtation will never ripen into anything" and desired to end it. And he added these significant words: "Called at Wesleyan College. Miss L. [Lucy Webb] not in." He was much interested in Lucy's whereabouts. He met girls, charming girls, but fancied that a country-bred girl such as Lucy would please him best.

In March, 1850, Hayes was sufficiently sure of himself to begin to rave after the manner of Bulwer, his favorite author. He wrote in Bulweresque:

I have not dared to put on paper, even in my sacred diary, much of my love. I have been afraid of profane eyes, and, with shame be it said, that one day I might blush to see it; not the love, but the repulse. Success, success even in affairs of the heart, is the thing which crowns and ennobles. For almost two years I have been in love with ———. She has been at times "coy and hard to please" and again yielding and kind, smiling sweetly upon my protestations of affection. . . . Shall I say to her "now or never?" This suspense must have an end! If I am wrecked and harried o'er the shoals of disappointment, I have elasticity and firmness and pride enough to quickly stand erect and free. . . . I'll talk to her—probe her yet again. . . . Foolishness! Shall I tear the page? No, let it stay a little while.

When his cool sense prevailed, Hayes was cautious, fearing entrapment. He spent an evening with Lucy and wrote in his diary, "Must keep a guard on my susceptibles or I shall be in beyond my depths." A prudent person, this Rutherford Hayes. He raved to his diary, not to Lucy.

In July, 1850, he finally terminated one flirtation, apparently that with Miss H. Hayes lightly told her that he could never dream of loving such a flirt as she had become, and they ended with a laugh. He was not hurt; it is to be presumed that the girl was not.

In the spring of 1851, the vital urge ran strongly in Rutherford Hayes, now beginning to achieve a place in Cincinnati. His thoughts, as usual, turned to Lucy Webb. He pronounced on her:

She is a genuine woman, right from instinct and impulse rather than judgment and reflection. It is no use doubting or rolling it over in my thoughts. By George! I am in love with her! So we go. Another bachelor's revery! Let it work out its own results.

It was fitting that the climax came in June. On a June night, Hayes rescued, or thought he rescued, a woman from a plunging horse—at least put his arms about her and pulled her out of danger. The act gave him unwonted courage, that courage with which a man walks on fate. He turned into the gate of the house where Lucy lived. She was there; the night was warm and fragrant. They talked familiarly of old things and friends, paid a call, returned to the house. Hayes grew a little sleepy.

Suddenly impulse possessed him—"unthought of, unpremeditated, involuntary." Rising from his rocking chair, he seized Lucy's hand and blurted, "I love you," no doubt trying to remember the Bulwerian formula, but bungling it. Lucy did not immediately answer. He repeated his declaration. She gently returned the pressure of his hand, and the joyful Hayes knew that all was well. He waited until she spoke. Finally she yielded modestly, "I must confess, I like you very well." Hayes felt the rapture of the triumphant lover of the fifties, and at once they plighted troth. He went home an engaged man; the great deed was done.

He, of course, was a victim, but he did not know it. His mother had chosen the girl for him and the girl knew that she was chosen; but Hayes was permitted to believe that he was a free agent. As is usual in such cases, his mother chose more wisely than he would have done, unassisted. The somewhat shrewd Sophie Hayes had sized up Lucy Webb as the right wife for her Rutherford, and her judgment was sound.

Lucy Webb was precisely the kind of a girl a man's mother picks out for him. She was warm-hearted, popular, religious, pretty, but not dangerously so. Her eyes were really beautiful, and Hayes, flatteringly, likened them to a panther's. She was rather quiet, perhaps a little shy. She had fished for Rutherford, whom she always admired, and she had done it skillfully.

Lucy Webb was quite unusual, but Hayes was not prompt to discover it. In an age when woman's education was rudimentary she had taken classes at Ohio Wesleyan University at Delaware, although women were not formally admitted. The college was a curious looking place, recalling the old Mormon tabernacle at Salt Lake City, but it supplied culture of a sort, and Lucy made the most of it. She made an excellent wife and probably was a large element in Rutherford Hayes' success in life. He patronized her, considering her mental endowments to be rather limited; but all that was limited about her was her gift for self-assertion. She became the vicarious sacrifice of Hayes's virtues. Hardly an ardent prohibitionist herself, she endured the ridicule of the first prohibition regime at the White House. People blamed her for it, ignoring or not being aware of the fact that Rutherford Hayes was a temperance advocate from early manhood.

Lucy Webb Hayes was gifted with greater power of winning

RUTHERFORD B. AND LUCY W. HAYES
At the time of their marriage, December 30, 1852, from a Daguerreotype

popularity than was Rutherford Hayes. Her ambition for him, higher even than his ambition for himself, lifted him several pegs in politics and her ready tact smoothed the asperities of many a political contention. She loved her portion in life: home, church, society, farming, flowers. When the Civil War arrived, she wished that she had been a man to go to it. As it was, she spent months in camp and endeared herself to the soldiers. She had accomplishments, being a singer of good voice. She was, all in all, very human, with no great taste for the Sunday-school adulation that trailed her. "I am not good," she once said. "I am bad. I am not religious. I'm not what you are. All I can say is, I do want to do to others as I would like them to do to me."

The deed was done, and Hayes waxed dithyrambic. He was forgivable in 1851; it would be inexcusable now. He wallowed in sentiment, writing:

To think that that lovely vision is an actual, living, breathing being, and is loved by me, and loves in return and will one day be my bride—my abiding, forgiving, trustful, loving wife —to make my happy home blessed indeed with her cheerful smile and silver voice and warm, true heart!

On December 30, 1852, Rutherford B. Hayes married Lucy W. Webb, at her mother's house on Sixth Street, Cincinnati. Professor L. D. McCabe, of the Ohio Wesleyan University, officiated. Fanny and Uncle Sardis were there to felicitate their Rutherford.

Rutherford and Lucy Webb Hayes lived together for many years, probably in greater harmony and satisfaction than is vouchsafed most couples. She bore eight children: Birchard, the bookish; Webb, the sportsman; Rutherford, the mild; Fanny, the serious; Scott, the adventurous; and three who died in childhood, Joe, George Crook and Manning. It was an age when fathers took thankfully all that the Lord sent, and consequently were plentifully blessed.

The Hayes children were brought up in the good old way, on the catechism and the rod. However, they were very fortunate children, with a wise mother and a father who entered into the spirit of childhood, sharing their games. While he was away from them in the Civil War, Hayes wrote tender letters from camp, grieving that he had to miss Birchard's birthday celebration; advising the children to study, but not too hard; telling them war stories; looking forward to the time when he would be at home and "Ruddy and Webby and you will gather around to listen to my stories, and how often I shall have to tell them, and how they will grow bigger and bigger as I get older."

Hayes himself, the vigorous and virtuous citizen, fitted well into the ideal picture of home life in Cincinnati. A handsome, broad-shouldered man, he stood five feet eight and a half inches tall, and weighed from 170 to 180 pounds. In maturity the fragility of childhood faded utterly away. His mobile features relied on his dark, deeply-set blue eyes for animation. The long, full beard which he assumed on entering the army, like his military bearing and the air of Unionist soldier, clung to him for the rest of his life. An elasticity in his step, a mildness of voice, a subdued style of dress gave an impression of pleasant, commonplace tranquility to his presence. He gained such measure of success as came his way because he was so much like the mass of American business men of his age. There was nothing out-of-the-way, no esoteric touch in his make-up.

His character had certain complications but, in the main, was simple. Imaginative and romantic in youth, life made him practical enough—perhaps too much so. He would have been far more appealing if he had kept a dash of his youthful dreaminess, if he had not been so entirely the model husband and father, the excellent business lawyer. Introspection always remained with him to a certain extent. He sometimes tried to snatch the mask from his personality and traced in his character self-confidence, common sense, a weakness for flattery and fame. Ambition was pronounced in him. In order to rise he had to overcome many difficulties. Diffident and rather unready as a speaker in youth, he mastered the art of clear and forceful presentation, but never became an orator in the meaning of that age, in which men swayed other men by the spoken word as musicians charm their auditors.

Although Rutherford B. Hayes was the first of his line to achieve distinction, and although he was in appearance the typical middle-class American of his time, he was not without pride of birth. He made many trips to Brattleboro to complete his genealogical studies. He was especially proud of the Scotch strain in his ancestry, which boasted hazy coats-of-arms. His stock was mainly early New England, strong, sturdy, successful in a solid way. He cannot be blamed for being proud of one of the best blood strains the world has ever known. He was free from snobbery; that he was well-descended was a matter of gratification to him, but he never made it a cause of offense to others.

Hayes was fond of people, read them well, wielded them. In traveling he liked to sit in the smoking car, where he could talk to men. Even as a youth he enjoyed the observation of human nature as it was revealed to him on trains and boats. Sometimes he put his observations pithily, as when he wrote of a trip from Boston to Oswego:

Old women with squalling children, and old maids with barking poodles, young men with foppish airs and young women with silly smiles and sillier tongues, crazy students, and all creation driven by the cold rains from Saratoga gambling home, complaining of all the ills of the flesh from the gout to the headache, groanings over lost umbrellas, crushed hat boxes and wet weather.

He made friends and held them. He and Uncle Birchard were much more than relatives; they were cronies. Then there was Guy W. Bryan, whose friendship weathered time, war and distance, and William Henry Smith, his John the Beloved. He was even close to that mollusk, John Sherman, to whom he wrote, "You were at the cradle and you have followed the hearse of this ambitious life." Hayes had other intimates: Carl Schurz, Stanley Matthews and General M. B. Force. He knew every President from Lincoln to Taft and found them all friends except Johnson and Arthur. He knew McKinley and Taft as boys, Roosevelt as an associate in reform movements. With Cleveland his relations were intimate, and Cleveland incurred censure by attending his funeral. Hayes had fine friendships with women, too—with such women as the beautiful Mrs. Herron, mother of Mrs. William H. Taft, Mrs. Davis of Cincinnati, Mrs. L. C. Austin of Cleveland and Mrs. A. H. Miller of Fremont. At home in the best society, he was also perfectly at ease with men of every class. A Michigan farmer said of him, "Why, he was just as common as any man I ever met." Could politician ask for higher tribute?

Hayes would greet his friends with, "Well, what do you know?" All his life long he had a keen scent for knowledge and at seventy attempted the Chautauqua course of reading. Once out walking he picked up a piece of conglomerate and, desiring to know why it was round, pursued the riddle for several blocks and up three pairs of stairs until he learned that attrition had worn the pebble smooth.

Hayes was no great speaker, but he was something better; he was the prince of listeners. It might almost be said that he listened himself into the presidency. One congressman declared that Hayes was "a most agreeable man to visit upon official business. You left him feeling that he was your friend and that if he could comply with your wishes and requests it would give him pleasure to do so. He was a statesman with a heart." _

A statesman with a heart! Not a bad summing-up of the political career of Rutherford B. Hayes.

Carl Schurz chuckled to himself that the Republican party in choosing Hayes for President had nominated a man without knowing it. Hayes had perhaps few great qualities, but he moved upon a level with a sure gait and he had a certain strength of will that was not discernible at first. Such was the man, the good, sound technical lawyer but mediocre speaker; the model husband and father; the public man of good intentions. Such was the man and such his background. What, then, were his beliefs?

Rutherford B. Hayes came of religious people—religious New Englanders. He had religious grandparents, a religious mother and a religious wife, but he was never religious himself. When he left Kenyon College he knew that he would never be. Deeply interested in all spiritual matters, religion neither convinced his mind nor touched his heart. Once when a revival at college had gathered in all but ten of the students, Hayes remained without the fold. Yet he was a lifelong churchgoer. At Harvard he attended church regularly, confessing that "the sermon, the music, the elegant church, and the fashionable audience are by no means weak attractions." He was, in fact, a Modernist.

Always skeptical, Hayes found himself entrenched in unbelief at Harvard, which in the forties taught doubt as a duty. Harvard prided itself on this; it believed that in teaching a skeptical attitude it was strengthening intellectual honesty.

"I am so nearly infidel in all my views," Hayes once said,

"that, too, in spite of my wishes, that only the most liberal doctrines can command my assent." In other words, Hayes would have liked to believe but, even in that age before the rise of science, he could not give intellectual acceptance to the doctrines of Christianity. He was never intimate with preachers. Once in camp during the Civil War he wrote, "The chaplain returned today—not an agreeable or useful person. I wish he had not returned."

As the husband of the well-doing Lucy Webb and the leading citizen of Fremont, Hayes was ever a generous contributor to religious causes, paying one fourth of the cost of the new church. He tolerantly watched his children join the church, no doubt wishing that he also could do so. He once said to his son Webb Hayes, "I hope that you will be benefitted by your churchgoing. Where the habit does not christianize it generally civilizes. There is reason enough for supporting churches if there were no higher." In time he came to be president of the county Bible society. "The true infidel," he explained, "in the offensive and objectionable sense is not the honest skeptic but the man who opposes all religion." And so he somehow snuggled into the fold.

Since Rutherford Hayes was a man of moral passion but no religious convictions, he had, like other men of his type, to seek a creed that would serve as substitute. Communists are fond of likening Christianity to a narcotic. They are wrong; the genuine narcotics are the reforms that men take up in place of Christianity. Christianity itself is the most overpowering stimulant humanity has ever known.

Hayes did not grope in the darkness to snatch some flimsy phantom of spiritualism, or strain eastward to a flame of faith from the Ganges. There was no quality he possessed that he was vainer of than his stolid common sense. Being a mundane person, he looked around him instead of above him for a creed and found his Lucifer in the saloon. He decided that he would be the first exalted apostle of temperance. Be it said to his credit, he chose a difficult course. Alcohol was the milk on which America had grown. The vast spaces, the isolation of country life in America put a premium on the cup that cheers; and the United States in the forties and fifties was the most drunken country in the world except England. Foreigners stood appalled at the quantities of whiskey that Americans consumed without blinking, raw. To oppose a custom so deeply rooted in American life required courage; to take the opposition to the White House in the seventies demanded something like audacity.

Hayes was right; the world was tending that way. The United States—the whole United States except New York and Massachusetts—was to see the light. But in 1850 to become a prohibitionist, or temperance advocate, as they called it then, was at least an indication of marked initiative.

The issue had not always troubled Hayes. In collegiate days nothing tickled him more than to tease stern Sophie Hayes with tales of debauchery as impossible as the adventures of Alice. Aside from jest, he sometimes drank alcohol—indeed drank wine until he entered the White House.

On going to Cincinnati his interest in temperance quickened. In 1850, he was the speaker on a temperance program in Columbus, though he was still graceless enough to offer currant wine to Uncle Sardis. In July, 1850, he attended a Sons of Temperance meeting with his mother and his niece Laura, but when the question of organizing a temperance party came up he opposed it. He continued to oppose it out of political sagacity. He became an orator of Sons of Temperance meetings; indeed, in the forum of this now forgotten organization he gained a great part of his early experience of public speaking. Prohibition never injured Rutherford Hayes. It strengthened his reputation as a model husband and father by exhibiting him as the possessor of a tender public conscience. His personal gain was that the void left in him spiritually by his inability to grasp religion was somewhat relieved by a concrete object of reform. One of the substitutes for the orthodox Presbyterian hell Hayes found in the reeking saloons of the Cincinnati of his day.

It was the year of fate, 1861. Rutherford Hayes's boyhood
dreams had been of war; he had reluctantly abandoned the hope
of taking part in the Mexican War. And now at last, all unex-
pected, dropped from the skies, was war! Hayes was flaming
enthusiasm at once, partly because he believed in the Union
cause and partly because he liked war.

It should be remembered that war is one of the things that
civilization has ruined; poison gas and high-power explosives
have played havoc with martial romance. Lindbergh and Byrd
have roused youth to the stainless glories of peace. But in 1861,
war was still the great adventure, the joyous vision of boyhood,
the test of mettle.

Hayes was somewhat tired of the dreary routine of the law,
and besides he had a certain taste for outdoor life. Once with
two friends he had adventured up Mount Washington,
equipped with two blankets, two bottles of brandy, pork pie
and bread, besides a bag of oats for the horses and an ax to cut
fuel. The roughness pricked even the boys' crude fancies. When
they had cuddled up on a door for a bed and pillowed their
heads on a stovepipe, the whistling wind defied them to sleep,
frightened their horses, and blew down the wall, but left them
none the worse for wear. Now Hayes was to go camping again,
and he relished the idea.

"Wolf, wolf!" had been cried so often that Hayes at the
beginning of 1861 was one of those who frankly refused to
believe in the reality of secession. In the presidential contest of
1860, he only yawned over the candidates; four of them and
not one worth the stirring of his stumping talent! He did make
a speech for Lincoln, but wrote Uncle Sardis in September that

he could not get up much enthusiasm over the contest. "A wholesome contempt for Douglas on account of his recent demagoguery is the chief feeling I have." This in reference to the candidate whose election would perhaps have spared the horrors of the Civil War! Too evidently Rutherford B. Hayes had no prevision of the boilings of the pot of Fate.

Later it was borne in upon him that the ultra-slave states, South Carolina and her satellites, were about to wrench themselves from the Union. But Hayes did not take it very seriously, thinking that the border states would not go with the Southern tide. Two months later, when they had seceded, he was ready to let them go. The twenty states left, stretching from the Atlantic to the Pacific, were stuff for a glorious nation. Better negotiation, better compromise than war. Let the erring sisters depart in peace!

Hayes in the early spring thought that separation had to come. He supported the government in enforcing laws, defending forts and collecting revenues, but had no idea of approving actual war with the slave states—a burdensome war, sucking up blood and shackling debt on the country. But of what avail is antebellum conservatism when a nation is gripped with the war fever and befogged with propaganda?

By May of 1861, Hayes had discovered that this was not a war of conquest but "to defend the rights of the Union"; that it had been forced upon the country and could not be escaped. He even swallowed the current notion that if the government had only frightened the impudent ones with the threat of force all the trouble might have been avoided, and that the new-born Southern Confederacy had sinister designs on Washington. So it would be a defensive war (since all wars are defensive), a proper chastening of naughty seceders.

At length Lincoln loomed as of greater stature than Hayes had thought at first, a kind, conciliating soul, sorely grieved at the conflict before him. Hayes spoke of the "nobility of this typical American. He possesses strength in reserve. This will be tested soon."

The hypnotism of the hour now made war seem to Hayes a sacred duty. "I would prefer to go into it," he declared, "if I knew that I was to die or be killed in the course of it than to live through it and after it without taking a part in it." "This is a holy war," he continued later, "and if a fair chance opens I shall go into it; if a fair chance don't open, I shall perhaps take measures to open one."

Hayes was city solicitor and would run again for the office if he did not go to war, though he expected to be defeated with the rest of the ticket. He had reaped from the office all that it could give him, experience and reputation. He left it, conscious of duty done, of never having been surpassed as a city solicitor. So public and private shackles fell off. The family did not object to the soldiering; Lucy wished she were a man and could go. Stern old Sophie Hayes thought that the war was a judgment on the country for its sins, and perhaps she was right. Rutherford Hayes found it an opportunity and a lark. Boyhood dreams had come true at last.

On April 20, 1861, the literary club was engaged in a new and quite unintellectual pursuit, turning scholarly heads in obedience to "eyes right" and "eyes left" and shuffling awkwardly in drill as a volunteer home company. A week before this the whole community had been jerked to its feet by the news of Fort Sumter and by Lincoln's call to arms. Rutherford Hayes never forgot the bracing shock of that night, the frenzied excitement of staid church members, the half-insane abandon of mass meetings. At the principal one of these he was chosen to write the resolutions.

And now politics yielded large dividends. Hayes, all innocent of military knowledge, was not to begin at the foot of the ladder but quite high up; in June, Governor Dennison offered him a majority in the regiment commanded by no less a colonel than William S. Rosecrans. All the field officers of this Twenty-third Ohio regiment came from Cincinnati.

At Camp Jackson, Hayes began the novitiate of war. He found his first sleep under canvas to be cool but refreshing; he liked canvas. Through this simple, well-ordered military life swept clean winds, gusts of courage. When Hayes saw the exaltation with which the oath was taken, a "swelling of the heart" possessed him.

In the absence of the colonel he once had an exhilarating taste of authority, being responsible for three thousand men. When a West Point graduate came to him for the orders of the day, he wore the mask of the shrewd uninformed as he instructed the officer to follow the usual routine unless the commander saw occasion to change it. Hayes like his colonel, with whom he shared a taste for pleasantry. Many a day after duty the regimental triumverate chuckled over the day's happenings.

Finally the Twenty-third Ohio was ordered to western Virginia, the section of the old commonwealth destined to become the state of West Virginia. Before going to that region, Hayes was allowed a short furlough at home. He had a hysterical welcome everywhere and departed for the scene of action in the best of humors.

He found soldiering to be much the lark he had expected. In the summer of 1861, the Unionists had rather easy fighting in the western mountains of Virginia. Those mountains were far more accessible from Pennsylvania and Ohio than from eastern Virginia. To reach the Kanawha River from eastern Virginia, the Confederates had to drag themselves for many weary miles over a few mountain roads. Supplies were transported with the utmost difficulty. The Confederate troops were

HAYES AS A UNION SOLDIER

untrained, their first generals amateurs. Exposed to a wet summer in the mountains, they suffered in health and their camps were filled with boys dying of the measles. It is little wonder that they did nothing and that Hayes conceived a certain disdain for them as soldiers. He was destined to revise that opinion before the war was over. Later Robert E. Lee was sent to western Virginia but almost ruined his military reputation by failing to overthrow Rosecrans, who confronted him with every advantage of supply base and equipment. Indeed, this campaign made Rosecrans and very nearly led to the retirement of Lee from active military operations.

It seemed to Hayes, curiously observant of the new life about him, that the war had brought out the good and evil of Virginia. The enemy, he thought, were very mixed in quality, part of them the cream of the country, the wealthy and educated, products of books and banks, "who do nothing openly"; the rest, the scum of the earth, the vagabonds and criminals. The Union adherents were of the middle class, "the law and order, well-behaved folks." They came in handy, these friends who were willing to aid Union expeditions. Hayes marked them as the "well-to-do people of the neighborhood, and usually are Methodists or other orderly citizens."

While there was no fighting on a large scale, there was sufficient excitement. The mountains, so lately roamed by wild beasts, were now full of armed men seeking murder. Blood was shed, and not all on one side.

The worst nuisance the Union army had to contend with was bushwhacking. Wagon trains were occasionally attacked and sacked; lone soldiers were likely to be cut off. Parties of scouts scoured the hills for these pestilential guerrillas and gradually cleared them out.

The outdoor life agreed with Hayes, and authority pleased him. He lamented with a pity bordering on vanity the lot of

his friends who were compelled to stay at home. In this mood
he wrote:

I know that we are in frequent perils, that we may never
return and all that, but the feeling that I am where I ought to
be is full compensation for all that is sinister, leaving me free
to enjoy it as if on a pleasure tour.

It speaks well for Hayes's manhood that he was able to look
on war as a picnic. Naturally a soldier, he would have learned
much of war if he had not spent his formative years in law, a
pursuit of a very different character. In camp for a long time
he served more as judge advocate in court martials than in
actual military operations.

The last of August, 1861, the regiment was ordered to Sut-
tonsville. With the Third Ohio, the Thirtieth Indiana, and
parts of other commands, the Twenty-third Ohio camped near
the head of Tygart's Valley at Cheat Mountain Pass. Condemned to leave comfortable quarters for the wild woods,
Hayes sacrificed his horse Webby to a footsore captain and
walked on ahead of the regiment. That night he kindled a fire
as best he could and warmed himself beside it without overcoat
or food.

Presently he joined Rosecrans, ridiculing a newspaper story
that the latter had been captured, for his regiment guarded the
general. Hayes was fond of Rosecrans and liked nothing better
than to be in attendance on him.

Finally there came the welcome news that three thousand of
the enemy were at hand. Battle! Hayes had the breathless feeling he was accustomed to at the beginning of an important case
in court; he laughed and chatted nervously with other officers,
waiting the order to go forward.

Told to take four companies and charge a hill, Hayes
snatched up his men and advanced through a cornfield to the

brow of a height overlooking the Gauley River, within less than a mile of the enemy's entrenchments. He was to hold the extreme left of the line at the beginning and was then to follow inspiration.

When Hayes's force reached the bottom of a thicketed hill, they mistook the rain and the river for the enemy. Crawling on hands and knees, the Unionists advanced toward a foe who did not respond. In the darkness the men began to fire blindly and hit friends, but there was no clash with the Confederates. In the morning a great shouting at the earthworks informed Hayes and his men that the enemy had fled, leaving tents, ammunition, even flags. Here was beginner's luck indeed; an adversary fleeing from the first battle. In truth, the Confederates had been in a false position, with a deep, rapid river at their backs, and they had retired just in time.

"The enemy are no match for us in fair fighting," Hayes gloated to Lucy in September. It had been but a scratch, for the Unionists had lost only thirteen killed and sixty wounded. The next day Hayes was assigned to another duty—to head off a company of recruits moving to join Governor Henry A. Wise, Confederate commander. Guerrillas hidden in the rocks made this experience more thrilling than the battle of the day before. It was strenuous campaigning; Hayes wrote that he had been in the saddle for nineteen hours of one day and had gone without sleep for thirty-six hours.

In September, 1861, he campaigned for some days along the Gauley and then, to his disrelish, was assigned a job as judge advocate. He much preferred to get away from law, become for the time nothing but a soldier, but his legal knowledge was more in demand than his military acquirements. As judge advocate Hayes went to General Cox's camp on Mount Sewell near Lewisburg, facing the Confederate position. He knew that the campaign was almost over, for the Unionists were too far from civilization and too near starving to hold on there. The unfortunate part, he lamented, was that the enemy might construe their departure as a retreat, which it assuredly was not. As it happened, both armies, being in the same boat, simultaneously gave up the hopeless task and withdrew.

Hayes expected to be sent to Kentucky, but the Twenty-third Ohio went into camp near Gauley Bridge on a turnpike leading to the White Sulphur Springs and so to eastern Virginia. Hayes himself proceeded to Rosecrans's headquarters at Camp Tompkins and resumed the practice of military law, trying twenty court-martial cases.

He himself was well pleased with his lot, declaring that the troops were "better fed, better clad and better sheltered than any other army in the world." Many of the men dressed better and lived better than at home. Of his superiors, however, he was critical. Lincoln, he commented, "is not perhaps all that we could wish, but he is honest, patriotic, cool-headed and safe. I don't know any man that the Nation could say under all circumstances is to be preferred in his place."

Hayes was not to spend the whole war in making presentations before court martials. Much to his satisfaction, his title of major and judge advocate were dropped for that of lieutenant-colonel and he was restored to the bosom of his beloved regiment. In November, 1861, he wrote his wife:

I am pleased as people in the army always are with my promotion. I confess to my weakness of preferring (as I must hereafter always be called by some title) to being called colonel to being styled major.

It is one of the engaging traits of Rutherford B. Hayes that he pleaded guilty to the charge of vanity. That is a virtue that most of us take some pains to conceal.

Hayes's regiment passed the winter sixteen miles from the

Kanawha River, a unit in a little army of fifteen thousand men kept to protect western Virginia from the designs of secessionists. Hayes himself was depressed at the prospect of continued inaction. He grumbled that it was a bore, that there was no danger except of starvation, a slow, tedious form of extinction. Where were the battles of yesteryear?

In the rough camp environment, Hayes admitted that he was reverting to the primitive. Since he had come to Virginia in July no razor had desecrated the beard that now hung in festoons around his face (it made him so lazy that he never shaved again, merely trimmed his whiskers); he never slept except with some of his clothes on and often booted and spurred; sometimes he slept on the bare ground, once in the snow; for months he had had no white collar or handkerchief or other white clothes. Because of this, he was hale and hearty. His kit was as follows: Portmanteau containing two pairs of socks, one shirt, a towel containing bread and sugar, a tin cup, a pistol in one holster and ammunition in the other, a blanket wrapped in India rubber, and a blue overcoat.

In September, Hayes had criticized the Southerners severely. Floyd's army, he declared, was made up of youngsters, genial and pleasant but lacking enterprize and endurance, or else of the scum, lazy and cowardly. The rebels told the negroes that the Yankees were going to sell them in Cuba to pay for the war. However, in saner moments it dawned on Hayes that the negroes were not the driven beasts of sun-weltered plantations as described in *Uncle Tom's Cabin*, but lazy, lovable dependents. "The negroes," he complained, "expect the North to set them free and see no need of risking their lives to gain what will be given them by others." He also discovered that the Confederates were "just like other folks." He showed kindness to prisoners, rescuing the young son of General Beckley from a crowded guardhouse and sharing his bed with the boy.

In February, 1862, Hayes went home for a brief visit. He came back, believing that the Confederacy was fatally wounded, and wholly enamored of war. Racing over the hills on horseback thrilled him. "Physical enjoyments like this are worth a war," he pronounced. It was a good world. McClellan would soon overthrow Johnston's army retreating from Manassas. After that, there would be only scattered parties of adversaries to disperse. The rebellion as a menace to the Union would be ended. It was the hour of optimism bred by Fort Donelson, the false dawn before the darkness.

At this time Hayes was in pleasant contact with the Beckley family. Mrs. Beckley came imploring that her husband, the general, might not be sent to Columbus, even if he had surrendered. Hayes found Beckley to be an agreeable sixty-year-old specimen of the Virginia colonel of the cartoon and stage type. However, when in April they all went off together, the only tears shed were feminine ones and they were poured for the Yankees themselves, who were "such fine men." "And we burned all their rails!" Hayes mused, dwelling on the strange amenities of war. These genial Virginia folk, who were kind to those so unfortunate as not to be born Beckleys or Tompkinses, exhibited a naïve vanity that was charming to plain Westerners. In October, after Hayes had held a court martial in one of the parlors of Colonel Tompkins's home, he confessed with twinkling eye, "I have profaned the sacred mansion and I hope that it will soon be converted into a hospital for our sick."

Now spring had come, and the Twenty-third Ohio once more took the field. Hayes was with the advance company that fell in with the enemy at Princeton. In twenty minutes the foe were put to flight at the expense of four men killed and seventeen wounded, before the rest of the regiment came up. Hayes talked to the wounded prisoners, "who seemed grateful for the kindness which I always gave them." He was kindly but he was also somewhat condescending.

But the Twenty-third Ohio was just under the enemy's guns and the enemy numbered three thousand. It was Hayes's task to take his command out of range, which he succeeded in doing. It was almost a miracle, he explained, and he was proud of the Twenty-third, of his horse, of himself. In this hour of danger he had experienced no fear or apprehension of death. He assured Lucy, "I still feel just as I told you, that I shall come safely out of the war."

In the early summer of 1862, Hayes was still confident that the end of the struggle was in sight. In six weeks they would stamp out the war in Virginia, and without that State the rest of the Confederacy would collapse. In July, rumors that Richmond had burned raised his hopes still higher; but these were soon mingled with tormenting reports that McClellan had been defeated. Hayes fretted at the idleness imposed on the troops in western Virginia. They made a few raids that were negligible in results, though these might have filled the newspaper columns of a more "literary regiment." Whether he had accomplished anything or not, Hayes grumbled, he had given two years to the cause, and two years were two years. That this was appreciated by the government, however, was evident when Rutherford Hayes was offered the colonelcy of the Seventy-ninth Ohio Regiment on July 23, 1862, an honor which he relished but finally declined because it would take him away from the beloved Twenty-third. He stuck by his regiment and in the end became its colonel.

Hayes was with the Twenty-third Ohio when that regiment was summoned to Washington in August, 1862. In the capital the men were fed, enjoyed applause for their drilling, felt flattered by their military sunburn. No raw recruits, these, but veterans. Later, the regiment defiled through Alexandria and found itself once more in Virginia but in a very different terrain. It was no longer a game to be played with half-armed, undrilled foes led by political generals; Lee, Jackson and Longstreet were in front, and there was nothing easy in the job that faced Pope. The regiment camped at Upton on August thirtieth, with the music of the cannon ringing in their ears. "There is one comfort here," Hayes commented. "If we suffer it is in the place where the decisive acts are going on."

It was a vivid pageant of war—the flags flashing from grassy hills; the white dome of the Capitol in the distance; the faraway boom of artillery; the long lines of wagons and ambulances; the hurrying columns of troops—it would have been delightful enough if only things had been going well with the Union, which they were not. Pope was having the worst of it, and assuredly the war would not be stamped out in Virginia in another six weeks.

Hayes was now querulous, affected by the change of scene from western Virginia, where all was serene confidence, to eastern Virginia, where all was doubt and confusion. He admitted the superiority of the Southern generals. Out of the fog of war Lee and Jackson towered, threatening Washington, the Union itself. As for the Union generals, when would they learn not to attack an adversary in a fortified position? Were all the generals whole-hearted? Was Tecumseh Sherman so when he said that he was "ashamed to acknowledge that he had a brother who was one of those damned black Republicans"?

Hayes, irritable, had a controversy with the dyspeptic Burnside. The general had gone off into a towering rage because soldiers had put straw on the ploughed ground they were to sleep on. It had not soothed him to hear that Hayes had acidly remarked, "I trust our generals will exhibit the same vigor in dealing with their foes that they do in their treatment of their

BATTLE OF SOUTH MOUNTAIN.   SEPT. 14, 1862

friends." The testy general demanded an explanation. Somewhat dismayed, the ever-diplomatic Hayes tried to win back the favor of his superior officer, for whom he had genuine admiration, but in vain. Burnside was not appeased.

Hayes presently saw the war from an entirely different angle; indeed the whole world did. Richmond was basking in self-complacent safety; Washington was in danger. Hayes discovered that the enemy had other advantages besides superior generals; to wit, superior cavalry, superior infantry, superior artillery. "We must have superior numbers to make success a sure thing," Hayes confessed.

By the middle of September the army had ebbed into Maryland, now invaded by the enemy. The Confederates (so far is reality from post-war romance) were pictured by Hayes as a horde of men, filthy and lousy, which perhaps they were, seeing that they had no kind government to issue them uniforms when needed but clad their patriotism gloriously in their rags. "Lee's Miserables" they later called themselves.

Now at last Hayes was cast into the cauldron of real war. He had hoped for this, longed for it, perchance prayed for it, for he had the true spirit of the fighting man. Out of it he came what he wished to be, a hero. He came out wounded, and even this may have been as he desired. Your real warrior enjoys his scars.

It was at South Mountain, September 14, 1862. McClellan had clasped a portion of Lee's army there, fought to devour it piecemeal before the remainder could intervene. Hayes was ordered to head the Twenty-third Ohio and capture a battery on a hill. He hesitated. "If I find six guns and a strong support?" he asked.

"Take them anyhow," Colonel Scammon snapped.

So Hayes went forward. Thinking to take the guns with one rush, the men halted only long enough to form and then ran up the hill. They were met by a storm of shot and shell and repulsed. Once more they formed and again rushed up the slope, this time driving the enemy away like a frightened swarm of insects.

Hayes had found glory at last. Just as he flung his line forward in the final, successful charge, a musket ball smashed his left arm below the elbow. He fell to the ground and lay there, weak and sick at stomach from loss of blood. A soldier bound a handkerchief around the wound, and Hayes's will asserted itself. He moaned out an order to an officer to bring a company up to face a threatened attack from another quarter.

The men began to fall back before the advancing enemy, and presently Hayes found himself sandwiched in between his command and the Confederates.

"Hallo!" he called out; "Twenty-third men, are you going to leave your colonel here for the enemy?"

Not those stout Ohioans. In spite of the near neighborhood of the Southerners, six of them ran to pick up Hayes.

"Oh, no!" they cried. "We will carry you wherever you want us to."

Their loitering was punished by a volley from the enemy, and it was left to Lieutenant Jackson to carry off the brave colonel, to give him a canteen of cool water and leave him for his brother-in-law, Doctor Joe Webb, to take to a near-by house.

Hayes did not know how severely he was injured and, while he lay on the field, confided a last message to his family to a wounded Confederate beside him. "We were quite jolly and friendly," Hayes related afterward. "It was by no means an unpleasant experience." Although hurt and badly shocked, Hayes's constitutional strength showed itself. After his wound had been dressed, he was able to walk half a mile to an ambulance.

Convalescence bored him greatly. Snatched from the struggle just when it was becoming thrilling, Hayes chafed at resting, was weary of being sick, tired of having nothing to do, hopeful that Lucy would come. Presently she came, and things were bettered by her soothing presence. Lucy was a real soldier's wife, at home in camp and hospital. She laughed with the wounded and turned her back to weep.

Lucy came to camp from time to time for long stays, bringing the children. One, born during the war, died there. She loved the soldiers and was loved by them for the many kindnesses she did them. When battle impended and she rode out of the danger zone, she cheered the marching men. Years afterward when she was in the White House, the regiment presented her with a gift in remembrance of the war days.

Hayes, after a short visit home, went to winter quarters, much cheered. He thought that things looked well for the North, that Morgan's raid into Ohio was the last spurt of a moribund cause. "Very queer," he assured his wife, "these last struggles of the Rebs. They are dying hard."

Hayes was again in the Virginia mountains, which in this year, 1863, became the state of West Virginia by a slight manipulation of the United States Constitution. Hayes was at home in West Virginia, where the Union cause was always ascendent; here he felt no doubts of ultimate success. In July, 1863, he sent out an expedition of two regiments to check Morgan the Raider. There was a fight at Gallipolis in which a few men were killed and forty wounded. Hayes thought the whole matter a joke and boasted that "The Rebs couldn't fight soldiers *very well* at all." Yet his promptness led to Morgan's defeat, and this was perhaps his most notable military exploit.

Presently he found himself under the command of one of the best officers of the war, George Crook, and was given Crook's first brigade of infantry, consisting of the Twenty-third Ohio, the Thirty-sixth Ohio, the Fifth Virginia (Union) and Thirteenth Virginia (Union) regiments. The brigade moved quickly from Fayetteville by Princeton and Poplar Hill to plunge into a small victory at Cloyd Mountain. A fort was stormed at the cheap price of twenty-five men killed and twice as many wounded.

In May, 1864, the brigade proceeded to New River bridge at Blacksburg through the Salt Sulphur Springs to Anderson's Ferry on the Greenbrier River. Here was glorious country—a land made for peace and laziness and laughter, heaped with fir-topped mountains, sprayed by chilly springs, perfumed with the fragrance of pale pink rhododendron. Hayes decided that when the guns had ceased to bark and the appetite for blood had been satisfied, he would bring Lucy here for another honeymoon. It is thus that men long for peace in war, as in peace the remembrance of war is alluring.

Hayes was in the valley of Virginia during the campaign of 1864. At times his partizanship was assailed by misgivings; the burning of the Virginia Military Institute did not please him. He deplored the casting out of Governor Letcher's family from their home on ten minutes' notice. The war, like all wars that last long, was becoming more and more barbarous. Hayes did not think that devastation was necessary. He reproved Lucy for speaking of "brutal Rebels," since there were brutes enough in the Yankee ranks just as there were humane Rebels. His sense of justice could not be obscured, and besides he felt that the end was in sight. "Whip what is now in the field," he declared, "and the game is ended."

On July 8, Hayes was ordered to Parkersburg and eastward, going to Martinsburg and spending a week with his family at Chillicothe before proceeding to camp near Sharpsburg, Maryland. Here the tide of destruction was gathering, ready to turn

the beautiful Valley of Virginia into a gutter. But Early was
there and defeated the devastators in battle near Winchester.
Hayes's brigade fell back to the Potomac. They went into camp
in Maryland, having had their full share of campaigning, having marched a thousand miles besides traveling by train, and
having taken part in five battles, not to mention such small
matters as skirmishes.

Hayes's military reputation was rising, even if he was a
minor figure, and politics now began to intrude on the war
field; he was being mentioned for the House of Representatives. He felt, however, that the hour had not yet arrived for
that. On July 30, 1864, he wrote Uncle Sardis:

As for the candidacy for Congress I care nothing about it,
neither for the nomination nor for the election. It was merely
easier to let the thing take its own course than to get up a letter
declining to run, and then to explain it to everybody who might
choose to bore me about it.

He thought well of McClellan as a soldier and a presidential candidate, and did not dread his election, believing that in
any event the war would go on as before. He was provoked
when the children prattled slanderously of McClellan, holding
that a brave soldier should not be judged by the company he
kept.

As to his own political aspirations, he wrote his famous renunciation letter, which was of much subsequent value, on
August 24, 1864:

Camp of Sheridan's Army, August 24, 1864.
FRIEND SMITH:—Your favor of the 7th came to hand on Monday, it was the first I had heard of the doings of the Second
District Convention. My thanks for your attention and assistance in the premises. I cared very little about being a candidate, but having consented to the use of my name I preferred

to succeed. Your suggestion about getting a furlough to take the stump was certainly made without reflection.

An officer fit for duty who at this crisis would abandon his post to electioneer for a seat in Congress ought to be scalped. You may feel perfectly sure I shall do no such thing.

We are, and for two weeks have been, in the immediate presence of a large Rebel army. We have skirmishing and small affairs constantly. I am not posted in the policy deemed wise at headquarters and I can't guess as to the prospects of a general engagement. The condition and spirit of this army are good and improving. I suspect the enemy is sliding around us towards the Potomac. If they cross we shall pretty certainly have a meeting.

Sincerely,

R. B. HAYES.

Wm. H. Smith, Esq.
Cincinnati, Ohio.

This was one of the most astute letters ever written. There can be little doubt that his patriotism was ardent, but to his shrewd mind it was evident that political rewards would come in time to soldiers who did their duty to the last. He was reconciled to waiting, especially as he was enjoying the war.

Sherman's terrible march through Georgia did not repel him; he thought that this vandalism was a "glorious course." With good judgment, he pronounced, "That is the best army in the world. Lee's army is next."

Sheridan's men had little reason to envy other destroyers, for the great cavalryman was outdoing Sherman in the Shenandoah Valley, cutting down crops, burning mills and private houses, leaving nothing but desolation. He exulted that a crow could not fly down the Valley without carrying its rations.

And now it was September, 1864, and fate was drawing close to the doomed Early, who with a small, badly equipped force was bravely opposing Sheridan's three-times larger array. Sheridan was assisted by men who are little known but who stand among the best soldiers America has ever produced,

Crook and Marcus Wright. Early was beaten on September 19 at Winchester and again a few days later. Hayes, with much truth, attributed the result to Crook, one of the ablest tacticians in the whole Union army. Hayes was in the thick of it at Winchester on September 19. He wrote:

My brigade led the attack on the left but all parts of Crook's command did their duty.

Hayes's flags were the first to enter Winchester. His men had crept within a hundred yards of the enemy, then plunged forward in the face of the furious Confederate fire until they found themselves in the protection of a deep, marshy ravine. Hayes's horse was mired and he had to abandon it and crawl ahead on all fours. The men struggled through the swampy stream and gained firm ground, to flank the Southern position. They advanced from three to five hundred yards in the teeth of a hot fire, driving the enemy before them. Hayes was bewildered by the swiftly moving drama, rather justifying Tolstoy's contention that battles soon get beyond the leader's control. After Crook was wounded, the command of his division fell upon Hayes, who did well in a position of much more responsibility than he was accustomed to.

At Fisher's Hill, some days later, Crook planned to turn the Confederate left, defying the advice of his colleagues and winning his point. Once more Hayes was in the thick of the fighting. "My division led again," he wrote Uncle Sardis. He thought well of Sheridan but declared that "Crook is the brains of the army."

Hayes was at Cedar Creek, the most remarkable battle of the Civil War. It seems among the deeds of romance rather than of verity that Early with his shattered force, slightly reinforced, should attack Sheridan's vastly larger army, flushed with victory, and almost win a glorious triumph.

Crook, for once, was completely beaten; the Confederates surged forward victoriously, capturing fifteen hundred prisoners. For a time it appeared that Sheridan's whole army would be routed. But the Confederates stayed their advance, giving Wright a chance to rally the infantry, and by afternoon the tide of battle turned. Sheridan helped by his famous ride, for his magnetic personality inspired the men. The battle closed with Early in retreat, having lost thousands of his troops.

Hayes had wisely deprecated political agitation in such times. His letter gained him more votes than a thousand speeches. Ohio was touched by the picture of the good soldier who refused to come home to run for Congress. The result was that, on October 17, 1864, Hayes's election to Congress by a majority of twenty-four hundred was reported. Patriotism was thus solidly rewarded.

Hayes continued with the army as a congressman-elect but acting colonel. After the battle of Cedar Creek, however, he looked on the war as practically ended. His health was excellent, his bones unbroken, though he had had some narrow escapes. Once his fine black horse was shot under him and tumbled head over heels to the earth, throwing the rider heavily. On another occasion Hayes was struck by a spent bullet. "I was hit fairly on the head," he explained humorously, "by a ball which had lost its force in getting, I suppose, through somebody else's."

From Cedar Creek to the end of the war, Hayes was mostly in garrison. On November 8, 1864, in company with Sheridan and Crook he marched docilely to the polls to vote for Lincoln. The whole army was marched to the polls, most of it to vote for Lincoln, by which means his reëlection was assured. Of Crook, Hayes was so fond that he named a son for him, the one who came to take the place of the lost infant, Joe.

There is no doubt that the influence of such men as Sheridan and Crook had much weight in securing a commission of brigadier-general for Rutherford B. Hayes, which was dated from the battle of Cedar Creek, October 19, 1864. He was not unduly elated at the somewhat tardy promotion. "I know full well that the honor has been conferred on all sorts of small people and so cheapened shamefully," he commented. He preferred being a good colonel to being an indifferent brigadier.

January 1, 1865, Hayes went into winter quarters near Cumberland, Maryland. He was delayed there on account of the confused state of affairs due to the absence of Sheridan, who had gone off with all the cavalry to destroy the railroads to Richmond. The war still lingered, chiefly because the mud and water of Virginia were the most faithful guardians of the Confederacy in this final hour; until a touch of spring came extended operations were impossible.

Hayes strongly desired to go to Washington. The war was nearly over, he was a congressman-elect, and the new field of action drew him. Besides he desired to witness Lincoln's second inauguration. He wished Lucy to go with him there. She would not have to dress up because "we are such little people that we can go strictly incog." It turned out, however, to be a good thing that Lucy did not go, because of the disgraceful weather and Andrew Johnson's no less disgraceful conduct. The country was treated to the new experience of a drunken inauguration speech; it would have been funny if it had not been sad. Hayes was glad that Lucy was not in Washington to be shocked by the intoxicated Vice-President. What a touch of the gallantry of the sixties!

It was now quite time for the audience to think of putting on their hats. There was nothing left for Lee to do but evacuate Richmond, which meant, of course, the fall of the curtain on the great drama. The victory clamor was hushed by the report of Booth's pistol. "Such a loss to the country!" sighed

Hayes. How would they get along without Lincoln—Lincoln who had got them where they were? Must Lincoln be given up for Johnson in the raw infancy of reconstruction? At all events Lincoln's place in history was safe; destiny had attended to that.

The war was over, and perhaps Rutherford B. Hayes regretted it. He was a true Nordic and fighting came naturally to him. He had enjoyed the war, which had brought him into prominence and taken him to Congress. He had spent four profitable years. He went home. "I intend to quit public life as soon as my term in Congress ends," he said. But he did not. Such men seldom do.

THE event of their lives was over for thousands of men, condemned henceforth to routine work and reminiscence. They would talk about it interminably at street corners, courthouse steps, lodge rooms, wherever men congregate and, later on, they would draw pensions on the strength of it. Hayes, on the whole, was satisfied with himself. He had won the name of a good soldier and had emerged from the war a brevet major-general and congressman-elect. His military title pleased him. When his knees became stiff with rheumatism, when his waist should be expanded by state dinners, it would be flattering, rejuvenating to be addressed as "General." Of all human titles, next to king this is the most tickling.

Early in June, 1865, Hayes resigned his beloved commission and went back to Cincinnati, parceling his time between his new activities as a congressman and his old, familiar duty of supporting a Republican candidate for office. This time he spoke for a former commander, General J. D. Cox, who was running for governor of Ohio on his military record. Hayes spoke for Cox at Marysville, at Grant's old home (which, after having looked on Grant as a kind of tramp, now felt honored at being his sometime home) and at other places. However, his pen loafed, his diary sank in dust, and epistolary spurts were few and frail. Perhaps Hayes was tired. This readapting one's self to work after a prolonged picnic has its difficulties.

Hayes's house at Fremont was rented until autumn. He spent some time in Chillicothe with his wife and children; in Fremont with Uncle Sardis, who was vastly pleased with him; in Delaware with his mother; in Columbus with his favorite niece, Laura Mitchell. Everywhere the chickens were slain to do honor to the returned warrior. Hayes finally established himself in Cincinnati in the law office of Stephenson and Noyes, in July, 1865, but not until he had consulted Uncle Sardis about his career, his family, his funds. Uncle Sardis was still the *deus ex machina.*

On November 30, 1865, Hayes came into the House of Representatives for the Second District of Ohio. He was a soldier honored by grateful constituents—of course, somewhat against his wishes. In the sixties it was still considered immodest for an office seeker to prowl abroad for his prey. If the office seeker practiced the demure artifices of a young girl decoying a beau, the office would usually seek him out. Hayes had been interested in politics from babyhood, thought politics, dreamed politics. Politics were the breath of life to him. He could repeat Webster's speeches verbatim. And now, at last, he held a place of some importance.

He was the child of luck. His timely Republicanism had given him the office of city solicitor of Cincinnati. His publicity as colonel of the Twenty-third Ohio Regiment had made him. When he was put up for Congress, he had no need to do anything at all. His banners strung across the streets of Cincinnati screamed: "Hayes is stumping the Shenandoah Valley. No humbug nor buncombe about our candidate." How could patriots resist such an appeal? Hayes's opponent was Joseph C. Butler, a banker, a capitalist, a most respectable citizen; but what chance had he against the military hero? It is true that the Democrats exhibited a picture representing Hayes as fleeing from rebel bullets, but this was a crass libel and fooled nobody.

Hayes entered Congress in one of its most interesting hours. The large Republican majority, exasperated by the long war and the assassination of Lincoln, clamored for revenge on the

South. The madman, Thaddeus Stevens, was the chairman of this inferno. A man so tolerant and sane as Hayes was here out of place, and he knew it. But he took care to say little. He did not like the policy of vengeance, but he realized that he could do nothing to check it and he had no intention of offering himself a sacrifice on the altar of reconciliation; he was not in the least a martyr, lacking convictions in the first place and possessing the instinct of self-preservation in the second.

The Southern States, under President Johnson's plan of Reconstruction, had elected members of Congress, and these congressmen-elect appeared, dubious but hopeful, in Washington at the beginning of the session. The Republicans were righteously indignant that late rebels should have the impudence to present themselves as members of the Congress of the United States without having been fumigated or purged in any way of the sin of rebellion, prodigals coming quite unrepentant and as if nothing unpleasant had happened since their States had last been represented in these halls. And it must be admitted that Johnson's methods were precipitate and tactless, though he was inspired by the patriotic and honorable motive of wishing to end the war now that military operations had closed. But wars seldom end for years after they have officially terminated.

A caucus of Republican members met; Hayes was present. "We agreed," he said, "to oppose the admission of any delegates from the Rebel states for the present." Already the Republicans were thinking of voting the semi-savage negroes *en masse*, for the Southern States presented a puzzling problem. Since the slaves were now free they counted as a whole man per head instead of three-fifths of a man, as formerly. In other words, freeing the slaves had merely accomplished the feat of increasing the number of members from the South in the House of Representatives. It was thus necessary to find some means of securing true and loyal Republican congressmen from the South instead of unpatriotic Democrats, or else the war would actually have strengthened the Democratic party. Besides, had not all Republicans proclaimed the equality of races? The Republican party might be saved by instituting manhood suffrage. In that case, if the liberated negroes had any sense of gratitude, several or all of the Southern States would be Republican. Humanitarianism would be justified of her children.

never!

In the caucus manhood suffrage was demanded by General Schenck, a confirmed hater of the South. It is significant that Hayes, modestly and quietly, sought to tone down the naked ferocity of Schenck's suggestion by offering an amendment proposing an educational test for voting. As hardly more than one negro in a hundred could read, his suggestion would have made the ex-slave in the South negligible for the time and yet would have opened the way for his eventual participation in politics when better prepared for such privileges. It is a pity that hate and partizan advantage as well as ignorance overrode Hayes, a pity for the South, much more a pity for the negro, for, if ever anyone was destroyed by his friends, the Southern black was by the Republicans. Hayes saw that moderation was impossible and he ceased to oppose the torrent of folly, which he could not dam but which might overwhelm him. He capitulated and at a later date not only accepted the Fifteenth Amendment, but aided in ramming it down the throat of Ohio.

The determination of the Republicans to force universal negro suffrage on the South, partly by way of punishment, more out of a desire to do justice to the blacks, brought the majority in Congress into conflict with Andrew Johnson, who now received the support of the Democrats. Johnson had been elected on the ticket with Lincoln, but he was a Democrat and had never pretended to be anything else. Egalitarian as he was in all his instincts, the lifelong foe of "aristocracy," he was appalled at the prospect of having great States come under the rule of ex-slaves, many of whom were still little less than savages and some of whom were but two or three generations removed from cannibalism. As a man of sense familiar with the South, this seemed to him to be sheer madness. If it had succeeded, instead of the strong, prosperous industrial South of today, there might be along the Gulf of Mexico a very different land. Forgetting his injuries and his animosities, Johnson strove to save the South, and in proportion as he labored Congress sought to destroy the South—at least the old South. Of course, it had some utopian dream of a new South, all perfect justice and equality, where a majority of the voters would be Republicans.

In this Congress, and the succeeding one, Rutherford B. Hayes sat, brooding, almost inarticulate. Out of place in the furious medley of passions which he did not himself share, unambitious to rival the orators who spouted day after day, he voted but did not speak. He always voted with his party, and for its worse measures, but his inactivity was his way of washing his hands.

What he did that was positive was mainly in the cause of culture; it was a pleasure to him to be able to do something that was not tarred with animosity. His chief committee assignment was as chairman of the Library Committee, an appointment entirely to his taste. In that quiet work he could do his bit for civilization while the herd about him raged and stormed. "While this is one of the no-account committees in a public sense," Hayes wrote, "it has some private interest." The committee, composed of gentlemen and scholars, brought Hayes into the gentle company of the bookish. In that bedlam that was Congress in 1865–1867, the Library Committee was a solace and a relief.

Hayes procured the passage in the House of Representatives of the Senate bill shifting the Smithsonian Institution's books to the Library of Congress. This may almost be said to have been the beginning of the Library of Congress. Hayes also opened the library to larger classes of readers, for at that time it was almost exclusively for congressmen. He moreover carried through an appropriation of one hundred thousand dollars to buy Peter Force's invaluable collection of Americana, one of the best investments ever made by the government. He also developed the botanical gardens, which at that time were a charge of the Library Committee.

All his life, Rutherford B. Hayes was politically wise, and he was never wiser than in his course in Congress. He did nothing to alienate his party, but at the same time he said nothing to win the hatred of the South; his silence may be said to have been platinous, for it was more valuable than gold. It did much to make him President of the United States.

A practical politician if there ever was one, Hayes let the orators talk while he worked inconspicuously but fruitfully. His specialty was in adjusting war claims of Ohio citizens; at one time he had seven hundred of these on his hands. He spent his time running to the departments and answering letters from soldiers. His time could not have been put to better use. He secured the payment of soldier bounties and pensions for many a humble Ohioan and gained the invaluable reputation of being the soldier's friend.

Not that Hayes was wholly self-seeking in all this. He was a man of kindly nature who sympathized with the woes of soldiers; and in those years there were many soldiers suffering from inabilities incurred in the war or imbued with a chronic distaste for labor gained in the free-and-easy life of the army. While he looked out for these unfortunates, he made himself politically in thus working for others.

Ohio could not spare her Samuel long to linger in the national temple at Washington. From time to time rumors that he was desired for governor had reached Hayes. This was quite acceptable news, though he wrote to his mentor, William Henry Smith, that he was dubious of the propriety of accepting such an office as long as he was under obligations to Hamilton County. This was fumbling for a loophole. Hayes confided to Uncle Sardis, in February, 1867, that he did not particularly enjoy Washington. "I have no ambition for congressional reputation and influence," he said, "not a particle. . . . If the nomination is pretty likely, it would get me out of this scrape, and after that I am out of political life decently." Once more he was retiring from politics. Only he didn't.

In truth Washington life did not make much appeal to the Hayeses. Perhaps they preferred to be larger figures on a smaller stage; perhaps they were victims of nostalgia; perhaps the series of losses in the home circle drew them back to Ohio. In May, 1867, little George Crook died; in September, Grandmother Webb; in November, Grandmother Hayes.

As usual Hayes got what he wanted. A tide of letters, and particularly the news that his regiment desired him for governor, removed his coy objections. The nomination came to him in June, 1867. His resignation from Congress was to take effect at the adjournment.

In reaching this goal the hurdles had not been high. Governor Cox had satisfied his appetite for office and was not a success as governor. The pestilential Democrats were raising their heads again and a vote-getter was needed by the Republican party. Rutherford Hayes embodied the proper combination of military record and peaceful ambition. More especially, he was popular with the soldiers, many of whom enjoyed bounties or pensions obtained through his efforts. It was felt that he was the man to carry Ohio for the righteous cause.

In his Democratic opponent, Allen G. Thurman, however,

Hayes faced a real man, one of the best men indeed that Ohio ever knew. Things were tending to go back to normal, and normally at that time Ohio was a Democratic State. In those days the majority of the best people were Democrats—the staid, solid, churchgoing people. Sane men, too, were becoming alarmed by the violence of the Republican majority in Congress; commonplace people were a little bored by the eternal, "Rally 'round the flag, boys!" They thought it was time for the war to be over. Appomattox was receding into the past.

Thurman was a better speaker than Hayes, knowing more and having more to say. In that garrulous campaign of 1867 he delivered seventy-one speeches. But Hayes had learned that it is necessary for a candidate in a close and uncertain campaign to talk, and he talked and talked. He talked as much in the Ohio towns as he had kept silent in Congress, delivering eighty-one speeches and finally wearing out Thurman. By dint of hard effort and endless practice, Hayes had become a fairly effective public speaker, having lost his dread of audiences and a certain unreadiness that had once handicapped him; but he never shone as an orator.

Manhood suffrage was one of the issues of that campaign. Congress was endeavoring to force universal suffrage (without any restrictions whatever) on the unfortunate South, though Ohio and most of the other Northern States had limited suffrage. Was it not consistent, then, for Ohio to throw open its elections to all male beings, twenty-one years old and over, who had never been convicted of crime? Hayes thought so; Thurman thought not. They debated, but reason lost. That prime curse of democracy, manhood suffrage, was not to be escaped. Hayes rang the changes on all the fallacies of the day, speaking such nonsense as "Color ought to have no more to do with voting than size," as if he actually believed it. But he had to say this; every Republican had to say it. It was the slogan of the day.

Hayes indeed talked negro suffrage to such an extent that he overdid it and gave his opponent an opening that the latter stupidly ignored. Had Thurman ceased talking about states' rights, for which nobody cared, and discussed equal suffrage and the Fourteenth Amendment to the Constitution, to which many people were still opposed, he might have snatched victory from Hayes and the Union army. As it was, the Union army elected Hayes by three thousand majority while the amendment to the state constitution was snowed under by fifty thousand. The legislature was Democratic and sent Thurman to the Senate.

Elated, Hayes sat down to compose his maiden inaugural address. It was to be a dwarf speech, the shortest ever delivered in Ohio. However, it carried three ideas: a compliment to General Cox; a courageous piece of advice against too much legislation; an urge for equal—that is, negro suffrage. As an afterthought he added a plea for Ohio to support the Fourteenth Amendment in spite of the repealers. Hayes sent the speech to Sardis Birchard to look over. It was probably the happiest task of the old man's life. He would not live until 1876.

The speech, however, as delivered contained additional thoughts. Hayes called the attention of the people to the fact that the state was the type of the nation, implying that the gubernatorial chair was a step toward the White House. Already, he was dreaming of that of which all American politicians dream to the end.

The people of Ohio were pleased with the new governor's concern for the treatment of convicts in prison, then unquestionably bad enough, and for the needs of the widows and orphans of soldiers. Hayes had made a good start.

The Democratic legislature was not in accord with Governor Hayes. It tried to recall the action of the previous legislature in ratifying the Fourteenth Amendment and sought to prevent negroes from voting in Ohio. At this time negro suffrage for the South was much more popular in the North than negro suffrage for the North.

The presidential election of 1868 shortly ensued. Hayes, who had become a vigorous bloody-shirt waver in the Ohio election of the previous year, continued to bewail an endangered Union. For the Republicans there could be but one possible nominee, Grant, since they counted on the soldier vote to keep them in power. In fact, the country had been really under military government since 1861, and under Grant that convenient method of administering affairs would continue.

The Democrats nominated the excellent Horatio Seymour, former governor of New York. It is to the credit—or discredit, if you will have it so—of New York that it is the most tolerant city in the nation. Even in the crisis of the Civil War it never attained that intensity of sectional hatred that characterized other Northern communities. It supported the Union faithfully, but it could not see why every personal right and every constitutional guarantee should be sacrificed on the altar of Mars. In his difficult position Seymour had acquitted himself well, doing his duty but refusing to let himself be bullied by the military. For this stand, and the still greater wrong of advocating mercy for the stricken South, he was denounced by Republican orators throughout the country, among them Hayes. Seymour accepted the presidential nomination under sufferance, realizing that he had little chance of election, but he did what he could for his party. He was one of those fair-minded and patriotic Northerners who, if they could have elected Douglas in 1860, might have prevented the Civil War and who, failing in this, did what they could to mitigate its evils and lighten its consequences. In regard to the office of President, Seymour was infinitely better equipped than Grant, but naturally the great general, the idol of the army, was elected by a considerable majority. Grant would have richly deserved the election if he had been capable of properly performing the functions of the office; but, as he was not, his elevation to the presidency was in the nature of a calamity.

The presidential election was over at last, and Hayes had time to devote to his duties as governor. The little that he did was good. He urged on the legislature a geologic survey and a proper registration of voters in order to prevent frauds and injustice. At that time registration requirements were almost non-existent in the United States, with the result that furious disputes took place at the polls when voters were challenged for one reason or another. Hayes also gave attention to the financial condition of the State, disregarded by the soldiers who had preceded him in office.

He had not accomplished a great deal in his short term as governor when, in 1869, another gubernatorial election came up. But he had supported Grant warmly the year before and the soldiers were more solidly behind him than ever. Besides, he was popular with the people generally, being regarded as a gubernatorial improvement. This time Hayes, against weakened resistance, carried the doubtful State of Ohio by 7,500 votes. It was a personal triumph and marked his emergence as a national figure. The feature of the campaign was the Fifteenth Amendment to the United States Constitution, which was enthusiastically supported by the Republican party, although it was one of the worst measures ever passed by Congress. The Fifteenth Amendment sought to place the negro in the South beyond the reach of State laws, entrench him forever in power. Hayes had little sympathy with this policy, intended both for revenge and to secure the permanent ascendency of the Re-

publican party in the South as well as to safeguard the ex-
slaves; but he was too wise to oppose it, since if he had done
so the Republican party would have promptly thrown him over.
In this election the Republicans had the soldier vote lined up
so solidly that they knew two weeks in advance just what
Hayes's majority would be.

Hayes found his inspiration for his 1870 inaugural in church
where, in lieu of any interest in religious ceremonies, he often
thought out his problems. In addition to urging the legislature
to adopt the Fifteenth Amendment and see that all negroes in
Ohio were privileged to vote as well as all disabled and indigent soldiers, Hayes wisely opposed increases in municipal
debt and taxation and suggested that statutory limitations should
be placed on them. He thus stands as one of the first public
men to protest against the orgies of waste that then distinguished
municipal government in the United States. Furthermore, he
asked for better provision for prisoners and the insane and
urged the foundation of an agricultural college. Later Hayes
pointed out that State taxes in a decade had increased 33
per cent, and local taxes 170 per cent. It was surely time to
call a halt.

Hayes was also one of those public men who viewed with
alarm the abuses of railroad administration, in those days so
marked. Rates, rebates, stock watering were then in their lusty
prime. In general, his administration was characterized by a
mastery of the problems of the day and a unique spirit of
opposition to the extravagance and graft with which American
government in that age was saturated.

If he was partizan in his attitude on the unhappy Fifteenth
Amendment, designed to place the Southern Anglo-Saxons at
the mercy of Africans, he was not in the least narrow in his
administration of affairs. He appointed Democrats on commissions and resolutely refused to oust a Democratic State

RUTHERFORD B. HAYES, 1869
While Governor of Ohio, 1868-1872

librarian who had given satisfaction in order to make a place for a hungry Republican office seeker. In that partizan age, this liberality was a revelation.

Always interested in scientific advance, Hayes secured a provision for a geologic survey of Ohio and selected for the work one of the best geologists of the country, at a time when such appointments were usually nothing but political "jobs." He also greatly encouraged the study of the history of Ohio, securing many important documents dealing with the early period. History was always a delight to him; he looked forward to an old age of historical research.

Hayes was making a growing reputation as an administrator, but at first his fame was local. In his second term as governor he had a chance to bring himself before the country and secure a measure of that newspaper publicity which is the breath of life to modern public men. His address at the Exposition for Textile Fabrics at Cincinnati, in 1869, was widely published.

He could have had a third gubernatorial nomination in 1871, as his popularity at this moment was great. But it would have violated the two-term tradition of the State, and besides Hayes had won about as much prestige as he could expect to gain as governor of Ohio. Moreover, he was far from rich and his private affairs needed attention.

His services to Ohio in the period 1867–1871 were important. Already on a small stage he showed the devotion to civil service reform, resumption of specie payments, and debt reduction that was to mark his administration as President. In his term in office the State debt was reduced by a fifth. Every year about five millions of dollars of taxes were harvested for the support of the government, for Hayes was a firm adherent of the "pay-as-you-go" system. There was about him a metallic method, a hardheadedness and economy anticipatory of Coolidge, whom he resembled not a little. To the people of Ohio, accustomed to war governors, soldier governors, uncivilian governors, this governor who spoke the language of the tribe, who could talk at need of the glories of 1861–1865 and defend the Fifteenth Amendment, and yet who was essentially civilian and business-like, was a happy change.

Some of the things he did were in advance of his crude age. The Ohio board of charities was, in reality, his creation and his dependent. When his term as governor expired it collapsed, only to be revived again when he became governor again. The Ohio Soldiers' and Sailors' Orphan Home at Xenia was his child. This was in part a needed reform, in part another bid for soldier votes, so sedulously cultivated by pension services.

Hayes struggled against the evil of election frauds, even urging the representation of minorities on election boards. He also carried the principle of minority representation into the appointments of members of public boards and commissions, a new idea in that age of party fanaticism.

All in all, Rutherford Hayes made an excellent governor and could have had a third term if he had wished it. At this time he expected to leave public life, but he found that it was quite impossible. Fate beckoned to him.

With Hayes out of the way, the Republicans nominated an ordinary politician, General Edward F. Noyes, who defeated the Democratic nominee, Colonel George W. McCook, by a majority of 20,000. In that period few men without military titles had any hope of securing office; it was the cue of the Democrats to nominate distinguished officers in the hope of taking a part of the soldier vote from the Republicans, for it was the soldier vote that determined matters then; united, it kept the Republicans in power; divided, it gave the Democrats their chance. In 1871, Hayes' success as governor and his personal popularity, in addition to the Fifteenth Amendment (which was fatuously supposed to have ended the Civil War instead of reopening it, as was the case) swept Ohio for the Republicans. Hayes took the stump for Noyes in this campaign and spoke effectively; it makes little difference that nearly everything he said in regard to party politics was wrong. The congressional measures he praised, instead of healing the wounds of the war, had profoundly inflamed them, and conditions in the Lower South were going from bad to worse. Consequently, Hayes's facile optimism, his typical American confidence in the power of curing any disorder by legislation, made him seem shallower than he was, for he did not actually believe in all this; he was merely a practical politician. Sometimes he spoke better than he knew, as when he said on August 24, 1871:

Hitherto Democracy has taught that, as a question of law the amendments were made by force and fraud, and are therefore void; that, as a question of principles, this is a white man's government, and that to confer suffrage on the colored races—on the African or Chinaman—would change the nature of the government and speedily destroy it.

The Democratic contention was true enough. Nothing, indeed, is clearer in American history than the fallacy on which the Fifteenth Amendment rests—that race makes no real difference in politics. It makes every difference, since in communities where races that do not mingle are nearly equal in numbers race becomes the sole party test. Hayes never appeared worse than in his advocacy of the measures designed to secure the negroes of the South in power. Insincere, not believing in such a policy, he upheld it because he saw that the mass of the people, swayed by propaganda, were determined to have it—at the time. Only a year later popular opinion had changed.

His political acumen, however, was never better illustrated than by an occurrence that took place early in 1872, not long after his gubernatorial term ran out. John Sherman was before the Ohio legislature for reëlection to the Senate and the Republicans were in control. But the cold-blooded Sherman was anything but popular with his fellow Republicans, some of whom were looking about for a rival candidate. Hayes was approached. A coalition between the disgruntled Republicans and the Democratic minority would bring about his election in Sherman's place.

Hayes was too shrewd to consider the proposal for a moment. He knew that a success won at the expense of party regularity always rebounds on the heads of those who win it. He knew that he could be a senator for one term, but that his political life would then end. On January 4, 1872, he published in the *Ohio State Journal* an editorial declaring that he was not a candidate. Even after this, politicians besought him to oppose the unpopular Sherman, but Hayes continued to refuse. Sherman was reëlected senator, but, by his self-restraint and shrewdness, Hayes had won something better—the presidency. He became known as a good party man, a man to be relied on. This reputation stood him in good stead when the Republicans, in 1876, desperately sought a winning candidate. And John Sherman, who could easily have blocked Hayes's nomination, remembering his fair dealing, gave him support instead of hostility.

There can be no doubt that Hayes desired to withdraw from politics, at least for a season. He was tired and in need of money and wished to take stock of things. But politics cannot be given up when one so desires unless one expects to make a final renunciation. It thus followed that Hayes, intent on retiring for a season to Fremont, which he had decided on for his home, found that inaction was impossible.

The presidential election of 1872 was coming on, and the sky was cloudy. Grant, acclaimed as the nation's hero four years before, and wafted into the White House by a great wave of feeling, had not renewed the glories of Vicksburg and Appomattox in the presidential chair. In fact, he had been a failure as chief executive, and the nation was aware that while he might be first in war he was not first in peace and was in some danger of not being any longer first in the hearts of his countrymen. Yet the Republicans had to renominate him, much as they grimaced at the idea, for the army still controlled politics, and the army was still for Grant.

The Democrats in 1872 were pessimistic, since they had no striking candidate to offer in opposition to Grant. Certain to be accused of "rebellion," no matter what they did, the Democrats waited on the dissatisfaction that was ripening in the Republican ranks and in the country at large at the corrupt and inefficient government of Grant. The Liberal Republicans, who were tired of army rule, bloody-shirt waving, and corruption, held a convention in Cincinnati the first of May. David Davis, one of the leading independents in the country, seemed a possible nominee. Charles Francis Adams, the famous minister to England in the Civil War, was another candidate for the Liberal Republican nomination. Carl Schurz was the mentor of the general movement. Hayes watched the proceedings with interest and sympathy. In reality, he was a Liberal Republican himself, but entirely too good a party man and too wise a politician to desert the regular Republicans on the eve of another victory.

The aims of the Liberal Republicans were wise and patriotic: civil service reform, reduction of protective duties, and withdrawal of the troops from the Southern States. Curiously enough, this platform was destined to be adopted by Hayes almost in entirety when he came into power, though he opposed it now. Stanley Matthews, one of Hayes's closest friends, was chairman of this convention. Matthews gave the note when he said: "As the war has ended, so ought military rule and military principles."

At this time there was little hope of reform. The army, under the leadership of a congressional oligarchy, ruled the country and the army was still bent on punishing "rebellion." In the face of its solidarity, probably no candidate could have been elected by the Liberals or Democrats. The Liberal Republicans, however, made a poor choice, nominating Horace Greeley, the great editor, a confirmed Republican, a lifelong opponent of the South, and a protectionist of extreme views. The two leading candidates were Charles Francis Adams and David Davis. Greeley was a third choice, brought forward when the supporters of Adams and Davis had, more or less, deadlocked. The Democrats endorsed Greeley's nomination, but to the rank and file of the party Grant was as acceptable as the editor of the New York *Tribune*. The Liberal Republicans, who were free traders, felt no enthusiasm for Greeley, the ultra protectionist. In fact nobody felt any enthusiasm for Greeley, who would never have been nominated if certain politicians had not obtained control of the convention.

Taking the contest to be a struggle between two parties and not the simulacrum it actually was, the country began to stir with excitement in the autumn of 1872. The hollow presidential elections of 1864 and 1868, decided by the army, had whetted the appetite of the people for a contest and they tried hard to believe in the reality of the election of 1872. Indeed, if the Democrats had possessed a great leader it might have been real.

Astute politician that he was, Rutherford Hayes found himself a delegate to the Republican convention at Philadelphia that renominated Grant. His growing prominence in the party councils was shown by his appointment to the platform committee. He was becoming an insider. In Philadelphia, with flags waving and bands playing, it was found possible to revive enthusiasm for the considerably discredited Grant. The politicians went home much comforted.

At home things were not so satisfactory. People who desired decent government and were sick of the war wanted a civilian candidate and showed, at one time, a tendency to turn to Greeley, who enjoyed the distinction of not having been a soldier in an age when every sheriff and constable had been at least a corporal in the home guards. These dissenters gave a certain measure of concern to the faithful, among them Hayes.

Hayes, expecting to take the stump for Grant as a party duty, did not desire another nomination to Congress. He did not like Congress and could see little to gain by remaining in it, but he was nominated with considerable enthusiasm and was much too shrewd a politician to refuse an honor the party insisted on giving him.

He campaigned vigorously for Grant and, incidentally, for himself. He made many speeches, most of them specious and insincere. He was too intelligent to think that Grant had made a good President or to believe that the Union would be endangered by the election of Horace Greeley. Occasionally he was led into what was perilously near falsehood, as when in a speech delivered on September 4, 1872, he said:

Notwithstanding the predictions of our adversaries, that to confer political rights upon colored people would lead to a war of races, white people and colored people are now voting side by side in all of the old slave States, and their elections are quite as free from violence and disorder as they were when the whites alone were the voters. . . . The watchword of the Republican party four years ago was "Let us have peace." . . . A survey of every field where the peace was then imperilled . . . and in the South, shows that the pledge implied in that famous watchword has been substantially made good.

This in spite of the terrible conditions in the South, with which Hayes was conversant! It was necessary, however, to delude the Ohio voters into believing that the reconstruction policy and, especially the Fifteenth Amendment, were successful; and when it was necessary he was not the man to stick at a political trick or an oratorical artifice.

More absurd even than this pretense that things were well in the South, almost inconceivable in its presumption, was Hayes's contention that Greeley was the tool of Tammany Hall. This is the ancient, the perennial device of the Republicans to conceal their own corruption, and has been used with effect from 1860 to 1928. McClellan, Seymour, Greeley, Hancock, Cleveland, Parker . . . everybody down to Smith except Bryan and Wilson have been the hirelings of Tammany in the preëlection declarations of Republican orators.

Hayes appears at his worst in this campaign of 1872. Sympathizing with the Liberal Republicans, ardently hoping for reform, he yet stood on the side of corrupt government because his acumen told him that the hour had not come for improvement and that the army was still in the saddle and would reëlect Grant in spite of everything.

He could not, however, secure his own election to Congress. Grant would go in again because he was a national idol, but lesser candidates felt the growing indignation at Republican misrule. The congressional election came a month before the presidential and Hayes was defeated by 1500 votes, though he was fortunate enough to run ahead of the rest of the ticket in Cincinnati, which was overwhelmed. Hayes had rather expected to be elected, and the disappointment, together with the strain of the canvass, left him weak and incapable of further effort. He went back to Fremont, where he stayed until the eve of the presidential election.

He was among those who rejoiced over Grant's second election. Grant immediately rewarded him for his faithfulness when many had faltered by offering him the office of assistant United States Treasurer at Cincinnati. But it was not a job that attracted Hayes, who decided instead to return to his place, Spiegel Grove, outside Fremont, which had been deeded him by his uncle and which he made his home for the rest of his life. It was a fine estate, but Hayes was far from wealthy and at times in the remaining years was somewhat straitened financially.

He amused himself for a while with real-estate developments and plans for founding libraries, for he was a sort of forerunner of Andrew Carnegie, believing that libraries are the best gifts the affluent can make their communities. The time passed busily and happily.

Early in 1874, Hayes met with one of the great sorrows of his life, when Sardis Birchard died. Birchard had been a father to him; the tie between uncle and nephew had always been of the warmest and most confidential nature. Birchard was a self-made man, beginning life with nothing and, by virtue of his Yankee wits and industry, coming at length to be considered the richest person in his community. It had been a long time since his first drove of hogs fed upon refuse grain in the yard of the Lamb and Hayes distillery at Delaware, Ohio. Because of Sardis Birchard, Rutherford Hayes had been reared in modest, easy circumstances, educated, comfortably settled in business, married, started in politics, and had enjoyed leisure for study, society and personal publicity. It was to Birchard that he was to owe the presidency, though Uncle Sardis did not live to see this.

In his last days the old man grew reminiscent, groping for the pearls of the life that was slipping from him. Hayes persuaded him to give a library to Fremont. Rather touching were Birchard's efforts to turn his nephew's mind toward religion.

"You have been a good boy," he said. "You always minded me. I fear you are not as correct in your religion as I wish you were. I know you are not religious." To Birchard religion was as simple and sweet as bread and air. He had no intellectual difficulties. He died saying how nice it would be to see those who had gone on before; "that is," he added, smiling, "if I go to the right place, and I rather think I shall."

The bulk of the Birchard estate went to Hayes, but there were financial drawbacks in his way. By good investments he had made some money for himself; in April, 1873, he counted his interests in or near Toledo at $143,000. In September of that year, he said, "I am now chiefly interested in providing a good estate for myself and family." In all the years since he had been elected city solicitor his expenses had always exceeded his salary, but his investments had saved him. Now Uncle Sardis's estate came to him. Yet the presidency seems to have cost him money, and he was not in very good financial circumstances when he died. The failure of the famous Jay Cooke hit him hard, and he had other losses.

At this time Hayes seems to have believed that he was out of public life, if a politician ever really believes that as long as the breath is in his body. Again circumstances forced him into the political arena, circumstances that were imperative: to wit, the needs of the Republican party.

As we have seen, in 1871 General Edward F. Noyes carried Ohio by a large majority in a campaign of hullaballoo and glorification over the Fifteenth Amendment. But things instead of getting better were getting worse; even with the party of high protection and artificial prosperity in power, the country in 1873 was in the throes of its most terrible financial panic. In the same year, Noyes, who had made a mediocre governor, was renominated by the Republicans, while the Democrats brought out William Allen, an old man of character and standing and an uncle of Allen G. Thurman. This time patriotic oratory fell before acute monetary distress, and Allen was elected by a small majority. To the Republicans, who thought that they had made Ohio safe by enfranchising negroes and indigent veterans, this was a prostrating blow. The Democrats also carried the legislature and reëlected Thurman to the Senate.

At first it seemed that the Lord was merely chastening those he loved, but worse was to follow. In 1874, the American people, smarting from the panic, rose in protest against army rule, corruption, and the horrible state of the South; the Democrats swept the country, carrying the House of Representatives by a large majority. It was in reality one of the most important elections ever held in the United States, since it saved the Lower South from destruction. It should be noted that the South was not saved by the South but by those Northerners who put justice and sanity before humanitarianism and even, in many instances, before party and voted the Democratic ticket. Notice was served on the Republic party that it could no longer gloss over its corruption, inefficiency and cruelty with the plea of having won the war and saved the Union. The people had at last become thoroughly tired of the war and it no longer served to defeat a Democrat that a Republican orator denounced him as being in sympathy with "rebellion and treason." It was no longer possible for Rutherford Hayes and his comrades to fool the Ohio people with assertions that the Fifteenth Amendment had brought peace to the South, for the smoke of its torment ascended to heaven and filled the nostrils of the nation.

In 1874, the Democrats carried Ohio by a plurality of 17,-000 in the State election and elected thirteen out of twenty congressmen. It was a bad prospect for 1876. What was the army to do? The ungrateful public, unmindful of its deeds, no longer thought that military services were the open sesame to every honor and the cover of every shame. The country, sick of Grant's misgovernment, was demanding a better rule.

Allen, in his administration, carried on the good work begun by Hayes, insisting on reduction of taxation and economy in government. With the State more and more tending to the Democratic party and an efficient Democratic governor in office, the outlook for the Republicans in 1875 was anything but hopeful.

No man had ever before been governor for three terms; but undoubtedly the best vote-getter in the State was Rutherford Hayes and, consequently, he began to be considered for the governorship again early in the election year. Noyes had been beaten and was plainly impossible, being nothing but a soldier in office. John Sherman was too unpopular to be used; Garfield had not yet come to the fore. The available candidate—indeed, the only available candidate—was Hayes.

The party leaders began to make overtures, but Hayes was shy; he flirted but held off a while. Another idea had begun to fill his head; he was dreaming of the presidency. No reward could be too great for a leader able to redeem Ohio from its heresy and bring it back to the straight and narrow path. Hayes denied to himself that he had such an ambition and, by his very denial, has let us know what was really in his mind. For on April 14, 1875, he wrote in his invaluable diary:

I am still importuned in all quarters to consent to run as Republican candidate for Governor. Several suggest that if elected Governor now, I will stand well for the Presidency next year. How wild! What a queer lot we are becoming! Nobody is out of the reach of that mania.

Shakespeare has described the dilemma:

Glamis thou art, and Cawdor, and shalt be
What thou art promised: yet do I fear thy nature;
It is too full o' the milk of human kindness
To catch the nearest way: thou wouldst be great;
Art not without ambition, but without
The illness should attend it: what thou wouldst highly,
That wouldst holily; wouldst not play false,
And yet wouldst wrongly win.

Hayes, not assured that his nomination would be wholly acceptable to his party, continued to decline. But it was not intended as a final declination, though some of the Republicans took it as such. Judge Alphonso Taft, father of William Howard Taft, was groomed for the nomination, and even old Ben Wade was mentioned with some wild idea of reviving the Civil War and appealing again to the soldiers to save Ohio.

The nominating convention met at Columbus early in June. Taft was the principal candidate and Hayes was there, ostensibly to aid him but in reality to get the nomination for himself. He had determined to have it, since now the presidential bee was buzzing in his bonnet; but as it seemed best to him to have the honor forced on him and not to angle for it, he appeared in the convention as a Taft supporter. The word that Barkis was willing was quite enough for the Republican leaders, who much preferred a vote-getter such as Hayes to Taft, almost certain to be beaten by the Democrats. Hayes was nominated by 396 votes to 151 cast for Taft. The people thus called their man to the front again, but Taft accused Hayes, with some little reason, of treachery. At least Hayes had used him as a stalking horse and obtained what he wished through him.

This charge, which was reflected in the newspapers, gave Hayes much annoyance. He denied that he was responsible for Taft's candidacy and claimed that he had steadfastly re-

fused to be a candidate against Taft, that the convention had
forced the nomination on him. It is the usual plea, and no
more or less sincere in Hayes's case than in that of other politicians.

Hayes, nominated for the third time for governor, had at
last become a recognized national figure. Ohio, in 1875, was a
very doubtful State, and the election there would have a definite bearing on the presidential election of the succeeding
year.

James G. Blaine, already angling for the Republican nomination, found it expedient to cultivate the rising Ohio politician, who had not yet appeared as a rival. On June 11, 1875,
he wrote Hayes:

And so our friends in Ohio thought it wise and well to take a
ready-made Governor—having gone through the fire twice, the
presumption is in favor of your salamander qualities.

I congratulate you very cordially and I congratulate the Republicans of Ohio still more—for I have no doubt that you can
pull a larger vote than any other man that could have been
named— And as to winning, that is a necessity— "Success is a
duty"—and I believe you always do your duty— We shall en-
deavor to set you a good example in our September vote in
Maine.

Pray advise me of the "situation" in Ohio as you see it.[1]

The Maine statesman might have been more sparing of con-
gratulations if he could have foreseen that Hayes would be
his principal opponent in the convention the following year
and bear off the prize. But in June, 1875, Hayes, to Blaine,
was only a politician to be sedulously cultivated with a view
to acquiring the votes of the Ohio delegation in 1876.

The campaign of 1875 had as its issue the question of the
resumption of specie payments. Hayes had come out strongly

[1] Hayes Papers.

for "sound money"—that is specie—while the Democratic platform called for a sufficient currency for the needs of business and opposed specie resumption. Both sides were right: the resumption of specie payments was eminently desirable, yet at the same time the threatened contraction of the currency in a country where there was an insufficiency of money for its growing needs was an evil—an evil that became prominent in the campaign of 1896 and was not remedied until the Federal Reserve System was founded. It is also interesting to note that in this election, as in others, the Republicans accused the Ohio Democrats of being the minions of the Pope because there was a sentiment for using some of the public money for parochial schools. The election was decided in favor of our public school system, from which moral and religious instruction is banned as if it were something inherently wicked and repugnant.

The campaign of 1875 was one of the warmest ever held in Ohio. Governor Allen had been renominated by the Democrats and, as he was an honest and capable executive, there was no good reason to unseat him. And indeed if Rutherford Hayes had not also been known to be honest and capable, Allen would have been reëlected, for in this year the plea of saving the Union was ineffective. Carl Schurz and Oliver P. Morton, of Indiana, aided Hayes in the canvass, as the Republicans were fully aroused to the necessity of redeeming Ohio.

The veterans again stood by Hayes and a large part of the civilian population, and he was elected by 5544 votes, a great triumph. The deciding factor in the election was Schurz, who strongly approved of Hayes's stand for "sound money" and reform and brought him the solid German vote.

Able to appeal both to soldiers and civilians, Hayes was recognized as an ideal candidate for the times. His success in carrying Ohio for governor argued the probability of his carrying it for President; and, since Ohio was a State that the Republicans must needs gain in order to win in 1876, Rutherford B. Hayes suddenly found himself one of the important men of the nation. His patience, industry, honesty and foresight were at length rewarded. Almost over night he had changed from a provincial politician, little known outside the limits of his own State, into a presidential possibility. And with Grant out of the way and no other overshadowing personality in sight, the chance of a favorite son—that is, the favorite son of such a State as Ohio—was anything but inconsiderable. Rutherford B. Hayes faced the future with hope, the presidential bee now humming loudly in his bonnet. If circumstances favored him, the miracle might happen.

AT the beginning of 1876 thinking men in the United States were in revolt. The whole world would come to the great fair in Philadelphia; and sensitive Americans were stung by the taunt, often repeated, that the only thing in which the United States surpassed the rest of the world was in corruption. America did not then stand, great and triumphant, as it does today; it was still passing through the fires of the Civil War era.

It had passed through civil war and the Union endured, although it was no longer a union based on consent but on force. The Union endured, and there was hope that the stitches by which the almost severed sections had been sewn together would heal in time, though the cicatrices were still raw.

The most terrible misfortunes of the human race attend its efforts to secure justice. Life is based on inequalities, and when we try, as we do, to remedy them by force, by violent adjustments, we often create suffering worse than the ills we seek to cure. Perhaps the most frightful tragedy in modern history was the Russian Revolution, which was humanity's most passionate reaching out for justice.

The American Civil War was partly the result of a striving to do justice to what was supposed to be an oppressed race. The harm came from picturing the negro slaves as injured and imagining that the usually mild servitude in which they lived was a system of cruelty and wrong, and that by destroying it Utopia would be established in the United States. There were indeed abuses in slavery, but there were also abuses in freedom, and there are still abuses.

As a matter of fact, the slaveowners and poor whites were the victims of slavery rather than the slaves, who absorbed nearly all the profits of the system. For that reason there were few rich Southerners, though the South created much wealth. Most of it was used or wasted by the slaves in an inefficient economic system.

The idea, however, was spread through the world by politicians and imaginative writers that American slavery was a monstrous thing, a delusion still cherished in spite of the increasing weight of evidence to the contrary. There was of course a strong moral argument against slavery. But the extremists postulated their opinions on the hallucination that race makes absolutely no difference between men, that differences are all individual, not racial. Thus the egalitarians of the fifties, sixties, seventies and eighties believed that negroes, whose savage ancestors had recently come from the Niger, were nearly as well equipped for the duties and responsibilities of life as Anglo-Saxons with centuries of self-government and Christian civilization behind them.

One of the dogmas of the age was that the sole distinction between white men and black men lies in the color of the skin. Even the practical Hayes subscribed to it. It was, therefore, inevitable that when the North overthrew the South full civil rights should be bestowed on the ex-slaves. Holding the thesis that most of the Republicans did, they could not avoid this conclusion. They would have stultified themselves, rendered themselves open to the charge of insincerity in the principles on which they had conducted the war, if they had denied the negro the ballot. Their mistake lay not in the conclusion to which their logic led them but in their premises. The negro was not an outraged victim of greed and cruelty; he was, in 1860, largely the beneficiary of a system that had rescued him from the darkest savagery and taught him the rudiments of civilized existence. Curiously enough, the negro leaders of to-day realize this better than the whites do.

That something was wrong in the egalitarian thesis became evident the moment the negroes were granted suffrage, in 1867, and put in power in the Southern States. If the only difference between whites and blacks lies in the color of the skin, the negroes should have been able to conduct governments almost as well as the Anglo-Saxons they displaced. But the governments run by negroes and carpetbaggers with the support of negro voters not only showed mental inferiority, which might be debited to inexperience, but moral inferiority, which was not to be expected of oppressed virtue. The negro and carpetbagger governments were not only incompetent but dishonest almost beyond anything known before in American life.

The South was not vitally injured by the Civil War, but it was nearly ruined by emancipation and negro suffrage. The blacks, ceasing largely from work, began to revert to savagery. They consumed nearly everything that was left and produced little, looking to confiscation and government bounties instead of to labor to provide for them. The carpetbag governments were unbelievably corrupt. Taxes were enormously increased in a land burdened by a disastrous war; bonds were issued in large amounts and the proceeds stolen. Thousands of farms were sold to pay taxes, and the white inhabitants of the Lower South faced ruin.

These terrible conditions led to violence, for which the whites have been solely blamed. In fact, both sides resorted to violence: the negroes and their white associates to stay in power; the body of the white people to oust them and restore civilized government. The efforts of the Southerners to end oppression were termed in Congress "the deprivation of the freedmen of their constitutional rights."

In spite of the urgings of such fanatics as Thaddeus Stevens and Oliver P. Morton to complete the destruction of the South, the white people gradually regained power in most of the Southern States as the United States troops were withdrawn and something like normal conditions restored. By 1876, Virginia, North Carolina, Tennessee, Georgia, Alabama, Mississippi, Arkansas and Texas were once more under white rule. Although South Carolina, Florida and Louisiana, where the troops remained, still groaned under carpetbag government, these States were also on the road to freedom. Louisiana, where possibly an actual majority of the whole body of the inhabitants were Democrats, had been held under Republican rule by force, by the inexcusable use of troops by General Sheridan. Finally, a compromise was arranged, by which the Democratic legislature was permitted to organize in turn for the recognition of the corrupt governor, Kellogg, who continued to hold office.

The year 1877 was destined to see the last of these governments by which the South was debauched and the nation disgraced. A quarter of a century longer the South was hampered by its unstable political equilibrium. Finally, the negroes were eliminated from politics—with the aid of the United States Supreme Court—and the one-party system substituted for white and black parties. Instantly the South began to go ahead; its progress in recent years has been marked by giant strides and by the prosperity of whites and negroes alike. The old South had two curses: slavery and politics. Modern business methods replaced the system of slavery; white men earned and saved money instead of having to make provision for the needs of negroes. The negroes shifted for themselves, with the result that some of them did well and others starved. The one-party system minimized politics, which in former times had absorbed the energies of the best men. The latter turned to business instead of to oratory. Deeds replaced words.

The Southerners passed through an ordeal that metamorphosed them from idealistic dreamers into the most practical materialists on earth. It was inevitable that they should pass through the ordeal. The age demanded the application of the egalitarian theory to the South, and the will of the age cannot be frustrated. It would have been far wiser to place property and educational checks on negro suffrage; but this was impracticable in view of the fact that manhood suffrage, in its utmost viciousness, prevailed in the North. It would not have been possible to have unlimited suffrage in the North and a rigidly restricted franchise in the South. The best solution would have been to change the Constitution by frankly acknowledging the inequality of men and giving the negroes minority representation. In that way they would have obtained protection and instruction in self-government without endangering civilization in the South. But in that age such a cutting of the knot was impossible.

The South endured and was saved, though hardly. It was saved by the conscience of the Northern people, who turned decisively to the Democratic party in 1874 and thus announced that South-baiting must cease. No party has ever rendered a nation a better service than the Democratic party of the Reconstruction, led by Seymour, Thurman, Hendricks, Bayard and Tilden. The Democratic party and the newspapers alone stood between the country and open military rule. The Democrats, in spite of constant defeat and detraction, continued to advocate the restoration of constitutional government, which the war had nearly wrecked. Under Johnson, Congress had deprived the President of most of his rightful powers. Under Grant, the soldiers and their associates were in the saddle and sought to cry down opposition. A congressional oligarchy really ruled.

The nation, as well as the South, was passing through a revolution—an economic revolution. Industrialism, as a system, was being planted on the ruins of the political power of agriculture. The result has been the most marvelous industrial development the world has ever seen at the expense of the farmer. We have glorious cities crammed with millionaires and an impoverished countryside.

But this marvelous development, which has made the United States the foremost nation on earth, might not have taken place if military rule had continued, for that is not favorable to peaceful growth. And in the Reconstruction there was danger that military rule might become the fixed government of the country—that is, that a congressional majority would rule and keep itself in power by the use or threat of force. If bayonet supremacy had continued indefinitely in the South, that expeditious method of government would have been extended to the North. If soldiers interfered to prevent the election of Democrats in Louisiana or South Carolina, force might have been invoked to keep "Confederates" out of power in Ohio or Indiana. The nation, as Lincoln remarked, could not endure half slave and half free. No more could it continue to be half military and half civilian. And so strong was the propaganda put forth, the natural resentment felt against the South for the losses of the war, that unless a party, able and devoted, had been in opposition, American liberty might have vanished and have been replaced by that dictatorship which is the natural rule of most nations. Since few others, Northerners or Southerners, have done so, I lay a tribute on the tombs of those Democrats of the North and Middle West who did so much to preserve the republic.

The men who strove for better conditions in that dark age were not Democrats only. The Liberal Republicans, who aided them, made reform possible and, by electing Cleveland President in 1884, prevented the political system of the United States from becoming some such farce as that of Mexico. To

Carl Schurz, especially, America is under deepest obligations.

In 1876, the results of war, violence, and unconstitutional rule had become painfully evident. Far more apparent were the consequences of the great and sudden industrial expansion, the conversion of the United States from a primitive, loose-jointed agricultural country into a nation of mills and factories; the rise of modern finance; the beginning of stock speculation; the creation of an immense railway system, the intoxication and corruption of a novel era, a new page in history. The world has had many deities. The seventies in America witnessed the orgiastic welcome to a new god—Machinery.

The country was rotten with graft and fraud, fruits of the revolution. So many public men were corrupt that to be in politics at all rendered one the object of suspicion. Grant was not to blame for the evil. If he had been in civil life the Titan he was in war, he might have checked it to some extent; but the only remedy for conditions so strange and menacing was a return to constitutional government, that is, the rule of civilians instead of the rule of soldiers or military politicians based on appeals to the passions of war. For the democracy, drunk with power and success, had inaugurated the industrial age by force and threatened to maintain it by force. Both national and municipal administration was demoralized. The greatest reproach of all was the swindling of the city of New York by the Tammany boss, Tweed.

Almost as bad and far more numerous were the scandals appertaining to the Federal government. Among a hundred stories that twist the nose awry the chief is that of the Credit Mobilier. The Credit Mobilier was a company organized to build the Union Pacific Railroad, that pet child of the government, that wonder of the age. Amply endowed with public-land grants and money for construction uses, the Union Pacific saw its resources disappear into the capacious maw of the Credit

Mobilier, which built the railway in the most extravagant manner and absorbed the assets. Credit Mobilier stock rose in value; part of it was set aside for the purpose of winning the friendship of statesmen. Blaine was on its purchase list but refused the bait. Not so with all; many reputations fell to rise no more when the inevitable revelations came.

Second only in fame were the Whiskey Ring frauds, which disgraced Grant's second administration and had something to do with keeping him from a third term. The Whiskey Ring, by bribery and intimidation, muzzled the lesser officials of the internal revenue department, especially at St. Louis, and stole millions. So powerful was the organization that Benjamin H. Bristow, Secretary of the Treasury, showed marked courage when he attacked it. Some of the head men in the conspiracy were brought to justice, but the amazing part was that General Babcock, Grant's private secretary, was implicated. Grant defended him stoutly, for Grant always stood by his friends, right or wrong, but finally let him resign. It was believed by some, though it is highly improbable, that Bristow aimed at Grant himself. The Secretary of the Treasury, by his prosecutions, made a great reputation and became a candidate for the presidential nomination of 1876. He was a man of hope to the plundered country.

Even more disastrous to the administration was the corruption brought home to Secretary of War Belknap. He had sold a post tradership in the Far West with profit to himself. Impeachment proceedings were begun in Congress but, when Belknap resigned, were defeated by the Republican members on the ground that an impeached officer of the government could not be convicted after resignation.

Bigger men than Belknap and Babcock were tarred. Schuyler Colfax, Vice-President in Grant's first administration and one of the most popular public men in the country, was driven from politics by the revelations concerning him. Many other national leaders labored under suspicion; charges and countercharges were bandied about with the utmost recklessness. Most of the accused were Republicans; but the Republicans, by way of retaliation, brought baseless accusations against Kerr, the Democratic Speaker of the House of Representatives. The greatest of the besmirched statesmen was James G. Blaine, the foremost public man of the country; the charges against him were destined to influence history. As the election of 1876 approached, the mass of the American nation was more deeply stirred than at almost any time since the firing on Fort Sumter, feeling that relief from existing conditions was vital. It looked to two possible saviors, the Democrats and the Liberal Republicans, both of whom stood stoutly for reform.

The Liberal Republicans had no intention of taking the field in 1876, being mindful of what had happened to them in 1872; but they had not decided whether they would return to the regular Republican fold or join the Democrats, who were expected to nominate the great reformer, Samuel J. Tilden. They were still free traders but they now placed emphasis on reform as more immediately necessary. One thing they were determined on: that Grant should not have another term. They meant to bend every energy to prevent that.

In this stand the Liberal Republicans rendered the country a vital service. Grant ardently desired another term, for he had found the presidency pleasant, the atmosphere of adulation agreeable; and he might have had four years more if the Liberal Republicans had not been so strenuously opposed to it. They declared that the government must be reformed and rather asserted than implied that it could only be reformed under another President. The great man, idolized as a soldier, seemed to them beneath contempt as a statesman.

Men's demerits are sometimes more fortunate than their virtues. It was so with Grant. If he had been a great administrator, able at least to check the abuses of the government, he would probably have been President for three or four terms and American liberty might have been endangered. For the man on horseback, the booted and spurred chief, does not find the ways of freedom palatable. The troops would not have been withdrawn from the South; the quasi-military national government would have continued, and the arbitrary measures to which the public had gradually become accustomed in the war period would have been the order of the day. Grant's prestige was so high, the magic he exerted over men's imaginations so compelling, that nothing less than a party revolt could have unseated him. The Democrats unaided could not have defeated him, for they were constantly handicapped by the condemnation they incurred at any course they took. But when the opposition was joined by some of the leading members of the Republican party and when the newspapers, Democratic and Republican alike, ventilated the scandals freely, the nation was profoundly influenced and turned from Grant. It was remembered that there was an unwritten law forbidding three terms to any man. Washington had had only two terms. Was Grant greater?

The Liberal Republicans sounded the note in a meeting they held at the Fifth Avenue Hotel in New York City on May 15, 1876, just a month before the Republican convention. The insurgents of 1872 were there, including William Cullen Bryant, Theodore D. Woolsey, the former president of Yale, Alexander H. Bullock, Horace White and Carl Schurz. Others present were Charles Francis Adams, Thomas Wentworth Higginson, Henry Cabot Lodge. It was a remarkable gathering of intellectuals, who felt a little helpless in a moron world but yet hoped to accomplish something. Again Schurz, that impractical genius fated to exert so profound an influence on

American politics, made his crusading spirit felt. The idealists condemned the "wide-spread corruption" which had "disgraced the republic in the eyes of the world." When Republicans so spoke Grant's third term vanished into air.

Reluctantly, Grant let it be known that he was not a candidate for reëlection, though he must have hoped, till almost the end, that the lightning would strike once more. He was taken at his word. The politicians soon ignored him, realizing that a new deal had come. Seldom has an immortal so suddenly descended from his pedestal. The nation was stirred into a greater interest in politics than it had felt at any time since 1860. A new President was to be chosen, and it was anybody's race, for this time there was no mighty figure overshadowing rivals and rendering competition ridiculous. As the summer drew on two men stood somewhat above other candidates, James G. Blaine and Roscoe Conkling.

Blaine had gained his leadership by ability, energy, endurance, audacity. He had been Speaker of the House of Representatives and won fame in that difficult position. As a debater and a party leader in Congress he had no equal in his day. Quick-witted and a past master of political arts, he has had few equals in any day. Impressive and commanding, if he had not been disfigured by the long beard which the statesman of that age wore as a symbol of masculinity, he would also have been handsome and winning.

Roscoe Conkling was Blaine's rival in Congress, though he sat in the Senate while Blaine was the genius of the lower house. Conkling, large of mold, looked with his long curly hair and long curly beard much like a gigantic Persian cat. Irascible and overbearing, he owed his position to his reputation as the leading criminal lawyer of the day and to his unbending hatred of the South; but outside New York, which he ruled with a rod of iron, he was anything but popular. He was a State boss of singular stature but he was not much more than a State boss.

In 1866, Blaine lost his temper in a debate with Conkling in the House of Representatives. Blaine sometimes lost his temper, which shows that even if he was an expert in political theory he was not perfect in practice. Worse still, he was a phrase maker, which is almost as fatal as being a humorist. Viewing Conkling's theatrical criminal-lawyer manner in a moment of irritation, Blaine commented acidly on his "turkey-gobbler strut." Unforgettable and unforgivable phrase! Conkling became Blaine's enemy for life. When Blaine finally, in spite of many scandals and a host of foes, ran for President in 1884, Conkling declined to take the stump for him, saying, stingingly, that he was "no longer in criminal practice."

In the winter of 1876, Blaine was in a strong strategic position, having behind him delegates from New England, the Middle West and the South. If he had not alienated Massachusetts men, by commenting in Congress in another moment of vexation on Massachusetts' secession tendencies in 1814—a painful allusion in an age when secession had become the unpardonable sin—he might have had the support of Bay Staters and gained the nomination. As it was, he hoped but doubted.

Blaine felt that he had one serious weakness: he had no military record, either in the field or in Congress. He had neither joined the army nor distinguished himself in the House of Representatives by ruthlessness toward the South. Conkling had sought to win the love and gratitude of the soldiers by advocating the entire destruction of the seceded states, while he, Blaine, had actually gone so far in the other direction as to kill a force bill introduced by the worthy "Beast" Butler and designed to render the Anglo-Saxons of the South still more prostrate under the feet of their ex-slaves. Blaine thought that his war history was unsatisfactory.

Accordingly, he rose in the House of Representatives, one day in January, 1876, in a debate on a general amnesty bill, and delivered what was perhaps the most offensive speech ever uttered in that body. It was an incredibly harsh attack on Jefferson Davis, whom Blaine accused of murdering the Union soldiers that had died in Andersonville prison. In an instant, the House was aflame with war bitterness.

Seldom is a wicked act followed by such prompt retribution as Blaine's bloody-shirt speech. He won vast applause from the veterans, his objective; but at the same time he gained the hatred of the Democrats in the House of Representatives, many of whom had been his admirers and some of them his friends. The Southerners, accustomed to being called rebels and traitors, were electrified at being denounced as murderers. In fact, Blaine had violated the ethics of politics, and he soon paid the penalty.

The Maine statesman had quite forgotten that people who dwell in crystal palaces should not indulge in the sport of hurling missiles. Indeed, he had no idea that he himself was vulnerable until hate found the unguarded heel. Like nearly every other prominent Republican he had been involved in some of the shady transactions of the age, but in reality he was probably more honest rather than less honest than the majority of his confrères. Before this time his private affairs had interested nobody, but now that he aspired to the throne shortly to be vacated by Grant his past suddenly became of importance, and there were matters in that past—matters that might be construed as dishonorable. He was charged with foisting worthless bonds on the Union Pacific Railroad, the victim or presumable victim of every politician, and of other improper deeds. Republicans were probably behind the exposure, but the Democratic majority in the House of Representatives appointed an investigating committee to see what could be made of the case.

So there was one more scandal to add to the Credit Mobilier, the Whiskey Ring, the post traderships, and the many others.

The evidence desired by the investigating committee consisted of some letters written by Blaine which had found their way into the hands of a go-between named Mulligan. Blaine trickily regained the letters and refused to turn them over to the investigating committee. Appearances were against him.

Then, on April 24, 1876, he staged one of the most dramatic scenes ever beheld in the House of Representatives, for he was a great actor. Taking the floor and flourishing a packet of letters, he said: "For some months past a charge against me has been circulated in private and was recently made public—designing to show that I had in some indirect manner received the large sum of $64,000 from the Union Pacific Railroad company in 1871—for what purpose has never been stated." He denied the charge and read extracts from his letters tending to exculpate himself. Finally, he turned on Proctor Knott, a member of the investigating committee, and demanded if the latter had received a certain expected telegram from abroad. Knott, dumbfounded, admitted that he had. Blaine then flashed at Knott, furiously: "I heard you got a dispatch last Thursday, completely and absolutely exonerating me from this charge and you have suppressed it." The Democrats sat paralyzed by his audacity. It was a magnificent performance, but after all it was only a performance. Despite the *coup*, Blaine was quickly involved in a bog of evasions, half truths and falsehoods that convinced a large part of the public that he had been guilty of wrong-doing. Actually, he seems to have done little more than all the Republican leaders did. But he was a Presidential candidate now.

Hurt as he was by the charges against him, Blaine was not yet wholly without the pale of reform as the delegates went their way toward Cincinnati. His luck, however, had changed with his evil stirring of the dark passions in Congress; he had brought a nemesis upon himself.

The Republican convention was to meet on June 14. On Sunday, June 11, a very hot day, Blaine walked to church in Washington. It was not that he desired to appear before the world in this hour of destiny as a churchgoer of unostentatious habits, for he had been a regular churchgoer. But Americans then, as now, liked presidential candidates to be churchgoers—that is, Protestant churchgoers.

Just as he was about to enter the church Blaine had a fainting fit. When he was brought home the physicians turned up their eyes and shook their heads ominously; but grim Zach Chandler, Secretary of the Interior, coming in, declared that Blaine would soon be all right if the doctors did not kill him. This diagnosis was sound; Blaine was perfectly well in a few days.

Many people called at the great man's house, among them Benjamin H. Bristow, the head and front of the reformers. Blaine believed that Bristow was behind the charges made against him, and Bristow, himself a budding presidential candidate, may have had hopes that Blaine would die at this convenient moment; but at all events he called and a disagreeable incident followed. Bristow went away with the idea that he had been affronted.[1] Such, at least, is Senator Hoar's account. The newspapers stated that Blaine and Bristow had an altercation the day before. The affair did not tend to draw the reformers, already seriously prejudiced against Blaine, closer to him.

Blaine's illness was joyfully seized on by his opponents in Cincinnati as the delegates poured into the convention city. They gave out that he was dead or dying, or at least paralyzed, to the consternation of the Blaine camp. Next to religious un-

[1] George F. Hoar, *Autobiography of Seventy Years,* I, 381.

soundness, nothing does a presidential candidate more harm than to be accused of ill health. In a day or so Blaine was able to drive out and send a reassuring telegram to Cincinnati. His relieved followers then attempted to make capital of his illness, asserting that he had been martyred by the "Confederate Congress," as Republicans (including Hayes) were wont to speak of the Democratic House of Representatives at Washington. The incident was not helpful to Blaine, since it raised the question of his physical fitness for the chief magistracy.

At the Fifth Avenue conference in May, the Liberal Republicans had once more sought to bring forward their hero, Charles Francis Adams, but plain politicians felt no warming of the heart toward the over-cultured Bostonian. In the interval between the conference and the Republican convention, the reformers found a better candidate in Benjamin H. Bristow, Secretary of the Treasury, who had endeared himself to them by so thoroughly exposing the Whiskey Ring frauds as very nearly to involve Grant himself. The man who had made a third term for Grant impossible was a real friend to reform. The recent breach between Bristow and Blaine did not brighten the latter's chances, for the reformers were powerful.

The extent of the injury done Blaine's prospects by the Mulligan letters is revealed in a letter of Carl Schurz to Hayes, written during the campaign of 1884.

. . . He received the impression that in your opinion the only reason for my opposition to Blaine was our difference on the tariff question. I wrote him that the tariff question had absolutely nothing to do with it, that I should have warmly and actively supported a protectionist like Edmunds or any other clean man; but that I oppose Blaine because I believe that the election to the Presidency of the United States of the man who wrote the Mulligan letters, and who stands before the country as the representative of the practices they disclose, would be a precedent fraught with incalculable evil—a fatal blow at the moral foundations of our republican government. It would be a terrible thing to teach our young people that such a record does not disqualify a man for the highest honors and trusts of the Republic.[1]

Truly the bloody-shirt speech was sufficiently avenged!

On the eve of the convention the principal candidates were Blaine, who might be called the congressional candidate; Conkling, on whom Grant's mantle had fallen; Oliver P. Morton, of Indiana, beloved of negroes, carpetbaggers and scalawags; Bristow, the man of the reformers. Then came a group of favorite sons: Hartranft, of Pennsylvania, Jewell, of Vermont, Hayes, of Ohio. At this time Hayes was only the first of the favorite sons and his nomination did not seem at all likely, but he had Fate and the most skillful politicians on his side. As to personality, he was overshadowed by the spectacular Conkling, the splendid Blaine and the sensational Bristow; but the positive qualities of these men raised objections that did not exist in the case of the negative Hayes.

Hayes's candidacy had been determined on soon after he was elected governor in 1875. The Ohio politicians were deeply interested in getting the great prize for their state, and Hayes offered them their chance. They formed, and still form, the most astute political group in the United States and the Presidents they made are known as the "Ohio Dynasty." Hayes was their first candidate and Harding their last. In both cases their methods were much the same.

A preliminary victory of importance was won when the Ohio strategists succeeded in having Cincinnati chosen for the convention city; in fact, it really decided the issue. Hayes would never have been nominated in New York or St. Louis or Chicago because in those cities he could not have commanded a

[1] Hayes papers.

tithe of the publicity given him in his home town and he was no national figure of large stature. In Cincinnati his name was on everybody's lips—in saloons, billiard-rooms, hotel lobbies, everywhere. This mass suggestion had its effect on the convention.

Grant is said to have mentioned Hayes as a possible successor, but this is doubtful, as he knew Hayes but slightly. In January, 1876, John Sherman began to suggest Hayes for the presidency, thus paying his own debt for retaining his senatorship. Another, astuter politician was soon in the field for Hayes —James A. Garfield, destined to be the second beneficiary of Ohio's superior skill in politics. Garfield wrote Hayes on March 2, 1876:

We should give you the solid vote of the Ohio delegation and await the break up, which must come when the weaker candidates drop out.

Charles Foster was a powerful supporter who early came over to Hayes. One by one, the Ohio Republicans trooped into his camp.

The Ohio State Republican convention, on March 29, 1876, unanimously declared for Hayes. The governor played the game carefully, cautiously and with many disclaimers of any ambition for the presidency, a universal pose in the seventies when the office was still supposed, theoretically, to seek the man. If Hayes was to be nominated it could be done only by management, skillful management, yet on May 3 he wrote:

You speak of management by my friends securing results. I think I can see that part of it impartially. If anything depends on management, I suspect my claims may be put down at zero.

On May 4, Hayes sent a letter of sympathy to Richard H. Dana, of Massachusetts, who had just had his feelings painfully jarred by being rejected by the Senate for the mission to England. Dana had been so unfortunate or foolish as to raise a feud with "Beast" Butler. When Dana was nominated by Grant as minister to England, Butler (save the mark!) brought charges of dishonesty against him. This picture of Vice rebuking Virtue convulsed the country; but Dana was rejected by the Senate. He was a leader in Israel among the reformers, and Hayes tactfully expressed his regrets at the inconsiderate action of the Senate.

All this time Hayes was presenting the picture of the perfect republican magistrate in his modest home at Columbus. His wife, daughter Fanny, and son Scott were all his family now. He had only a servant and a half—an establishment that commended him to reformers aghast at the extravagance and corruption of the country. At least the governor of Ohio had not enriched himself at the public expense.

Hayes rose early, between five and seven, and wrote letters until breakfast at 8:30. From 9 A. M. to 1 P. M. he was at his desk and again, most virtuously, from 2 P. M. to 5 P. M. He was in good health but stayed so closely in the office that he suffered a little from lack of exercise. But duty is duty, and voters like to see office-holders work or appear to work. Not that Hayes merely appeared to work; he was always a toiler.

Several days before the meeting of the national convention, the rival managers were on the scene in Cincinnati endeavoring to beguile into their respective camps the incoming delegates. It was a convention of amazing contrasts and included many notables. Near each other sat George William Curtis, Richard H. Dana, James Russell Lowell, John Sherman, James A. Garfield, Robert G. Ingersoll, Nelson Dingley, Matthew S. Quay, John A. Logan, Zachariah Chandler, Ben Wade, Frederick Douglass. There were 1,500 delegates and alternates, about fifty of whom were negroes, a curious composite of various interests and different social strata. It was, indeed, one of the most interesting and colorful conferences ever held in this country. Then, as always in Republican conventions, famous men hobnobbed with negroes, drank with them, patted them on the back, brothered them—and on adjournment instantly forgot them.

Already, on June 12, two days before the convention met, the shrewd politicians who managed Blaine's campaign realized that the danger to their candidate came not from Conkling but from Hayes. The Conkling managers endeavored to win over the carpetbaggers and scalawags on the ground of their candidate's extreme hatred for the South but made little progress. Indeed, they made no headway anywhere, for Conkling was popular only in New York. In early June, when it was believed for a brief time that Blaine was incapacitated, various contestants attempted to qualify as his legatee. Morton, especially, counted on having Blaine votes turned over to him. Already the managers of the other candidates were combining against Blaine, who was easily the favorite of a majority of the party. But it is another thing to be the favorite of a majority of the party leaders.

Bristow was prominent and powerful, actually holding the key to the situation though having absolutely no chance for the nomination himself. The reformers were for Bristow, and the reformers were strong enough to make themselves felt from the first. They had done Blaine much harm but could not, by such means, bring success to their own candidate. It remained to be seen if they were strong enough to break Blaine, the idol of his party, the foremost figure in the country as Grant faded away. The fight, first and last, was negative, to defeat Blaine, not to nominate anybody in particular.

On June 13, the Bristow men busied themselves in unsuccessful conferences with Morton and Conkling, by which they hoped to name their own candidate or, at least, determine the choice of another candidate. The Hayes managers approached the Vermont delegation with the proffer of the second place to Marshall Jewell. Both the Conkling and Blaine workers came to Hayes with the offer of the vice-presidency, showing his strong position. Hayes remained coyly uncommittal. With many currents running his way, why should he not have the first place?

On the eve of the convention it was found that Blaine had largely recovered from the shock of his illness; that Bristow was strong but could not be nominated; that Conkling had no chance, as he had no delegates but those of New York and Pennsylvania; that Morton was not taken seriously; that Hayes was the dark horse in a race between the favorite and a field of selling platers.

Hayes had for his manager one of the shrewdest of Ohio politicians, General Edward F. Noyes, which is to say that he had about as good an agent as could be found in the world. But the real Warwick, the man who secured the nomination for Hayes, or did most to that end, seems to have been Stanley Matthews. Matthews was a Bristow leader but he was also close to Hayes, for his sister had married Doctor Joe Webb and he was always an intimate friend of Hayes. Hayes had in Matthews an associate to take advantage of any change in Bristow's camp, and all the more useful because Hayes himself was generally reported to favor Bristow's candidacy. This Hayes could well afford to do because all wise politicians knew that Bristow would not be nominated; he might unearth some more frauds. The office-holders had no intention of naming the Great Rectifier.

The convention came to order at midday of June 14, 1876. It was held in one of the vast and crazy barns in which thousands of people were jammed in those days, and with safety, since men chewed tobacco then instead of throwing lighted cigarette ends on the floor. According to the New York *Tribune*, the convention hall covered "over four acres, its architecture that of an ambitious and disappointed railroad depot, its decorations those of a country barbecue on a four-acre scale, its rafters innocent of any tint except that of age, and its roof an unsightly mass of beams and rafters." But this was a fine setting for a picnic, and was not a political convention in that age a picnic?

A picnic, for that is a kinder word than "spree." At least it was a glorious occasion. Cincinnati was crowded to its hotel limits by a mob of politicians and office-holders, accompanied by satellites, ward heelers, touts, loose characters of every sort. Across the front of the hotels ran enormous streamers bearing the names of candidates. Bands played and torchlight parades of delegates, bebadged, sometimes uniformed, threaded the murky, gaslit streets. Orators held forth on steps or in hotel lobbies. The glittering bars in the hotels were thronged with happy statesmen, who firmly planted their feet on the rail and quaffed gargantuan drafts of whiskey without that wretched modern fear of being poisoned. It was a good time to be alive —for people not over-æsthetic and not over-sensitive to the prevailing corruption in the government and to the flaunting vice of the cities. Indeed, the air was electric. The Centennial Exposition in Philadelphia was drawing all eyes to the United States and filling the crude American of that day with pride of country.

For the first time since 1860—and that was far away—the rank and file of Republican politicians were having a good time at a convention. They were no longer automatons assembled to ratify the already determined nominations of Lincoln and Grant. This time they were going to name the candidate themselves, and if they had been left to themselves they would have nominated James G. Blaine with a shout. But they were not left to themselves. Why have leaders if delegates are to vote as they like?

Stanley Matthews was to have been made temporary chairman but he was finally passed over because he was a Bristow man. When the convention came to order, one T. M. Pomeroy, of New York, became temporary chairman, emerging from obscurity a moment and then returning to his native nothingness, never to reappear.

The Conkling delegates were turning their minds toward a second choice, for it was evident that their leader had no chance. That Conkling was Blaine's rival in this convention and prevented his nomination is one of the myths of political history. Conkling had little importance apart from the fact that he had a block of votes that could be thrown to some one else when the time came.

Noyes made an adroit welcoming speech, at once hitting at Blaine and recommending his own leader. He said:

As to the candidate of this convention, we of Ohio, ask only this. We fight nobody. We assail no man's reputation. Whoever you nominate we will try and help to elect him (Applause). All we want is a man, in the first place, who is honest (Cheers). In the second place, we want a man of comprehension enough to know what is right and what is wrong (Applause), and in the third place, we want a man who is brave enough and strong enough to carry out his convictions (Cheers). Give us a man of great purity of private life and an unexceptionable public record, and count on Ohio next November (Great applause).

"A man of great purity in private life and an unexceptional public record"—that is, Rutherford B. Hayes!

A noisy demonstration greeted reform resolutions presented by George William Curtis, showing how the wind blew. For the first time in years bloody-shirt oratory failed to elicit howls of approval. Old-fashioned orators were nonplussed and old soldiers felt doubts of the rightness of the universe. They did not understand that the convention was controlled by the reformers and that the reformers were weary of the war. The world was going forward; a new generation was coming on the stage. The past was beginning a little to be past.

On June 15, the presentations came. The best speeches were made by the reformers George William Curtis and Richard H. Dana in seconding Bristow, whose supporters intellectually, morally, socially dominated the convention and awed the plain delegates from the rural districts. The reformer, George F. Hoar, presented a woman suffrage petition. Plainly, the world was moving away from the Civil War.

Hayes's name was presented by Noyes and seconded by old Ben Wade. Reformer the governor might be, but his backers were practical politicians of the most practical kind. Noyes spoke in the vein of practicality. Hayes, he claimed, was "brave, honest, unpretending, wise, sagacious, a scholar and a gentleman"; but, warming up, he added what was upmost in his heart, that Hayes could "carry Ohio, Indiana, Illinois, and New York as well as all the rest." Cheers greeted this flattering assertion.

Conkling was nominated by a soldier, who spouted war oratory and won no applause. Of all the candidates, Conkling indeed fell the flattest. Morton's nomination was seconded by a mulatto from Louisiana bearing the Dickensian name of Pinchback. Morton was mildly cheered.

The event of the day, unquestionably, was the presentation of Blaine. The Maine statesman really represented the new generation; his frantic waving of the bloody shirt merely proved that he felt he must belong, in some sort, to the older, military order of things that was beginning to pass away and yet hung on tenaciously. He was young and virile, or had been virile before his June attack. If he became President, it might be possible to end the Civil War; but would the reign of post-war graft end also? The reformers shook their heads. They did not trust Blaine.

The emotional outburst of the convention came when Robert G. Ingersoll nominated Blaine. Ingersoll, chosen for the purpose, was as noted then for his oratory as he was later famous as the leading enemy of God in the United States. His silver-tongued elocution conquered the awful acoustics of the barn and his turgid rhetoric was the kind that stirred American hearts in the seventies. Even the delegates could understand his speech, which gained for Blaine his sobriquet, for Ingersoll spoke of him as a "plumed knight" tilting with his enemies. Americans of that age seemed to adore knights: Knights Templar, Knights of Pythias, Knights of Labor, Knights of the Ku Klux Klan. The word was a part of the popular vocabulary.

When the flood of oratory ceased, it was close on six o'clock in the afternoon, and the delegates were tired, hungry and thirsty. The Blaine men wanted to begin the balloting, but the lighting apparatus was out of order, perhaps intentionally, and the rival managers succeeded in adjourning until the morrow. By doing so, they defeated Blaine. His nomination had been greeted by such a burst of applause as had seldom been witnessed in a political convention, and if the voting had begun immediately he might have carried everything before him. It was his chance.

That night there was little sleep in Cincinnati, and none among politicians unless they were so unfortunate as to be overtaken in their cups. The Blaine leaders frantically dickered for votes, offering almost anything. The enemies of Blaine, now fully realizing his popularity, foregathered to find a way to defeat him.

In reality Blaine was already defeated, as the New York newspaper correspondents had discovered. The crisis had come when Blaine's men had offered the second place to Bristow and Bristow had telegraphed refusal. That meant a fight to the finish between Blaine and Bristow, and that meant Blaine's defeat.

The Cincinnati press had something to do with the result. Just before the convention met, Murat Halstead, leading American journalist after Greeley's death, had given a dinner to newspaper correspondents. The ubiquitous Stanley Matthews was there. Perhaps of prearrangement, perhaps spontaneously, the Republican newspapers of Cincinnati, at the moment of crisis, came out with a new publication of the Mulligan letters accompanied by editorials declaring that Blaine was unfit for the nomination for the presidency. This undoubtedly had some weight with the delegates. If Blaine could not command the support of his own party organs, what hope was there of his election?

More important than the pronunciamentos of the press was the agreement reached that night between the managers of Bristow, Morton and Hayes to throw the support of the other contestants to Hayes as the most available candidate. It is said that John M. Harlan, Bristow's manager, was promised a place on the Supreme Bench for bringing the Kentucky delegation to Hayes.[1] Never were politics better played than by Noyes and his lieutenants that memorable night. When morning came Hayes was as good as chosen unless a stampede, an irresistable emotional outburst, should bring the nomination to the man who had done the most to win it and who was really the party's choice. But it was precisely for that outburst that these seasoned politicians made provision. They had loaded the dice against Blaine.

[1] Matilda Gresham, *Life of Walter Quintin Gresham*, II, 459.

Hayes himself doubted but hoped—hoped strongly. His managers cheered him with the news from the convention. On May 19 he had written in his diary:

I still think Blaine is so far ahead in the number of delegates he has secured and is securing that his nomination is not improbable. He has not been greatly damaged by the investigations. As a candidate before the people, his newly acquired wealth, his scheme for getting the nomination, and his connection with the money interests depending for success on legislation, will damage him. But with two or three hundred delegates in his favor, will not all of the loose odds and ends gravitate to him? It so seems. If he fails, the next [probability] is a combination of selfish ends to make a candidate among the friends of the leading candidate. This would not be in my favor. My independent position, aloof from the bargaining, puts me outside the list from whom the managers will select. It is only in the contingency of a union between those who look for availability in the candidate and those who are for purity and reform in administration, that I am probable nominee.

In his slightly Pecksniffian way Hayes had said it: If he was nominated, he would be the candidate of availability and reform. It was in the night before the balloting that the managers decided that, in the first place, he was available and, in the second place, that he was a reformer or, at least, a substitute reformer.

To win over the reformers was the hardest task the Hayes workers had to accomplish; everything depended on this. Had Hayes not satisfied the reformers, they would have brought forward another man as the legatee of the Bristow votes and, if they could not have nominated him, would probably have turned to the Democratic party. So this situation was critical not only for Hayes but for the Republican party as well. Bristow could not be nominated; would the Liberal Republicans accept anyone else in his place or would they go over to the Democrats with far better chances of success than in 1872? The reformers decided to accept Hayes, and this decision determined not only the nomination but the presidency.

Noyes and Stanley Matthews must have argued, promised, manfully lied that June night to bring over the reformers to Hayes, for he had supported Grant, the patron of corruption, in 1872 and had done everything in his power to carry Ohio against Greeley. Indeed, if Greeley had really been the reformers' choice, they would never have taken Hayes to their hearts; but Greeley had been nothing but a makeshift, a sacrifice offered up in place of the unacceptable Adams, and the reformers cared little that Hayes had been against him. Hayes was firm on "sound money," and that was a vital consideration. He was not in any way implicated in the scandals of Grant's administration because he had never been a part of the administration. He was not noted as a waver of the bloody shirt, since the speeches he had made to stir the soldiers' hearts had all been delivered in Ohio and the reformers knew little about them. He was moderate on the tariff. He had a good war record without being eternally a soldier. All in all, he suited the reformers much better than Morton, who could be counted on to continue the war for all he was worth, or Conkling, who was close to Grant and therefore anathema to all true reformers. In fact, when the reformers looked around they found that Hayes was the only avowed candidate they could support.

Hayes's local prominence and national obscurity were his assets. He was too little known, too recent a candidate of consequence to have many enemies, and there was no time now to rake up a scandal with which to blacken his name. If he had been regarded as a serious contender for any length of time before the convention, there can be little doubt that charges of some sort would have been made against him; but he was a surprise candidate, and for that reason he succeeded.

Yet the reformers had thought of him in a quiet way for some time. George William Curtis had opened an indirect correspondence with him in May. When a newspaper inadvertently announced that Hayes was a Blaine supporter, he hastened to deny the injurious allegation. Still Hayes sent Blaine a message more than consolatory on the occasion of the latter's sudden prostration. He wrote:

I have just read with the deepest sorrow of your illness. My eyes are almost blinded with tears as I write. All good men among your countrymen will pray, as I do, for your immediate and complete recovery. This affects me as did the death of Lincoln. God bless you and restore you!

The tears may indeed have been tears of sorrow—Hayes was a sincere man. But at all events, he wiped away the tears and proceeded to take counsel how he might get the nomination.

The balloting took place on the third day of the convention, June 16. The first ballot ran true to expectations:

Blaine	285
Morton	124
Bristow	113
Conkling	99
Hayes	61
Hartranft	58
Jewell	11
Wheeler	3

Blaine was far in front, as had been foreseen. Conkling, so far from being Blaine's chief rival, was only fourth and he received his largest vote on the first ballot.

The next four ballots failed to show much change. On the

fifth ballot, Michigan went over to Hayes, whose vote rose to 104.

On the sixth ballot the expected break to Blaine began. It was evident that his nomination was imminent unless strategy were invoked to defeat the will of the majority, for the majority favored Blaine and was drifting toward him. Hayes made little gain in this ballot. In the interval between the sixth and seventh ballots, Blaine's enemies decided that the time had come to unite against him. It was now or never.

On the seventh ballot Blaine continued to gain. But Indiana cast 25 voters for Hayes and Kentucky voted unanimously for him. Then the drift to Hayes continued until he received a majority, 384 votes. Blaine was not far behind with 351.

Blaine was supported by most of the Southern States, Illinois, Iowa, Maine, Maryland, Missouri, New Jersey, Wisconsin and a large part of the Pennsylvania delegation.

Hayes had Michigan, Mississippi, North Carolina, Ohio, Tennessee, Texas, part of Pennsylvania, as well as Indiana (Morton), Kentucky and Massachusetts (Bristow) and New York (Conkling), transferred to him according to the agreement of the night before.

Conkling did not defeat Blaine, for he did not have the strength to defeat Blaine. His New York votes aided Hayes greatly, but Hayes would have obtained the nomination if the New York delegation had been split. The followers of Bristow and Morton were responsible for Blaine's defeat. Bristow was for Hayes because the latter was at least a quasi-reformer. Morton was for Hayes in order to keep the presidency in the Middle West. Men stood together in the Corn Belt.

What really determined the issue was the reformers' distrust of Blaine, the widespread belief that he was dishonest. Back of that was another feeling, unrecognized, subconscious —the envy of ineffectual politicians for the idol of the hour.

The hounds pulled down the stag. It is harder for a rich man to enter the kingdom of heaven than for a camel to go through the needle's eye. It is almost as hard for a great man to be elected President of the United States. His superiority really defeated Blaine. The men who frustrated him were George William Curtis, Richard H. Dana, George F. Hoar and their like—scholars in politics. James Russell Lowell declared that New Englanders defeated the New England candidate. They gave (at least in part) the presidency to Hayes because he was not splendid and dominating, a masterful leader of men. The political genius made those self-esteeming scholars feel small. How could they forgive that? Stanley Matthews, the bridge between the reformers and Hayes, was the chief figure in the situation. He actually brought about the result. The nomination was a beautiful demonstration of the combining of the little against the great, a lesson in the art of defeating the will of the majority. A convention, two-thirds of whose members knew next to nothing of Hayes, accepted him instead of the man of their desire.

The New Yorkers were now informed that they could name the Vice-President, the reward for Conkling's votes. They bandied the office about among themselves in caucus. "Take it, Chet," said one to Chester A. Arthur. "You take it, Cornell," another said to A. B. Cornell. Finally some one proposed, "Let's give it to Wheeler." So William A. Wheeler, a second-rate politician, was nominated.[1] Hayes had awaited the outcome of the contest, eager but calm. At 8 A. M. on June 16, he wrote in his diary:

Early in the struggle my friends were very hopeful. But on the 13th, Blaine became decidedly the prominent man—his prospects deemed almost a certainty. There has been a gradual change on the 14th and 15th, and now it seems something more

[1] Statement of Colonel Webb C. Hayes, who was present.

than a possibility that he will fail. If he fails, my chance, as a compromise candidate, seems to be better than that of any other candidate. So we are now in suspense. I have kept cool and unconcerned to a degree that surprises me. The same may be said of Lucy. I feel that defeat will be a great relief—a setting free from bondage. The great responsibility overpowers me.

It was with joy, tinctured with pride and fear, that Hayes heard the news of his nomination. Blaine's congratulatory telegram moved him deeply; he could appreciate the great man's magnanimity in the face of a killing disappointment.

The politicians piled out of Cincinnati on trains and steamboats in a happy, confident mood. The reformers, even Carl Schurz, were satisfied that a reform candidate had been named. The practical politicians believed that a practical politician had been chosen. Hayes had been represented as all things to all men so shrewdly by his managers that everyone saw in the candidate what he wished to see, whether that was better government or jobs and contracts.

Probably Hayes was a sounder choice than Blaine. If the latter had been a party to a disputed election, the Liberal Republicans would have been against him and might have turned the tide. On the other hand, Blaine was far better known, incomparably more popular than Hayes, and might have carried New York or Connecticut. The veterans loyally accepted Hayes and the Ohio soldiers (with grateful acknowledgments of pensions) were enthusiastic for him; but his almost unknown named aroused no such emotions as that of the general of Vicksburg, Missionary Ridge and Appomattox. The soldiers were no longer led by a great soldier.

The Democrats, gathering in St. Louis in July, presumed too much on the fact that a new epoch was coming in. They forgot that Mars dies hard, that the military era still lingered in the act of departure. The ticket they nominated, Samuel J.

RUTHERFORD B. HAYES, 1876
When Candidate for President

Tilden, of New York, and Thomas A. Hendricks, of Indiana, overshadowed Hayes and Wheeler. Rarely indeed have two men of such eminence and character been associated on a Presidential ticket. Nevertheless, the Democratic nominations were a mistake, in that they were based on the premise that the Civil War was over, while the war was not yet quite over.

Tilden was the greatest reformer the United States had as yet produced. He had been the chief figure in the overthrow of the powerful and dangerous Tammany boss, Tweed, and the little less vicious Erie Canal ring in New York State. He had made honest government respectable, almost fashionable. But he had one fatal disqualification for the Presidency: he was a complete civilian. He had taken no part in the war either as a soldier or as a Republican politician. Consequently, brilliant and courageous as he was, he was looked on by the soldiers as an enemy, a "rebel." Wise men might have foreseen the result. Tilden would have been installed by a landslide, but only by a landslide.

The Democrats would have done better to nominate one of the other candidates, Winfield S. Hancock. Hancock would hardly have been regarded by the veterans as a "rebel," even if he was a Democrat. In the event of a close election there would not have been the bitter feeling against Hancock that there was against Tilden, murmurs that with him as President, Jefferson Davis would rule. The Democrats hardly could have seated a civilian in 1876; they might have put in the White House the eminent soldier, Hancock.

It is to be observed that in this year, 1876, the Republicans found the brand of presidential candidate that best suits their genius. They nominated two great men in Lincoln and Grant; they have never nominated another great man except under protest. Most of their candidates have been average men, susceptible to advice, open to the opinions of party leaders: Garfield, Harrison, McKinley, Taft, Harding, Coolidge. Two first-rate men, Blaine and Hughes, they did not elect, and their greatest man after Lincoln, Roosevelt, almost wrecked the party. In the Republican system the President is only the head of the hierarchy, a pope well served by a college of cardinals.

In Shakespeare's play of *King Lear,* elemental forces usurp the action, dwarfing the human figures. It was so in the Presidential campaign of 1876. Tilden did, it is true, remain the head of his party and directed the storm, so far as it could be guided; but Hayes was nothing but a symbol of the powers behind him. These were steered by the practiced party leaders.

Preëminent among these was the national chairman of the party, Zachariah Chandler, Secretary of the Interior, a creature of energy, cunning and entire lack of scruples. Hayes accepted Chandler as chairman, though he declared plainly his objection to taxing office-holders for campaign expenses, the orthodox method of raising money in that day. Chandler paid no attention whatever to the candidate's conscience, levying freely on government employees and raising thereby a campaign fund, though not a very large one. It was, however, larger than the Democratic fund, which came chiefly from Tilden himself; if this had been ampler, there might not have been a disputed election.

Hayes was happy in his ignorance of the campaign management. It is hard to say what he would have done if he had been aware of the iniquities of a presidential contest. *The Nation* said:

All sorts of bad characters were usefully employed in the service of a candidate of spotless reputation, under an ingenious arrangement by which he profited by their activity without incurring any responsibility for their rascality.[1]

[1] February 1, 1877.

Neither party had much money and therefore, perforce, both parties had to wage a warfare of abuse. There was this difference: the Democrats had abundant ammunition furnished by Republicans out of humor with Republican maladministration; Grant's reign went beyond anything known in America for waste and corruption. Since the Democrats had been out of power for years, the Republicans were driven to depend on slander, which they did with an energy seldom surpassed.

The Republicans were fighting for place and power: jobs, contracts, prestige. If they lost they might be out in the cold for a long time, since they had given a classic example of misgovernment. A decent administration would shine by contrast. For the Democrats, too, victory was important. Business was beginning to become consolidated behind the Republican party because that party remained in power; the Democrats must win a presidential election soon or sink, by force of gravity, into a mere opposition.

Between the candidates and parties there was not much difference in principle. Hayes was for "sound money" and so was Tilden, though the latter might decline to commit himself too openly out of tenderness for the Greenback element of his party. Hayes had no very definite opinions on the tariff; Tilden was a moderate tariff reformer. Tilden was strongly for reform in government and for a civil service; so was Hayes. Tilden would withdraw the Union troops from the Southern States and leave nature to restore white rule; Hayes did withdraw them. Tilden would, of course, repudiate (though not openly) the Fifteenth Amendment. Hayes killed the Fifteenth Amendment. The struggle lay more between ideas than between issues. Republicans believed that the election of Hayes meant security for the Union, the continuance of soldier government as under Grant, the renewed repression of the South. Democrats thought that the success of Tilden would bring a new liberalism into the government, reform, salvation of the prostrate South. What Tilden would have done, if he had been seated, we do not know. Probably he would have done very much as Hayes did.

The Democrats found, ready-made, an abundance of campaign material. There were the hundred and one scandals of Grant's administration. More important, there were the hard times, for the country had not yet recovered from the panic of 1873. Scandals are forgiven for the sake of prosperity—as witness the election of 1924—but both scandals and poverty are a weighty load for any party to carry.

The Republicans, hard put, countered by launching a campaign that for violent vituperation has had few equals in American annals. They centered on two things: the Civil War and Tilden. The attempt, a thousand times repeated, was made to identify the Democratic party with the Confederacy. The bloody shirt was frantically waved in every city and town in the North and West; the soldiers were stirred to the core. The healing wounds of war were torn open afresh as the familiar designations of "rebels and traitors" were once more hurled at the Democrats.

This was to be expected; the Democrats had become used to it and the public did not respond as quickly as of yore. What was not quite so familiar was the storm of slander directed against Tilden. It was not enough that Democrats were rebels; their chief must be made out to be a scoundrel. The politicians of that age were past masters in the art of mud-slinging; bad as is our own age, it is incomparably less savage than the seventies. At least we have some sense of shame; they had none then. Greeley, in 1872, had been stunned by the vile abuse heaped on him, yet what he endured was as nothing compared to the slanders coined by fertile brains against Tilden.

In 1876 the Republicans were in danger and aroused. Tilden

was a leader of men, a millionaire, a publicist much in the limelight. Consequently there was material for libel. He was a reformer; for that reason it was necessary to show that he was a blatant hypocrite. He was opposing a corrupt government; therefore, it was well to demonstrate that he himself was a grafter. No matter how bad the Republicans might be, the country under Tilden would be infinitely worse off. Such were the Republican tactics.

To be specific, the Republican press accused Tilden of being a liar, a traitor, a hypocrite, a briber, a conspirator, a thief, a counterfeiter, a defrauder, a perjurer, a robber, a swindler, a railroad wrecker—in fact, there was hardly a crime save murder of which he was not charged by the regular Republican newspapers of the country.

This may not be believed. Read then the advertisement of a campaign pamphlet in the New York *Times Supplement* for May 18, 1876 and many subsequent dates:

TILDEN

1. A SECESSIONIST
   His Rebel Sympathies
   He invites Civil War
   Promotes Treason
   Declares the War a Failure
2. AN ALLY OF TWEED
   Promotes Electoral Frauds
   Mr. Greeley's Letter
   The Robberies He Facilitated
   His Share in Tweed's Conventions
   How He Stood by the Ring
3. A SHAM REFORMER
   His Canal Reforms Analyzed
   Great Cry and Little Wool
   A Lying Pretense of Economy

4. A SWINDLER OF LABOR
   Michigan Shinplasters
5. A WRECKER OF RAILROADS
   The Indiana Southern
   St. Louis, Alton and Terre Haute

The charge most in evidence, filling not columns only but whole pages of newspapers, was that Tilden had made a false income return for the year 1862. There was no direct evidence that he had done so; but ingenious journalists, by computing what they supposed was Tilden's income for 1862, demonstrated to their own satisfaction at least that the Democratic candidate was guilty of perjury and defrauding the government. This accusation, endlessly repeated, had some effect.

Another favorite slander was that Tilden had emitted early in the war a kind of makeshift currency, familiarly called "Michigan Shinplasters," though at that time, owing to lack of money, many people put out a kind of temporary small currency. Since he was rich, he was inevitably represented as being a harpy, without bowels, grinding the poor, increasing his wealth by every malpractice. Fortunately, Tilden was of sterner stuff than Greeley or he would have sunk under the weight of filth heaped on him.

More effective in a broad way than the attacks on Tilden's character was the grand revival of the Civil War staged by the Republicans. Soldiers swarmed at Republican speakings and soldier conventions were nothing but Republican mass meetings. The Grand Army of the Republic, then generally known as the Boys in Blue, greatly encouraged the orators of the Bloody Shirt, of whom Blaine was now the chief. To crowds of cheering veterans they declared that Tilden's election would mean the turning over of the United States to Confederate rule. One absurdity, which Tilden felt called on to deny, was that the Democrats intended to pay the Confederate debt.

Oliver P. Morton, grim politician now approaching the end of his violent career, declared: "The rebellion was as much a Democratic rebellion as the St. Louis convention was a Democratic convention, actuated precisely by the same feelings."

Answering the Democratic charge that the Republicans made outrageous use of the bloody shirt, Benjamin Harrison said, "I prefer the old gray army shirt, stained with but a single drop of a dead comrade's blood, to the black flag of treason or the white flag of cowardice."

The New York *Times* spoke as follows of the personnel of the soldiers' convention at Indianapolis in September:

John C. Robinson, who gave the rebels a leg at the Wilderness . . . there was Edward F. Noyes, of Ohio, who also gave the Democracy a leg; Ben Spooner, who gave it an arm; Ben Harrison, who faced its bullets from the beginning to the end of the war, and Tanner, who surrendered to the Democracy two legs at Bull Run.

Even Hayes fell into this strain of an endangered Union. At this Indianapolis convention, Noyes read a letter from him:

I am grateful to my comrades of the Union Army, assembled at Indianapolis, for their hearty greeting. The men who maintained the cause of national unity and freedom on so many battle-fields are not willing to see the results of the war imperilled by neglect or misconduct at the ballot-box. Their example will be very influential with all intelligent and patriotic people.

R. B. HAYES.

On September 23, the New York *Times* spoke as follows of the manner of conducting the Republican campaign in Indiana:

The general drift of the argument has been that the course of the Democratic party during the last session of Congress, in the House of Representatives, proves that it is really the Confederate party; that the nomination of Wade Hampton in South Carolina, the shot-gun policy in Mississippi, Louisiana, South Carolina and Florida, mean the inauguration of a new rebellion and the first step toward a new establishment of human slavery. . . . Between them all Democracy has been shown to be a sham, Tilden a fraud, Hendricks a cheat, their cry of reform a delusion and a snare.

Never has such an array of orators been put in the field as the Republicans summoned to stem the tide. In the long list were James G. Blaine, William M. Evarts, Carl Schurz, Benjamin H. Bristow, Robert G. Ingersoll, John A. Logan, John Sherman, Edward F. Noyes, Eugene Hale, Marshall Jewell, James A. Garfield, Benjamin Harrison, George William Curtis, Chauncey Depew, and even Mark Twain, who amused the country with a humorous campaign speech. Schurz was particularly effective with the Germans, who were beginning to show signs of desiring to break the Republican yoke. He painted the sins of the Democratic party as vividly as, in 1872, he had denounced Republican corruption. As a matter of fact, Schurz's liberalism was perhaps a little dubious; he was sufficiently a regular Republican if he happened to be on good terms with the Republican candidate.

Indeed, the Liberal Republicans were well satisfied with Hayes. They had been animated more by hostility to Grant than by any acute purpose to secure better government; and now that Grant was gone or going, they had no difficulty in reconciling themselves to the Republican party and working hand-in-glove with such unregenerate spirits as Blaine and Morton.

The Democrats attempted to retort to the abuse of their

candidate by attacks on Hayes, but there they felt the advantage the Republicans enjoyed from the obscurity of their candidate. Hayes's conduct as governor had been unexceptionable, and little was known of him before that. A slander was finally coined, to the effect that he had drawn and appropriated the pay of dead soldiers in his regiment, but this transparent fiction soon fell to the ground. In fact, the battle was not that of party with party but of the Republican party with Tilden. Seldom has a candidate more wholly transcended his party than did Tilden; seldom has a candidate been more completely submerged by his party than was Hayes. It was a curious contest.

Democratic meetings were more enthusiastic than Republican speakings because the under dogs realized that at last they had a chance to win. Years of scandals and scandal-airings had turned numbers of independents against the Republican party. In almost every city and town in the United States in that hectic summer of 1876, torchlight parades wended their way along the muddy streets to the strains of brass bands while transparencies proclaimed "Tilden and Reform." It was more than reform the people hoped for, and Tilden, like Hayes, was a symbol. The American masses, sick of war propaganda and misgovernment, were passionately turning away from military sway to civilian rule. But for the soldiers and their dependents, who stood squarely on the single issue of the Civil War, Tilden would have swept the country. The Republican party rested on the soldiers; the election of 1876 was the last scene in the Civil War drama.

Business tended more and more to array itself with the Republican party and Hayes's firm stand for "sound money" commended him to financiers; but business was not centralized then as it is now; the tariff issue was not sharply drawn; Tilden was a corporation lawyer close to captains of industry; and many commercial men, especially those who preferred a productive Democratic South to a Republican desolation, favored him. Farmers almost everywhere tended to the Democratic party that year because of the economic distress, though the bloody shirt made many of them vote for Hayes.

Tilden, who managed his own campaign, sought to strengthen himself by having worthy candidates nominated for State officers. He would gladly have joined hands with the Liberal Republicans; but they were not prepared to desert the Republican party for reform and few orators denounced the reformer Tilden more savagely than Schurz. Schurz had ambitions of his own.

One of the Liberal Republicans, and only one, showed that he put reform above party. It is not without reason that the Adamses of Massachusetts are looked on as the greatest American family, for they have shown a certain rigid integrity that is above personal interests. Charles Francis Adams was finely educated and impractical, but he had principle; facing a tempest of abuse, he stood by Tilden, who had him nominated for governor of Massachusetts by the Democrats. This helped Tilden in the East, where Adams was greatly respected, for people knew that he would not support Tilden if the latter were the criminal he was represented by the Republicans to be.

In New York, Tilden was not so fortunate. An August convention nominated Horatio Seymour for governor against the latter's protests. Seymour was too ill to run. A second hurried convention put up a quondam Republican, Lucius Robinson, who was elected. Everywhere Tilden sought the best men for candidates, regardless of past party affiliations. In this hour his genius shone as he gave unity to a party made up of a dozen factions.

Tilden indeed is one of the most singular figures in American history. What is the secret of the enthusiasm with which he filled the poor, the oppressed in that summer of 1876?

Cadaverous, tallow-faced, prematurely aged, infirm, almost tottering, he yet inspired the strong with hope. Unimaginative, secretive, sad, he nevertheless held his followers with a devotion such as few others except Bryan have ever inspired; but Bryan was young, bold, robust, splendid. Was it that Tilden had some vision of a better America arising from the crude, war-torn, corrupt republic of the seventies?

The torchlight processions, the blaring bands, the crowded meetings were for the North. In the South there was no such spirit of pageantry, for the election seemed to the South to be a matter of life or death. Tilden meant freedom from the white man's burden crushing the South. Hayes appeared to be only a lesser Grant and stood, in Southern eyes, for negro domination upheld by bayonets, misgovernment by alien adventurers, humiliation and despair. The South had not hoped greatly in 1872, though it had mainly supported Greeley. Grant carried Virginia. But what was there to choose between Grant and Greeley, both enemies? Tilden, however, was neither soldier nor persecutor; he was a friend, and the God-forsaken South had need of friends. A passion of hope moved it to new life.

Of the seceded States, eight had regained autonomy. Virginia, North Carolina, Georgia, Alabama, Tennessee, Mississippi, Arkansas and Texas had emerged from the welter of the Reconstruction and conducted their affairs without active Federal interference—bankrupt, wasted, suffering but free. In these States the white people looked forward to a better future. Yet that future was threatened by the presidential election, for an active enemy in the White House could turn back the clock and restore the carpetbag misgovernment. Virginia, North Carolina, Tennessee and Texas had white majorities and were safe (Virginia had been specially favored by Grant) but the case of Georgia, Alabama and Mississippi was dubious. It was only by nullifying the Fifteenth Amendment that these states had returned to civilization. If the Fifteenth Amendment were rigidly enforced, their new state governments, representative of Anglo-Saxons, would be swept away and ignorance would again be enthroned. The process of dispossessing landowners by unpayable taxes would be renewed and continued until the Gulf States would be one with the Niger and the Congo. Yet if the Lower South were allowed—as it was doing—to nullify the Fifteenth Amendment, democracy would be frustrated. The world would witness the outrage of a civilized minority ruling an uncivilized majority. Would a new Republican President, elected on the Civil War issue—the only issue on which he could be elected—permit this wrong?

The summer waned and Hayes said nothing to indicate that he had any thought of mercy for the South. He seemed *en rapport* with the bloody-shirt wavers, who must elect him if he were elected. Overshadowed by such famous public men as Blaine, Schurz, Sherman, Harrison, Morton, Bristow and Evarts, he wisely held his peace, or nearly held it. He thereby gained in reputation, much as Coolidge did, for the public easily believes the legend of the "strong, silent man."

The Nation said sardonically:

As soon as he [Hayes] had accepted his nomination he retired into the innermost recesses of the conventional privacy. He cautiously avoided showing his hand in the canvass in any way. No ingenuity of interviewers was sufficient to extract from him any expressions of opinion on any topic having the remotest bearing on the Presidential contest. He recognized nothing, and neither authorized nor repudiated anybody. According to the newspaper accounts he would hardly go further in political discussion than to accede to the proposition that there was a republican form of government and that this was the hundredth year of the national government.[1]

[1] February 1, 1877.

Only once did Hayes emerge from obscurity. Late in October he went to the Centennial Exhibition at Philadelphia for an Ohio celebration. He was surprised, almost overwhelmed by the interest he inspired. Crowds followed him wherever he went, eager to gaze upon the Republican candidate. Tilden's sober, scholarly face was well known, but Hayes was quite unfamiliar to the public as yet. Receptions were held at the Ohio building, and Hayes shook hands until he was exhausted, not being yet inured to such homage. The spectators were rather disappointed in him, for his appearance did not uphold the traditions of presidential candidates—much as Smith's brown derby in 1928 displeased the conservative. Dignity may be waived by mere governors; it is demanded of Presidents. One altogether friendly observer grumbled at Hayes:

Truth to say, His Excellency's personal appearance was more informal than any of those who crowded to pay their respects to him, for he wore a dreadfully shabby coat and a shockingly bad hat, all brushed up the wrong way.[1]

But then Hayes had never been well dressed; his clothes were always ill-fitting and his long beard was almost uncouth, even if it was fatherly. A kind man he looked, the sort one seeks in trouble, a good neighbor and friend; but he was not a figure to inspire interest and admiration. After the gaunt, weird and most impressive Lincoln, and the small but powerful-faced Grant, Hayes merely looked the proprietor of a store in some town or a country doctor. And such is human folly, such is its preoccupation with externals, that this man of profound significance is almost forgotten, partly because of his mediocre, commonplace, middle-class appearance.

The Republicans seem to have been reasonably confident of the outcome of the election until October. And the first elec-

[1] New York *Times*.

tions of that month favored them. Much bloody-shirt oratory had had its effect in New England; Vermont and Maine went Republican by majorities much larger than those of 1874. Ohio, too, was safely Republican, and everything seemed right with the universe. But Satan was still powerful, for Indiana, counted on by the Republicans, stumped from end to end by their best orators, passed over to the Democracy, expelling that notable politician, Benjamin Harrison, from the governorship. The worm had turned. The Indiana populace was weary of Morton and the Civil War and much drawn by Hendricks and the beautiful Greenback theory of finance. So the Hoosiers "went rebel."

This was the turn in the campaign. The Republicans had hoped to carry nearly all the Northern states, by dint of the Civil War, and therefore to have no need of Southern electoral votes. But it was now evident that Indiana inclined to vote for its favorite son, Hendricks, just as New York favored Tilden. New York, Indiana and the Solid South looked like victory for Tilden. Immediately, the three Southern states that still had Republican governors and still enjoyed the protection of the Federal government became of supreme importance to the Republican leaders.

The Republicans had, of course, considered the possibility of needing help from the South; for this reason, as well as to facilitate bloody-shirt oratory, the Southern states had been much in the public prints all summer. South Carolina, partly as the mother of secession, partly as the scene of a fierce racial struggle, was particularly prominent.

The best ammunition available for Republican oratorical guns was found in Southern "outrages." Some outrages there were, for race war existed in the South; but they were fewer than might have been expected, considering the intense provocation to violence created by conditions utterly irritating to

Anglo-Saxons. And of the outrages perhaps a half—at least many of them—were committed by the negroes, though on the subject of crimes of blacks against whites Republican newspapers were singularly silent. They sought to create the impression that the Southern white people indulged in the pastime of making unprovoked assaults on peaceful, humble freedmen. Violence occurred in Mississippi, Alabama, and perhaps other States, but it was not reported as thrillingly as the violence of South Carolina. This last State quite overshadowed the rest of the South in public interest.

South Carolina was paying for her distinctive social characteristics. There the truest aristocracy that has ever existed in America flourished before the Civil War. The planters who formed it had raised themselves decidedly above the small white farmers, called "Sand-Hill Tackies" and by other slighting names, and governed herds of negroes only slightly tinctured with civilization since many of them had recently arrived from Africa. Living in Charleston much of the year, the planters combined urban with rural life in a manner that made them the most cultivated and charming group of people in the United States.

They also ruled the State and ruled it with ability if with too much audacity, since they precipitated the Civil War by seceding. When the planters were overthrown at the end of the war, the mass of South Carolinians had no other leaders and found themselves in evil case; the carpetbaggers and scalawags were busily elevating the ex-slaves to a position above that of the poor whites. The latter had suffered at the hands of the planters, but the planters were civilized white men while the new masters were Africans and ex-slaves. These whites, almost pure-blooded Anglo-Saxons, rebelled at the horrible fate that awaited them and finally rescued South Carolina from negro rule. The planters themselves acquiesced in negro suffrage and Wade Hampton, their leader, pledged himself to respect the Fifteenth Amendment, a pledge honorably kept; but the mass of whites would not have it so and never rested until every vestige of negro power was swept away. It was in this struggle that "Pitchfork" Ben Tillman began his stormy career.

The class hiatus in the South was curious enough. That terrible organization, the Ku Klux Klan, which did so much to defeat Reconstruction measures by a system of terrorism the most scientific ever devised, was largely the agent of the poorer whites. The planters generally looked for relief to the Democratic party of the North and showed a self-restraint remarkable under the circumstances. The poor whites, directly menaced by negro government, placed their reliance on naked force—on intimidation where intimidation would do, on violence when that was necessary. Their measures proved effectual; they saved their racial supremacy. It was one of the most notable victories ever won by common people of the Anglo-Saxon breed. In the process they finally shoved the "aristocrats" aside and seized power themselves.

Nothing is stranger in American history than South Carolina in the Reconstruction. It was a tragic farce; if the consequences had not been serious, the performance would have been ludicrous. Everywhere were suffering and misery and death, and yet laughter was excited rather than tears. It was horrible.

The negroes did not desire to contend for power; they were driven to it. Noble idealists and scoundrels from the North urged them to stand up for their rights, to vote, to pass laws, to govern. Was not a black man as good as a white? What was color in the sight of God? It was the same old nonsense, repeated ten thousand times. Eventually, it sounded like sense to the negroes, who came to believe that the power was theirs since they were in the majority and since the soldiers of a paternal government were at hand to protect them. So they voted and were elected to office. They began to govern.

In the capitol at Columbia—in the midst of the blackened ruins of the evacuation fire—negroes fresh from the plow, illiterate, without racial experience in government, made laws under the guidance of adventurers and fly-by-nights who might have stepped out of a comic opera. It could, of course, be nothing but a frightful travesty on government. In that ruined place, among a population starving and naked, the savage legislators and their white associates wasted, rioted, embezzled, stole with an abandon seldom witnessed in America. A bar was kept in the capitol where the negroes guzzled, *gratis*, fine wines and liquors. The old government had cost little; landowners now found that the Reconstruction regime threatened them with ruin, for taxes took on seven-league boots. The government of the Fifteenth Amendment was an Old Man of the Sea, an unbearable burden to a population struggling to recover from the results of a lost war.

A first Radical governor, Scott, was succeeded by Moses, who is still remembered as one of the most picturesque scamps in American history. Moses was followed by a man of very different type, Daniel H. Chamberlain, who set himself to the Sisyphean task of reforming the government. When Moses and a venal negro named Whipper were elected judges by the negro legislature, Chamberlain refused to commission them. This was an act of virtue for which he was loudly praised by a population astonished at the spectacle of an honest Republican. The new governor made it plain that the reign of graft and theft had come to an end.

In fact, Chamberlain was holding out the olive branch to the white people, or Conservatives, as they were called then; the party designation of Democrat was little used in the South until after 1880. In all this Chamberlain was simply following nature, though he did not know it. Savagery, ignorance, poverty could not always rule civilization, knowledge, property; more than this, Africans could not always rule Anglo-Saxons. Gravity wins at last, spiritually as well as materially. Chamberlain was a cultivated man, Yale-Harvard finished, and he was weary of being a social outcast. There was one remedy: to go over to the Conservatives. He prepared to go over, with certain reservations—negro suffrage must be respected. The Conservatives listened, even flirted. But in proportion as Chamberlain won favor with the white people by honest administration he lost countenance with the negroes, who had reveled in the waste and graft of former administrations. Their complaints reached Washington; presently Chamberlain found himself being denounced by the tribune of freedmen and carpetbaggers, Oliver P. Morton, as that monstrous thing, a Democrat.

Chamberlain was now in a quandary. He was a Republican falling out with his own party and looking for support to the Conservatives on the eve of a presidential election. The vote of South Carolina might be important. It is difficult to say what Chamberlain would have done if the Conservatives had made him an outright offer; but they did not do so and he began to consider the advisability of taking measures to make the electoral vote of the State safe for Hayes, who would carry South Carolina if the negroes were allowed to vote as they pleased.

Resistance to negro suffrage was growing as the burden of the government grew and as the sufferings of the white population increased. The State was worse off in 1876 than it had been in 1865; conditions were approaching the impossible. The once timid negroes had been armed and formed into militia companies by the Republican state government, which refused to sanction white militia; and with numbers and force on their side, the blacks would soon have a mastery that would no longer depend on the bayonets of United States troops. Appalled by the danger of an armed negro populace and infuriated by the insolence the freedmen now began to exhibit, the whites prepared to defend themselves by forming illegal militia companies usually known as "rifle clubs." The organization to which Ben Tillman belonged was called a "saber" club. These rifle clubs were denounced by Grant as unlawful, but they were the sole means of defense of the whites against the negro militia. The poor whites were resorting to intimidation to control the blacks, who threatened to get entirely out of hand. Violence increased to such an extent that Chamberlain finally called on Grant for more troops. It was really a part of his play to carry South Carolina for Hayes, but there was certainly need of soldiers to restore order.

The summer of 1876 was a terrible season in South Carolina. The negro field hands in the eastern counties were on strike for higher wages and bands of them roamed the country, interfering with the laborers who remained at work in the rice fields and sometimes using violence upon them. Robbery was common and more serious offenses occurred. One outrage, the murder of an aged couple by negroes, led to a no less horrible retaliation on the part of the whites, who seized and shot six blacks arrested on suspicion.

Worse was to follow. In July, in the negro town of Hamburg, a riot broke out in which one white and five blacks were killed. This was the "Hamburg Massacre," to which the Republican newspapers devoted whole columns as an example of "shotgun rule" in the South.

Chamberlain sent a considerably distorted account of the Hamburg affair to Washington. His statement is too inherently improbable to be accepted, for he represented the disturbance as beginning with the insulting by two young white men of a negro soldier company drilling in the streets of Hamburg. It is most unlikely that any two white men, drunk or sober, would in the heated year 1876 have insulted a negro militia company with guns in their hands. The truth seems to be that the truculent attitude of the negro militiamen aroused the resentment of the whites, who attacked them and slew five with the loss of one of their own number.

Chamberlain's complaint removed any doubt of his party orthodoxy entertained by the Washington authorities but, on the other hand, brought to an end his support by the Conservatives. When these held their state convention, they nominated for governor the leading citizen of South Carolina, Wade Hampton, a noted Confederate general and a member of the planter aristocracy. This nomination was unfortunate for Tilden, in that it gave color to Republican charges that the Democrats were "Confederate"; but, as a matter of fact, Hampton was not an opponent of negro suffrage and was as just and fair a man as could be found in the State. Still he had been at the head of Lee's cavalry in 1864, and this could not be overlooked by the Republican press. If the Conservatives had nominated Chamberlain, the Radicals would have named a candidate of their own, in which case Tilden might have received the vote of South Carolina. Hampton's selection definitely killed that chance.

Chamberlain, now bereft of hopes of Conservative support, turned again to the negroes; in a convention marked by disorder and fighting he succeeded in obtaining the Republican nomination once more. There was no longer anything to be gained by propitiating the white people who had rejected him and he prepared to carry South Carolina for Hayes by Federal intervention.

In August and September, riots broke out in the rice fields. Strikers attacked and beat workers, and the negro militia, when called out, fraternized with them. Chamberlain made little effort to restore order, seemingly desiring a good excuse for calling on Grant for troops.

As the election approached, law hardly existed at all in South Carolina. In September, the streets of Charleston were held for a day or two by rioting freedmen engaged in attacking Democratic negroes; for, contrary to the usual belief, many blacks desired to join the Conservative party just as many white men, if left to themselves, would have been Republicans. The effect of race solidarity was to drive all negroes into the Republican ranks and all whites into the Democracy, since politics had become simply a struggle between the races for control. Dissenters in the negro ranks suffered threats and violence; with the whites, social ostracism was the powerful weapon used to prevent desertions.

In Charleston, where the negroes were numerous and counted on the protection of the troops, it was hardly safe for a white man to walk the streets. In the country, where the whites were armed and organized in rifle clubs, it was dangerous for negroes to show signs of political activity.

Two riots furnished Chamberlain with ample reason for demanding troops. At Elberton, negroes began a disturbance by attacking a white woman and child. When a posse of white men attempted to arrest the leader in the assault, the blacks gathered to resist. Skirmishing took place in which one negro and two whites were killed. An armed mob of white men moved on Elberton, where the negroes had massed. A battle was probably prevented by the arrival of United States troops. The whites were terrorized by the negroes, the negroes by the whites. At a political meeting a little later a fight took place in which a number of whites and negroes lost their lives; this occurrence was described by the Republican press as an unprovoked assault of whites on freedmen and no mention was made of the former who were slain.

These disturbances, for which the blacks were certainly partially responsible, were reported by Chamberlain as attacks of armed white men on unoffending negroes. In mid-October he made a formal demand for troops to restore order in South Carolina. Need of order there was; but since the request was made on the eve of a presidential election and since it was requisite for Chamberlain to show zeal for the Republican cause, politics unquestionably played the principal part in his action. Grant was sympathetic, for he also desired to carry the State for his party. However, it is likely that the election would have been a farce without the presence of troops, since the poorer whites, now thoroughly aroused, were bent on driving the negroes from politics and were resorting in many places to intimidation.

The troops came in response to Chamberlain's demand and were dispersed through the State in small squads. Their presence alone prevented much bloodshed on election day, November 7. The day was one of tremendous threatenings but few outrages. In Charleston the polls were thronged by negroes, who attempted to drive away white voters. In the afternoon the streets were scoured by a mob of blacks; they tore up trees and fences to provide themselves with weapons and insulted and sometimes assailed white men. One white was killed and others were wounded. The disorder grew so great at last that General Hunt, in command at Charleston, accepted the services of the rifle clubs to protect the peace. For this act of prudence he was relieved of his command by Grant.

In the country, the intimidation was on the Conservative side. Armed white men patrolled the polls in some precincts and scared negroes away. Of actual violence there was little, but this was due to the presence in the State of a considerable number of troops and to the menacing attitude of the whites. Before their grim determination the courage of the negroes wilted and many of them refrained from voting and did not even approach the polls. However, in precincts where the negroes were protected by troops, the Republicans did not hesitate at unblushing frauds; repeating was practiced on a large scale. So the sun sank on this election of intimidation and trickery.

There were two charming States in the old times, South Carolina and Louisiana. Because this was so, the powers that envy human perfection reserved for those two commonwealths the largest of the vials of wrath poured out on the South for being agricultural and non-industrial. The fate of Louisiana was even worse than that of South Carolina.

The Northern people did not understand this, did not understand the South at all, because looking as they did on the negroes as brunet Anglo-Saxons, they could not comprehend the objection of the Southern white people to being ruled by them. The Northern people did not realize until Grant's second administration that the negroes were not Anglo-Saxons at all, but that they were tropicals and that terrible things were happening in the South under the Fifteenth Amendment. No other American community has undergone the fearful experience of Louisiana in a regime of pure democracy.

Louisiana differed from all the other Southern States in being partly Latin, for there the French admixture was and is large. Louisiana was even more tropical than South Carolina and it was among the richer and more luxurious Southern States; those States were poor because of the presence of a very ignorant, half-idle, irresponsible African population rather than because of the institution of slavery. Slavery was an evil, a great evil, because it was the chain that bound the white race to the black; but the supreme evil was the alien race itself. It was the alien quality of the African that made the continuance of slavery possible, indeed almost imperative, since men tend to put up with familiar devils rather than to fly to evils that they know not of. The dread of that uncomprehending multitude from another continent, another climate, another race experience—actuated by other thoughts, swayed by other ethics, filled with a different soul—finally drove the Southerners to choose secession rather than to permit interference.

The other-world atmosphere of Louisiana, the presence of herds of slaves, the most savage in all the South, bred the habit of violence; Louisiana was the one romantic spot in America. There Latins and Anglo-Saxons clashed, laboring, speculating, making love, running for office, living an exotic life amidst the perfume of tropical flowers. There men waged and lost plantations or scores of slaves in a single poker game. There men gayly shot each other for imaginary insults. There men lived well if not wisely, with a curious lack of sanity that was charming even if it was unhealthy. Decent New England and the Middle West could not permit such communities to exist in the model republic, hence the Civil War. It is difficult to imagine in our standardized, mechanized America of to-day that these vital Latins were ever citizens of the United States. Hot life—that is one thing we cannot understand today.

New Orleans, the single interesting city of the United States, was beginning a little to recover from the ruin of the Civil War, regaining a shadow of the cotton trade that had made it populous and prosperous, when the blighting curse of the Reconstruction fell upon the unfortunate community. The slaves, some of whom still practiced the fetish religion of their African ancestors, were with great suddenness invested with suffrage and had turned over to them the government of a once great and rich State. This was the supreme human sacrifice offered on the altar of democracy.

The details of that sordid tragedy need not detain us. An adventurer named Warmoth was elected governor by the enfranchised freedmen. Under his enlightened rule the debt of Louisiana increased forty million dollars in the four years between 1868 and 1872, most of the money wasted or stolen. Then a curious thing happened. Warmoth, with a cynical humor that has no parallel, became a reformer, denounced the venality of Grant's administration and arrayed himself with Schurz's Liberal Republicans, coming out for Greeley.

This show of conservatism drew the wretched white population to him, and a fusion of Liberal Republicans, Reformers and Democrats put in the field a State ticket headed by one McEnery. The Republicans named a ticket, led by the most spectacular desperado of the Reconstruction, William Pitt Kellogg, on which the candidates for lieutenant-governor, secretary of state, auditor, attorney-general, superintendent of education and treasurer were all negroes. In other words, the government of Louisiana under the Republican party was becoming an outright negro rule. If it had continued, the white inhabitants of the State would have been without representation.

In an election marked by intimidation, fraud, disorder, and every known crime against the dignity and purity of the ballot, the Democratic candidate, McEnery, was elected by a substantial majority. The Republicans, contesting the election, appealed to Cæsar, that is, to Grant. Warmoth was removed from office by a court order and the mulatto Pinchback took his place. Grant, with a rather shameless partizanship, declared for the negro; McEnery was refused the office he had won in a contest in which the Republicans had outdone the Democrats in fraud. Supported by the bayonets of United States troops, Kellogg was finally installed as governor; it seemed that Louisiana faced another season of violence, graft, theft, all corruption.

The white people, maddened by their wrongs, formed the White League, an armed organization having some of the qualities of the Ku Klux Klan but differing from it in being supported by the best men and in being responsible for its acts. It did not practice the arts of midnight murder. Much more objectionable than the White League was the negro State police, which attempted to rule Louisiana. On September 14, 1874, the White League rose in rebellion against the negro masters and overthrew the Kellogg government after a battle in the streets of New Orleans in which sixteen whites and eleven blacks were killed and a large number of both races wounded. Among the leaders of the negroes was General James Longstreet, Lee's famous lieutenant. In after years a monument was raised to the men who died for white supremacy on this notable day in Louisiana history.

Kellogg was now dispossessed and in danger of his life, and in every way he was anathema to the white population. At this juncture, however, General Sheridan went to Louisiana and, violently partizan, denounced the white people of the State as "bandits," urging the support of the negro administration headed by Kellogg. Grant accepted Sheridan's representations and the white government was ousted by bayonets in favor of the black.

Anarchy, however, really reigned. Under the forms of peace race war existed. Wholesale intimidation was practiced by the whites; officers of the government, both negroes and white Republicans, were murdered. The negroes, for their part, robbed, burned houses and murdered. In short, the State of Louisiana exhibited the symptoms of a community degenerating from civilization into savagery.

Open war was prevented by the presence of the troops. Finally the terrible state of affairs drove the Conservatives to accept a compromise by which Kellogg continued to act as governor while the legislature containing a majority of Conservative members was recognized. So bad were conditions that it is possible that the Republican government of Louisiana would have been abandoned by Grant before this if he had not had hopes of carrying the State for the Republican party in the approaching election.

It was generally felt that the campaign of 1876 would be decisive, and the Conservatives were grimly determined to win the election by any means, fair or foul. Faced by a government which held in its hands the electoral machinery of the State and practiced every kind of fraud, the Democrats had to resort to intimidation and force if they were to have a chance to rescue the commonwealth from conditions that were almost unbearable and threatened to become worse.

The Republicans nominated for governor S. B. Packard, a carpetbagger, and renominated the negro Antoine for lieutenant-governor. The Democrats put up for governor General F. T. Nicholls, an ex-Confederate who had lost an arm and a leg, and for lieutenant-governor, Louis A. Wiltz, the speaker of the house of representatives.

The election was notable in that the Democrats made an effort to win over a part of the negroes to them by promises and active campaigning, hoping to carry the day in this way. If the negro vote were divided they would win, for the white race with few exceptions was enlisted in the Democratic party. In some parishes, where the negroes were consolidated and universally Republican, the Democrats resorted to intimidation. A few cases of violence occurred, but these seem to have been unauthorized; the White League apparently refrained from assaults for fear of giving the Republican election managers an excuse for throwing out precincts, and the government at Washington the opportunity for further nullifying elections and bulldozing the white people of the State. Thus there were not many outrages, but in the sequel much was made of such as occurred. As a matter of fact, the election of 1876 was the most orderly that had taken place in Louisiana in several years, probably due to the fear of the negro population for the White League and to the efforts of the league to prevent violence.

Florida was the third Southern State so unfortunate as to be still under Federal supervision. It was the classic commonwealth of the Reconstruction, the field of the most picturesque knavery, the scene of the most characteristic doings of the Ku Klux Klan.

Florida was not a community in which the freedmen were intimidated by the white population. The boot was on the other foot; in Florida the whites were overawed by the negroes and their carpetbag and scalawag leaders. For Florida was not a negro State; a majority of the people were white, and, under a fair system of registration and balloting, Florida would have been Conservative like Virginia and North Carolina. But there was anything but a fair system of registration and balloting; by one device and another, the Republicans managed to get the commonwealth in their hands, to loot it, to make it the victim of great frauds and finally the battlefield of an outraged and enraged population.

Florida began its reconstruction from an old-fashioned community of peace and plenty into a progressive State of corruption, violence and anarchy under the supervision of United States soldiers; they saw to it that a new constitution was adopted admitting to suffrage the simple savages who had rather enjoyed their condition as slaves in a climate and amid surroundings perfectly suited to them. When the first legislature under the improved government convened, there were but twenty-three members elected by the white majority, while nineteen negroes and thirty-four carpetbaggers and scalawags represented the black minority. This speaks well for the resourcefulness of the Republicans in that State. The fifty-four Republican members, together, owned less than $1,000 of taxable property; but when they gave up legislating, their share of this world's goods had considerably increased. In no State were the politicians thriftier, considering their opportunities, than in Florida. The Republican legislature, fearing that the State would "go white" in 1868 and cast its electoral vote for Horatio Seymour, passed a law depriving the people of the right to vote for presidential electors and then chose Grant electors. A beautiful lesson in democracy, taught the people of Florida by their carpetbag task-masters! More than this, the carpetbag governor, Reed, had a law passed creating a secret police in order to reproduce in an American State the methods of Tzarist Russia—another valuable demonstration of democracy. Deprivation of the presidential ballot and police terrorism—surely, Reconstruction was for Florida a cornucopia of gifts! However, Reed vetoed a bill compelling railways and hotels to accord the same treatment to blacks and whites, and this brought him into ill favor with the more Radical element. Always in the Reconstruction era the negroes tried to force social equality on the white race by means of mixed schools, hotels and churches opened to both races alike, and other devices; but generally the carpetbaggers and scalawags opposed them, fearing that the victims might rebel.

An attempt was made to impeach Reed, and every year or so during his stormy tenure of office he was impeached or almost impeached; but, in some way, perhaps by superior cunning, perhaps by bribery, he managed to keep his place.

Graft had begun with the installation of the negro government, but the real looting now took place. A suave adventurer named Littlefield came down from the North and showed the simpler-minded carpetbaggers the approved methods of modern finance. An act was passed by the legislature sanctioning the issue of railroad bonds, ostensibly for improvements. The act filed and published as the law was not the act as passed, but a forged document which eliminated a clause intended to protect the State. Littlefield went to New York with $4,000,000 of bonds, which were sold to unsophisticated Europeans for seventy cents on the dollar. Of the almost $3,000,000 thus raised, nearly the whole went to the rascals who arranged the deal, Reed receiving about $225,000. Of the entire amount, only $300,000, about a tenth, was spent in bettering the railways. This operation stands as a model in the art of graft.

In the election of 1870, the negroes attempted to terrorize white voters by gathering in armed mobs at the polls and to prevent them from voting by creating disturbances and thus causing delays. In spite of these efforts, the whites asserted their natural strength and Florida was carried by the white candidates for lieutenant-governor and congressman-at-large. However, the State canvassing board, erected for the purpose of keeping the Republicans in power and entirely controlled by that party, counted out the Democratic candidates and declared the Republicans returned. The Democratic congressional aspirant contested the election and, after a long fight, was seated.

Owing to the canvassing board, the Democrats were unable to win an election because, no matter what the polls showed, the Republican candidates were invariably declared elected. After Reed passed from the scene, the governor was another carpetbagger, Marcellus L. Stearns. It was now 1871; and the carpetbaggers and scalawags, fearful of losing power, stirred up racial hatred to the last degree as a means of keeping the negroes consolidated in the Republican party.

But the white people of Florida, defrauded, robbed, downtrodden, were about to rise against their oppressors. After all, they were Anglo-Saxons and there were limits to the wrongs they would endure at the hands of altruists bent on establishing the rights of man. Here the Ku Klux Klan performed a work that was not without its beneficent side despite its oc-

casional horrors. In the Sherlock Holmes story, "The Five
Orange Pips," Conan Doyle has told of the weird warning sent
by the hooded order to carpetbaggers and scalawags in Florida.
If the offender, after receiving a message that so many days
were allowed him, accompanied by some orange pips, did not
leave the State, he was "visited," with sinister results to himself. That, with some romantic exaggeration, this was true is
evidenced by the testimony given by a scalawag in 1871:

It was just eight days after the election that I got up one
morning and found a piece of paper lying inside of my gate informing me that if I remained three days longer I was in danger. . . . I went to the store and there was a negro man standing on the store steps with a gun in his hand. There was a big
notice on the store that they would give me 24 hours to leave.
. . . It was signed 'K.K.K.' and made up of little words cut out
of paper, not in writing.

The race war in Florida was begun by the inflammatory
speeches of Republican politicians, who felt the need of solidi-
fying the negro race, since the blacks were in a minority. It is
notable that the struggle passed from a contest between blacks
and Southern whites led by the Ku Klux Klan into an outright
race war between blacks and whites. On an occasion in 1869,
a party of United States troops were ambushed by negroes
(though the troops were there to protect them) and one soldier was killed. In retaliation the troops "shot up" the negro
section of Jacksonville.

The acute struggle began when negroes at a picnic were
fired on and a man and child were killed. The negroes retaliated
by firing at night upon a group on a porch in Marianna and
killing a girl. At this the Ku Klux Klan became active; there
was a short reign of terror in Marianna in which a few blacks
were slain, not many. The Ku Klux Klan in Florida did not

aim at killing negroes so much as at driving white Republican leaders away. Several attempts were made to assassinate carpetbaggers and scalawags and in the end a number of white leaders of the blacks were expelled from the State. The white majority in Florida then asserted itself; the State passed into Democratic control, and outrages ceased. It is not possible to compute the number of lives lost between 1868 and 1876, but it probably was not large.

Excitement rose high in Florida as the campaign of 1876 opened, since the white people there, as in all the Lower South, looked to the election of a Democratic President as the means of salvation from intolerable oppression. The Republicans were just as determined to hold Florida, for the electoral vote of the State might be important. They had hopes of carrying Florida as well as South Carolina and Louisiana because all three of these States had Republican governors and the electoral machinery was in the hands of the Republican party. It was the control of the electoral machinery and not the presence of troops in the States that inspired the Republicans, since the troops did not dominate the election and could not have done so. The election returns in Florida and Louisiana were Democratic, but in both of them the Republican canvassing boards reversed the decision. The main reason for the presence of the troops was to protect the canvassing boards in the processes by which they produced Republican majorities. If the canvassing boards had been in the hands of the Democrats, the performance would have been reversed.

In Florida the Republicans held their State convention in June. They were now badly divided, but the convention was terrorized by a mob of drunken negroes, probably in the pay of Stearns, and the governor was renominated. The "reform" faction of the party nominated one Conover. The latter withdrew before the election, leaving Stearns as the sole Republican candidate, but the Republicans did not heal their dissensions. The Democrats, united, thus went into the campaign with confidence, having an actual majority of the voters of the State. They nominated George F. Drew, a New Englander long resident in Florida and thus not a carpetbagger. Well organized and opposing a party rent by factions, the Democrats faced the election with hope. They had not yet learned that a majority can always be turned into a minority by manipulation. Troops were brought into the State and dispersed in squads. Order there would be on election day—and protection thereafter to the canvassing board.

As November 7, 1876, approached, a greater excitement seized the American people than at any time since Lee's surrender. The Republicans, arrogant, claiming that they were the only patriots and that their opponents were traitors, relying solely on the fact that they had won the war, now more than ten years past, were exceedingly uneasy over the outcome. The thousand scandals of Grant's administration, the bad financial condition, the state of the South, which so far from benefitting they had almost ruined, all argued against their continuance in power. On the other hand, the Democrats, really hopeful for the first time since 1860, looked forward to the election of Tilden as the escape from oppression, corruption, and all the evils of the military rule under which the country had groaned since 1861. And if the campaign had turned on reform, the Democrats would have swept the country. It did not; it was mainly a rehash of the Civil War. *The Nation,* in commenting on the complaints later made by the Republican politician, William E. Chandler, against Hayes, said:

The substance of "Bill's" accusation against Mr. Hayes is that he was distinctly nominated and elected as a "bloody-shirt" candidate; that he so understood it himself, as was shown in his letter of acceptance and the letter he wrote Nov. 8 when he thought he had been defeated, deploring the fate of the poor negro under Tilden. Chandler further truly remarks that the "campaign was carried on, as far as methods and utterances were concerned, in no respect differently from the campaigns of 1868 and 1872." [1]

The New York *Times* was foremost in charges that Tilden had evaded his income tax in 1862; it claimed that Tilden's real income was $80,000 in excess of his declared income and that the government had lost several thousand dollars of taxes through perjury. The violent and abusive language employed by the *Times* in supporting this accusation has rarely been exceeded.

The Nation, moved by the statements made by the *Times,* examined the matter carefully and came to the conclusion that Tilden had been slandered for political purposes. Its comparison of the *Times'* charges with Tilden's defence showed that income earned in 1861 had been included in the former as due in 1862 and that most of the other items cited by the *Times* had been assumed or imagined. When the *Times'* abuse was supported by attacks on Tilden by prominent members of the government on the very verge of the election, *The Nation* did not conceal its indignation. It said:

The practices which Jayne and his custom-house spies, with the aid and support of the late Administration and men like Mr. Conkling, have introduced of late years, seem to have so accustomed people to arbitrary measures that such documents as Mr. Bliss's letter hardly attract any attention or cause any indignation. They furnish, however, another proof of what using administrative machinery for party purposes inevitably comes to: it begins with filling places with "faithful men," and ends with the publication by high officials of the Government, in party newspapers, on the eve of a Presidential election, of

[1] July 3, 1877.

charges of fraud and perjury against the opposition candidate, based on evidence which is not known to exist and which no honest attempt has been made to discover.[1]

As the summer waned it was generally calculated by observers that Tilden would certainly carry all of the Southern States except South Carolina, which was classed as doubtful. Florida was as confidently put in the Democratic column as Mississippi or Virginia; 131 Southern votes were set down for Tilden. On the other hand, Illinois, Iowa, Kansas, Maine, Massachusetts, Michigan, Minnesota, Nebraska, New Hampshire, Pennsylvania, Rhode Island, Vermont, Wisconsin, 129, were conceded to Hayes. This left 109 votes in doubt, including those of Ohio and Indiana. New York was doubtful. After the October elections, Ohio was put in the Hayes column, Indiana in the Tilden. *The Nation* said, on October 19, 1876:

We put down as certain to go for Tilden the entire South except South Carolina, 131 votes, with the addition of Indiana, 15 votes. This gives him 146 votes, and makes it necessary for him to get 39 votes to carry the election.

These estimates are important in view of the fact that two Southern States, practically conceded to Tilden, had to be claimed for Hayes in order to make a majority for him. On the eve of the election, it was not known how the Far West would go, though Colorado had been carried by the Republicans in a local election; Connecticut and New Jersey were classed as doubtful, along with New York. The unusually heavy registration in New York City caused uneasiness to the Republican managers, though they shared in the increase. As the election neared it was evident to them that they would have difficulty in piling up a sufficient majority upstate to over-

[1] November 2, 1876.

come the Democratic majority in the city, for Tilden was popular all over the State and, besides, he was a New Yorker contending with an unknown outsider. The situation was more clouded and dubious than for many years; the readmission of the South to presidential elections had restored the balance of parties. Indeed, with all the Southerners voting again, it was generally felt that there were now more Democrats than Republicans in the United States.

AUTUMN drifted on toward November. As the great day approached even the calm Rutherford Hayes grew nervous. He wrote in his diary on September 24:

I am looking anxiously forward to the end of the contest. It is now almost one hundred days since the nomination and only about forty-five to the election.

He was apprehensive of the October elections but refused to read in them the omens that disturbed the Republican leaders, feeling relieved that Ohio stuck by him and not being overly depressed at the defection of Indiana. He declared he thought that Tilden's chances were better than his but there was an element of self-contradiction here. He really was quite confident of the result, quietly confident. He expressed concern for the South in case he was defeated, and this note was sincere. He always thought that he could do more for the South than Tilden, and he was right. Tilden could not have saved the South; Hayes did save it.

At length November 7, 1876 dawned. The election of this day was probably the most exciting that the United States has ever witnessed. Contrary to received opinions, it was a comparatively honest election. The campaign funds of both parties were small; consequently, bribery was not prominent. Zach Chandler had begun the process of obtaining election funds from business concerns, but this abuse was in its infancy. No State seems to have been carried by the use of money. Probably more people expressed real preferences in this election than in the elections for many previous years, for war inhibitions were weakened. The country was beginning to veer to civil rule again; the Mexican period of American history was approaching the end.

The two parties were very evenly divided, and everyone knew that the election would be close. The Republicans were the more confident of winning because they had won so often, and by such decisive majorities in the elections of 1868 and 1872, that it was difficult for them to visualize defeat in a presidential contest; they had all the advantages that the party in power enjoys in such case.

There was a bitterness that we simply cannot understand today, since there were few important differences in the principles of the contending parties. In that age party membership was a lifetime allegiance, a matter of pride, an article of faith. It was an earthly complement of religion; just as a man saved himself in the future world by belonging to the true church, he saved himself in this world by being a member of the right party. The Republican regarded the Democrat as a quasi-criminal, and the Democrat returned the sentiment with interest. It was not until the advent of the big-hearted, large-minded Grover Cleveland that Americans began to understand that membership in the opposing party need carry with it neither mental obtuseness nor moral obliquity. That time had not come in 1876.

All day of November 7, old soldiers went to the polls to vote for Hayes, fervently believing that they were doing their part to save the country from the rebellious, traitorous, evil and abandoned commonwealths of the South, which would enter on the control of the administration if Tilden were elected. The Democrats went to the voting booths, grimly hopeful that the day would see the end of military rule and of the corruption that pervaded nearly every department of government. Turn the rascals out! Never was the famous cry more loudly bawled than on this notable day. On neither side was there any clear conception of the issues involved, nor were the apprehensions of either party justified. Hayes was honorable and patriotic; so was Tilden. Both candidates were well prepared for the duties of the office, particularly Tilden, who was one of the ablest public men of the country, if not the ablest. As it turned out, Hayes made one of the best Presidents the United States has ever had. But the voters on that November day so long ago did not foresee this; they felt that the destiny of the republic rested with them. Voters did not realize then how much of a quadrennial farce our Presidential election is.

The sun sank on a feverish country; everywhere the telegraph wires began to buzz with news and rumors. All over the land the people watched the returns with bated breath, and in the South they watched with tears and prayers. It might be the salvation of the Lower South, apparently destined to the fate of the jungle.

Crowds gathered before the bulletin boards in a hundred cities. It was long before the day of the radio, even before the day of the telephone. All news came by telegraph and in many towns and villages the returns, as they were brought into some party headquarters, court house or other gathering place, were read aloud. In New York the crowds began to gather at nightfall; the voting in the city had been unusually peaceful. The customary rows at the polls had been conspicuous by their absence. A vast milling mob filled City Hall Park all night and groaned or shouted as the news, favorable or the reverse, was shown on the newspaper bulletin boards. All night long hope and fear rose and waned as seldom before and never since in American history.

The early returns that came drifting in from a few precincts here and there were so favorable to Tilden that the Republicans were astounded, fearing that they foreshadowed a Democratic landslide. New York, which had been regarded as doubtful, more and more inclined to Tilden as the normal up-state Republican majority failed to materialize. Connecticut and New Jersey, which ordinarily go with New York, were likewise seen to be in the balance. As the returns continued to flash in, it was evident that Indiana had repeated its October heresy and gone for Tilden and Hendricks. With New York, Connecticut and Indiana apparently Democratic, Tilden's election seemed probable, for it was certain that most, if not all, of the Southern States were Democratic. If the Solid South of a year or so later had existed then, Hayes would have had no chance.

Probably the Republicans would have conceded defeat if there had not been bright patches in the gloom. California, considered doubtful, was reported for Hayes, and Oregon also was believed to be Republican, though still in doubt. Pennsylvania, with its customary Republican fanaticism, had gone for Hayes, rather on Civil War issues than on the tariff, for Pennsylvania was distinguished for its hatred of the South—perhaps because it was so near. New Hampshire, Vermont, Massachusetts, Rhode Island were Republican because of the invaluable bloody shirt. Ohio, after a brief season of doubt, was seen to have voted again for its favorite son. Illinois, mindful of Lincoln, was Republican, as were Michigan, Wisconsin, Iowa, Kansas, Nebraska. But these did not outweigh Virginia, North Carolina, Georgia, Alabama, Mississippi, Arkansas, Missouri, West Virginia, Kentucky, Tennessee, Texas, all of which had gone for Tilden. As the evening wore on to midnight only hardened Republicans still hoped.

That raw, disagreeable autumn evening Hayes listened to the returns in his home in Columbus, marking time by the procession of telegraph messenger boys bringing him the dispatches as these came in. Mrs. Hayes and an admiring group of

friends hovered over him. He wondered what New York
would do, staking his faith on that wabbling giant, which more
and more leaned toward Tilden. At one time it even seemed
that Ohio had gone back on Hayes. Lucy, more malleable, less
controlled than himself, as soon as she had finished serving
refreshments to her guests, escaped to her room with a headache that was a heartache. Her husband's consoling talk restored
her a little, but she did not return to the parlor. Hayes himself
went back, grimly determined to be cheerful. As the returns
from New York showed Tilden distinctly ahead, Hayes's prospects seemed to melt into nothingness. "From that time," he
confessed in his diary, "I never supposed there was a chance
for Republican success." At midnight he went to bed, feeling
that he had lost.

All over the country Democrats, browbeaten, oppressed, denounced as they had been for fifteen years, rejoiced in what
seemed to be a great victory. Yet as the night wore on toward
morning the usual did not happen; Tilden's lead did not grow
but rather dwindled. It was apparent that he had been elected,
but elected by a small majority. The situation offered all sorts
of possibilities. The final outcome of the election was determined, in great measure, by a newspaper, the New York *Times*.
This journal had distinguished itself in the campaign above a
thousand other partizan sheets by its persecution of the Democratic candidate, whom it libeled in every possible way. The
early returns had convinced nearly all the newspapers—or all
—that Tilden was elected, and the New York *Tribune*, bitterest of the Republican press, conceded it in its first edition
on November 8.

That the New York *Times* did not follow suit was the result
of a deliberate plot to snatch the election from Tilden and give
it to Hayes, the first and only instance of the kind in American
history. Anyone who has followed the course of the *Times* in

the campaign of 1876 will hardly fail to come to the conclusion that the able and unscrupulous men who managed it would not have hesitated at any means to bring success to their cause. In the night of November 7, 1876, they were desperate, as the indications strongly pointed to Democratic success, but they had not despaired. About midnight Abram S. Hewitt, Democratic national chairman, sent a message to the *Times* asking what majority it conceded to Tilden and was met by the defiant declaration of John C. Reid, managing editor, "None!"

In the editorial council held soon afterward a momentous decision was reached. In the dirty office littered with proof sheets, the weary and distracted editors gathered—editor-in-chief, John Foord, John C. Reid, the managing editor, George Shepherd and Edward Cary—to consider what should be said in the first edition, soon to be prepared. Of these men the most dominating was Reid, who had spent some time in Libby Prison, Richmond, in the war and had conceived an insane hatred for the Democratic party. However, the man who decided the issue of the moment was Cary, who persuaded the others not to concede Tilden's election.

This determination was strengthened by an event which shows that the gods smile on those who dare and have no scruples. About 3:45 A. M. the *Times* received the following dispatch from Democratic headquarters:

Please give your estimate of electoral votes secured for Tilden. Answer at once.

D. A. MAGONE.

Such apparently are the facts in the case, though the message has also been attributed to Senator Barnum and to Arthur Pue Gorman.[1] The communication was a blunder, in that it showed the astute men in the *Times* office that Democratic headquarters had not received definite news from some of the States supposed

[1] Haworth, 47; Elmer Davis, *History of the New York Times,* 136.

to be for Tilden. As a matter of fact, the returns from some of the Southern States were behindhand, and this gave the political strategists in the *Times* office an opportunity they would not otherwise have had. There are indications that the first reports from the Republican managers in Louisiana and Florida conceded those States to Tilden but that the telegrams were suppressed.[1] In other words, the Democratic managers in South Carolina, Louisiana and Florida had not sent in reports, and in the absence of these the Republicans could claim the States and might be able to substantiate the claim. Both Louisiana and Florida had been practically counted for Tilden for weeks and the Republicans had not expected to need them; but the fact that New York and Indiana were reported to have gone Democratic revealed to the *Times* editors the desperate nature of the situation and the necessity of securing votes from the South if Hayes was to win. There was nothing to go on but nerve, since the only news from Louisiana at all authentic was an Associated Press dispatch that the Democrats claimed the States by 20,000 votes and the Republicans by 4,000, which shows plainly enough how the wind was blowing.

The *Times* editors knew, however, *that the Republicans still controlled the canvassing boards of South Carolina, Louisiana and Florida and thus could produce any majority they desired.* On this fact the whole election turned. The returns indicated that Oregon had gone Republican, which gave the conspirators their chance, for if that State had been carried by Tilden the entire vote of the three Southern states would not have saved Hayes. If the canvassing boards of the three States could be induced to give Hayes the votes of those States, he would be elected—or the votes of South Carolina and Louisiana at least. South Carolina was known to be genuinely doubtful and the evil reputation of the Louisiana canvassing board, im-

[1] E. Benjamin Andrews, *The United States in Our Own Time*, 215.

plicated in several frauds, offered a good ground of hope. Possibly Florida would not be needed.

The first thing to do was to induce the Republican managers, who had practically given up the ship, to claim the election. If that were done, the claim could be made good by the canvassing boards. John C. Reid took on himself the task of seeking the Republican leaders and showing them the opportunity before them.

Reid hastened through the still stirring streets—the New York streets of the seventies, with their cobblestones and telegraph poles and low buildings, so utterly unlike the present—to the Fifth Avenue Hotel, Republican headquarters. He found the committee rooms deserted, as the committeemen and their associates had gone home, convinced that Hayes was defeated. And indeed on the face of the returns he was defeated. It is probable, as stated before, that the first telegraphic dispatches to Republican headquarters from leaders in Florida and Louisiana conceded those States to Tilden.

But what is a majority if you have control of the electoral machinery and can manufacture majorities? The Republicans, having control of the electoral machinery of South Carolina, Florida and Louisiana, might well hope. At least Reid so reasoned.

The journalist started down to the hotel office to find the number of National Chairman Zachariah Chandler's room. The latter must be made to realize the possibilities of the situation before it was too late. An admission of defeat would be fatal; an assertion of victory might mean the election. It was a time when every minute counted, one of the tensest and most gripping situations outside the realm of fiction.

On his way down Reid ran upon a small man muffled in an overcoat and reading the New York *Tribune,* in which Tilden's election was described. This was William E. Chandler, of New Hampshire, only less conspicuous than Zachariah Chandler in his devotion to the Republican party and in his lack of scruples. Chandler believed that Tilden was elected, but Reid showed him the dispatch from Democratic headquarters and pointed out that this indicated the uncertainty of the Democrats themselves. He urged that the Republicans should claim the election first and substantiate the claim afterward. The two men, proceeding to William E. Chandler's room, went over the vote carefully, State by State, and counted it as was finally done by the Electoral Commission, giving Hayes a majority of one.

The conspirators then went in search of Zachariah Chandler, whom they found after several embarrassing intrusions on wrong persons. Loud knocking at length produced the chairman, who opened the door clad in his nightgown—it was before the degenerate days of pyjamas. Chandler, dazed by the labor, anxiety and disappointment of the day, comprehended only with difficulty. He finally authorized William E. Chandler to do what he thought best under the circumstances.

William E. Chandler and Reid hurried to the hotel telegraph office, which they found closed at this late hour. Obtaining a carriage, they drove to the main office of the Western Union. There messages were sent to Governor Chamberlain, of South Carolina; to S. B. Conover, Tallahassee, Florida; to S. B. Packard, Republican candidate for governor of Louisiana, and to others. One sent to South Carolina was typical:

Hayes is elected if we have carried South Carolina, Florida, and Louisiana. Can you hold your State? Answer immediately.

The implications of this message are evident, for at the time the returns from Florida and Louisiana indicated that those States had gone Democratic. It was thus left for the men who controlled the electoral machinery to produce the necessary results. If that were done, Hayes was elected. The telegrams were charged to the *Times*.

The first edition of the *Times* on November 8 was cautious. It did not assert too much. The following editorial was written by Cary.

A DOUBTFUL ELECTION

At the time of going to press with our first edition the result of the presidential election is still in doubt. Enough has been learned to show that the vote has been unprecedently heavy; that both parties have exhausted their full legitimate strength; that the peculiar Democratic policy for which such extensive preparations were made in the large registry in this city, and in Brooklyn, has had its effect, and that in some of the States where the shotgun and rifle clubs were relied upon to secure a Democratic victory, there is only too much reason to fear that it has been successful.

The method by which the *Times* went on to claim the election may be observed in subsequent editions. Without having reason to do so other than reliance on canvassing boards, the *Times* put South Carolina and Louisiana in the Hayes column, though according to available estimates Tilden had carried the latter State by a considerable majority. Florida, however, was not claimed at first because that State appeared to be safely Democratic and, besides, it was not certain that it would be needed in order to obtain a majority for Hayes. The first dispatches indicated that New Jersey was in doubt, and the Republican majority manufacturers in the *Times* office hoped that Hayes had carried it; if so, the nauseating work of the canvassing board in Florida would not be necessary and the State might be left to Tilden. But by morning it became clear that Tilden had carried New Jersey; immediately Florida became of supreme importance because it alone stood between Hayes and defeat.

The second edition of the *Times*, published at 6:30 A. M.

on November 8, conceded Tilden 184 votes, one less than a majority; and claimed 181 for Hayes, including Oregon, Louisiana and South Carolina. Florida, it stated, was in doubt. The next, and final, process was to claim Florida, thus giving Hayes 185 votes, a majority of one.

Zachariah Chandler at last learned the lesson, so painfully taught him by Reid. Early in the morning of November 8, he sent out his famous dispatch:

Hayes has 185 electoral votes and is elected.

Nothing more brazen than this has occurred in American history, but it was less bold, less revolutionary than it seemed. The Republicans had every chance of winning the election, *if they claimed it*. Reid's hardest task was to induce the national chairman to make the claim. This done, measures might be taken to secure the claim; that was in the realm of practical politics. In such a contest the Republicans had every advantage: the possession of the executive power, carrying with it the control of the army, an army accustomed to intervene in political affairs; the ex-soldiers and their dependents, numbering millions; the cry that the republic was endangered by rebels; the support of great business interests; the majority of the newspapers in the North and West; the sympathy of all those who feared a change; the austere dignity of the Senate, the body that has so often masked special privilege with the toga. The Democrats had only two supports: the House of Representatives and the conviction of the majority of the American people that their cause was just. But what is justice in politics?

However, the Republican leaders sadly needed stiffening in the morning of November 8, since they had ventured on an audacity common in Mexican politics, where elections are decided by the army, but new in American politics, where elections are usually determined by election judges, more or less fairly but not grossly. The men at headquarters communicated with Grant, in Philadelphia, over Jay Gould's private wire, for that paramount beast of prey was an ardent Republican. Grant probably gave them comforting assurance of support.

The battle was half won when the Republicans claimed the election. The Democrats were certain to resist, but would they actually fight? That was the question. The Republican leaders did not think so; they hoped that the Democrats would quietly submit when the Republican canvassing boards produced the necessary majorities in South Carolina, Louisiana and Florida. This they were certain to do unless the Democrats offered bribes of enormous size. The Republicans had money enough to offer and offices as well; besides, the canvassers were nearly everyone Republicans and naturally sided with their party. The only chance the Democrats had in the three States at issue was in bold, splendid bribery. Anything else would fail. The Democrats tried law and evidence, and failed. They dabbled with bribery but apparently made no real offers of large amount; so here they failed again. But they did not submit to the Mexican methods of the Republican party; and, by refusing to play the rôle of gentle resignation and humble submission, as in the Civil War period, they nearly brought on an armed conflict. The turning of the worm is not without danger.

Zachariah Chandler continued to intone his defiance to the will of the majority:

Hayes has 185 electoral votes and is elected.

And such is the effect of reiteration, of impudent claims confidently asserted, that the Republicans, convinced the night before that they were beaten, believed by the night of November 8 that they had won, though there was no basis for such faith except Zach Chandler's boundless assurance. Chandler claimed the election and dared the Democrats to do their worst. Such a situation had never before arisen in the United States in the many changes in power following presidential elections.

When Jefferson defeated Adams, he was seated though only after a contest with his fellow-Democrat, Aaron Burr. Jackson replaced John Quincy Adams without disturbance; Harrison succeeded Van Buren; Polk, Tyler; Taylor, Polk; Pierce, Fillmore. Only when Lincoln followed Buchanan was there trouble and then no one sought to prevent Lincoln's inauguration. The Southern Democrats might have found counting Lincoln out in the election better than secession, but they did not attempt it. No effort had been made to reverse an election until 1876; it shows how military control grows on men and colors their action with violence, or the threat of violence, that the Republicans tried it then. The lesson of American history is that anything may be done within the Union, any crime perpetrated, any injustice enthroned; but that the body of the people will not sanction an attempt against the Union. Few more honorable public men have appeared in American life than Jefferson Davis, but his name is still anathema to millions of Americans because he is supposed, mistakenly, to have been the head and front of the secession movement.

The Republican leaders based their hopes on the canvassing boards of South Carolina, Louisiana and Florida, the three Southern States still under the enlightened government of the Fifteenth Amendment and therefore communities where anything could happen. Majorities meant nothing in those states, where everything was settled by force or fraud. The Republicans, reflecting on this truth, were comforted. After all, they had done well in conferring suffrage on the freedmen. It was true that Georgia, Alabama and Mississippi had escaped from the politics of the jungle and reverted to Anglo-Saxon government; but while South Carolina, Louisiana and Florida remained, all was not lost. Once having claimed the election, the Republicans would probably have gone on to bare usurpation if necessary; but they hoped that the canvassing boards would spare them the necessity of violating the forms of law as well as the spirit of justice. There is much virtue in legal forms: they put the mask of right on wrong.

All eyes now turned to the three Southern States, which the Democrats claimed by virtue of the trifling fact that the face of the election returns indicated that they had certainly carried two of them. The Republicans had no scruples whatever in obtaining the desired results from the canvassing boards by an inversion of the election, since they looked on the Southern States as so much territory filched from them. They had hoped that negro suffrage would secure them the Lower South forever, and negro suffrage was proving to be a broken reed. The net result of negro suffrage was the strengthening of the Democratic party until it was able to contend on equal terms with the Republicans. Anything that could be won in the South seemed to the Republicans to be so much gain.

Soon after the election the Republican leaders made preparations to secure favorable results from the canvassing boards of the three disputed States. Grant lent them aid by an order issued on November 10 to General Sherman to prepare to send troops to support the canvassing boards in their labors. Under patriotic verbiage, this was really a warning to the Democrats not to interfere with the functions of the canvassers, who were perfectly well understood by the Republicans to be ready to secure the electoral vote of the three States for Hayes.

The troops were not intended merely to coerce the Democrats; it was even more important to coerce the canvassing boards. The weakness of the Republican position lay in the venality of the canvassers; they were nearly all scoundrels, and scoundrels seldom put fidelity to party above personal interest. There was nothing to prevent some canvassing board from deciding in favor of Tilden if sufficiently bribed, thereby embarrassing the Republican leaders immeasurably; and a round sum—say, a million dollars—would probably have overcome the virtue of a majority of a board. But with troops at hand it was far more difficult to bribe and be bribed, and this is possibly one reason why the bribery overtures failed. The Republican leaders, understanding the weakness of human nature, were prepared to offer counter inducements. It is probable that much money changed hands; at all events, nearly every official concerned in the transference of the votes of the three States to Hayes received a good Federal office. The laborer is worthy of his hire.

Shortly after the election a number of anxious Republican politicians went to Florida to see that the canvassing board did its duty. Among them were William E. Chandler; Edward F. Noyes, friend of Hayes; John A. Kasson, of Iowa; General Lew Wallace, the romantic novelist; and Francis C. Barlow, distinguished in that period as an honest man. Not to be outdone, the Democrats also sent emissaries to look after their interests: C. W. Woolley, of Ohio, and John F. Coyle; Manton Marble, of New York, and others. These "visiting statesmen," as they were called, acted as counsel and busied themselves in taking affidavits and other evidence. It was a game of wits in which the sole chance the Democrats had was to use money and much money.

In South Carolina, under the carpetbag law, the board of canvassers had power to canvass the returns for all offices except governor and lieutenant-governor, which were canvassed by the legislature. The board consisted of seven members, all Republicans: three negroes, three candidates in the election. Consequently, the Democrats here evidently had no ground of hope. Still the State supreme court, composed of Republicans opposed to Governor Chamberlain, candidate for reëlection, attempted to interfere with the work of the canvassing board. The return as finally canvassed gave the Democrats the control of the legislature (and thus the governor and lieutenant-governor) but the presidential electors to Hayes. A sop to Cerberus. On December 6, 1876, the Republican electors met and cast the vote of the State for Hayes.

It cannot be said that the South Carolina board of canvassers did an injustice in awarding the electoral vote to the Republican candidate. He had carried the State and, in an absolutely fair election, would have carried it by a large majority.

The case of Louisiana was somewhat different. Frauds had been committed on both sides impartially, and Tilden had carried the State by a considerable majority. But the Democrats had intimidated the negroes in some of the parishes; a few cases of shocking violence occurred. By throwing out the returns in nearly all the parishes that gave marked majorities for Tilden and refusing to throw out the returns in parishes in which the Republicans were shown to have committed frauds, the canvassing board finally, after much labor, succeeded in producing a majority for the Hayes electors. It would have done so if Tilden had carried the State by a hundred thousand majority. The visiting statesmen who aided the canvassing board to manufacture the Hayes majority, or attempted to prevent it, were of large calibre. Of Republicans there were John Sherman, James A. Garfield, Eugene Hale, others. The Democrats sent to Louisiana John M. Palmer, Lyman Trumbull, Samuel J. Randall, Speaker of the House of Representatives, J. R. Doolittle, and Henry Watterson, under instructions from Abram S. Hewitt, Democratic national chairman.

The Democrats might have spared themselves the trouble of coming to Louisiana unless they brought unlimited funds and the will to use them. It was idle to expect justice from such a body as the canvassing board of Louisiana, a place in which carpetbaggers and scalawags had outdone themselves in violence and corruption. The president of the board had been called by General Sheridan "a political trickster and dishonest man." The other white member was corrupt. Two members were mulattoes, one of them a confessed thief. This board had been severely criticized for its earlier performances by a committee sent by Congress to investigate the election of 1874.

It is indeed difficult to understand why the Democrats did not make a resolute effort to bribe this board, for Tilden's majority in the State was so large that the board would have found it easy to declare for him. That negotiations went on there can be no doubt. Cipher telegrams, delivered to the Republicans or stolen from telegraph offices by them, showed that W. T. Pelton, acting secretary of the Democratic national committee and Tilden's nephew, had some abortive dealings with the canvassing board. It does not appear that Tilden had any knowledge of these proceedings. If he had seriously desired to bribe the board, it is almost certain that he could have done so, as he was wealthy and the board utterly venal. But he did not attempt to buy the place which he thought was rightfully his.

The canvassing board not only received affidavits but oral testimony as well. This was done to justify the wholesale throwing out of precincts by furnishing dramatic proof of Democratic intimidation. Much of the testimony given by negroes was false but some of it was unhappily true. One woman on the witness stand showed frightful wounds she had received at the hands of white ruffians. The most was made of the few cases of actual violence that had occurred in the election. This evidence, telegraphed to the Northern and Western press, was stressed as examples of "shotgun rule" in the South.

The Hayes electors, meeting, cast the vote of the State for him. The Tilden electors, refusing to concur in a most partizan verdict, cast the vote of the State for the Democratic candidate. Thus two returns were sent to Congress.

William E. Chandler said, enlighteningly, of this election:

In Louisiana there had been thrown into the ballot box over 7,000 more votes for the Tilden than for the Hayes electors, and to make him President it became necessary for the Returning Board, acting under peculiar local laws, to throw out more that 7,000 Tilden votes on account of alleged murder, riot and intimidation in preventing a fair and free election in certain parishes. To perform this extraordinary, even if justifiable, work in the face of an armed and infuriated Democracy, required men of undaunted courage; and such courage the Returning Board possessed. It required also that the Board should have assurances that the national exigency demanded its performance.[1]

Tilden carried Louisiana, and the canvassing board produced a Hayes majority only by the most flagrant manipulation. Yet in an absolutely free election it appears that the State would have gone Republican, so it cannot be said that an actual injustice was done when the canvassing board, venal as it was, gave Louisiana to Hayes. Two members of this board were later prosecuted for fraud and were convicted by a jury containing two negroes, but were pardoned.

The situation in Florida was another matter altogether. In Florida both parties were guilty of fraud, but the Republicans far outdid the Democrats in this respect. Both parties attempted intimidation of voters; and if in this branch of practical politics the Democrats surpassed, it was not for want of will on the part of the Republicans. In spite of the grossest Republican repeating, Tilden carried Florida by a fairly substantial majority.

He had a majority because he had a right to it. Florida was not a black State like South Carolina and Louisiana. It was a white State, since it had a majority of white people. Moreover,

[1] *The Nation*, July 3, 1878.

the white race was now unified in the Democratic party to a greater extent than the negro in the Republican party. The latter party was rent by dissensions. Consequently, the canvassing board, in giving Florida to Hayes, not only falsified returns but ignored the potential majority. Thus the case of Florida was utterly different from that of South Carolina and Louisiana.

A Northern visitor to Florida thus described the election of 1876:

From the precinct ballot-boxes to the Tallahassee state house, the place of voting, the precinct officers who receive the vote, the officer who records the vote, the county officers whose judgment affects the certificate of the vote, the state officers who by law canvass the county returns of the vote, all are Republicans or under Republican control. Such is the law, such is the fact. The Florida Democratic Committee are unaware that county returns have been stolen from the mails, which are under Republican control.[1]

Dr. W. W. Davis, who has given the deepest research to the subject, states that:

General Francis C. Barlow of New York became disgusted with his work before it was over. He confessed to his fellow Republicans that the Democrats had fairly elected the State ticket and probably the presidential ticket. Barlow lost favor among his fellow Republicans and became a suspect from that moment.

The conclusion reached by Dr. Davis is that:

The affirmation sometimes made that a fair election would have resulted in a Republican victory is not supported by the

[1] William Watson Davis, *The Civil War and Reconstruction in Florida; Columbia University Studies in History, Economics and Public Law, 1913.*

more patent and fundamental facts in the case. A fair election would have resulted in a more complete Democratic victory.[1]

As stated before, it is impossible to resist the conclusion that the canvassing board not only falsified the returns but ignored the potential majority in giving Hayes the vote of the State. *Tilden carried Florida, and was elected by a vote of 188 to 181.*

The following table shows how the vote should have been counted in the election of 1876:

HAYES

California	6
Colorado	3
Illinois	21
Iowa	11
Kansas	5
Louisiana	8
Maine	7
Massachusetts	13
Michigan	11
Minnesota	5
Nebraska	3
Nevada	3
New Hampshire	5
Ohio	22
Oregon	3
Pennsylvania	29
Rhode Island	4
South Carolina	7

[1] The chief monograph on the dispute is *The Hayes-Tilden Election,* by Paul Leland Haworth. This is a valuable work, and Haworth's conclusions are substantially sound for South Carolina and Louisiana. They are not so good for Florida. Haworth did not use Davis's monograph, and thus missed the best work of this period of the history of Florida. Haworth's conclusion that the action of the Florida canvassing board was fair is absolutely at variance with Davis's contention, and Davis's research was deeper and his reasoning much more convincing. It is difficult to escape his logic.

Vermont 5
Wisconsin 10
                                 ———
                    Total   181

TILDEN

Alabama 10
Arkansas 6
Connecticut 6
Delaware 3
Florida 4
Georgia 11
Indiana 15
Kentucky 12
Maryland 8
Mississippi 8
Missouri 15
New Jersey 9
New York 35
North Carolina 10
Tennessee 12
Texas 8
Virginia 11
West Virginia 5
                                 ———
                    Total   188

In the case of Florida, like that of Louisiana, the Tilden electors refused to concur in the decision of the canvassing board and cast the vote of the State for their candidate. The Republicans made no serious effort to contest the election of Drew, the Democratic gubernatorial candidate, who was elected together with a Democratic legislature. The canvassing board, in making the State over to Hayes, had done all in its power. It was quickly succeeded by a new canvassing board, which counted the vote for Tilden. Thus there were two duly certified returns for Florida—the one made by carpetbaggers and scalawags, the other by representative Floridans. Furthermore, the legislature declared that the Tilden electors were elected. If mere legality were very important—which it is not—Tilden seems to have had the better title as well as the moral claim. But the Republican leaders were determined to secure the election, and Zach Chandler reiterated his cry:

Hayes has 185 electoral votes and is elected.

In the excitement immediately following the election, Hayes never entirely lost hope. On the morning of November 8 he went to his office in the state house with the intention of doing a day's work. There was something not unheroic in this poise in the midst of the fiercest political agitation ever known in the United States. However, Hayes did not work on November 8. A stream of callers—friends, politicians, newspaper correspondents—took his time while breath-catching messages from headquarters made hope rise and fall.

A false report that New York had gone Republican raised the temperature of the Columbus street throngs to fever heights. Hayes came to the door to tell the crowd that it was a pleasure to know that he had such loyal friends, a solace in case of defeat. He even rallied his companions on their despondent looks. Stanley Matthews had groaned of November 7: "I seemed all day to walk through the valley of the shadow of death. I felt as if a great conspiracy of ignorance, superstition and brutality had succeeded in overthrowing the hopes of Christian civilization represented and embodied in the Republican party." *Christian civilization represented and embodied in the Republican party!* One smiles. Yet one should remember that to thousands of intelligent Americans the election of the distinguished and honorable Tilden meant the triumph of evil. So much for political partizanship in the seventies!

In this welter of hysteria Hayes bore himself normally. The *Ohio State Journal* of November 9, 1876, said of him:

His manner during the day, however, was such that the ordinary habitué of the capitol could not tell from his appearance whether he was a candidate for any office or not. He received those who called in his usual cordial manner and was very unconcerned while the greatest office on the American continent was trembling in the balance.

Hayes would have been less than human if he had not been greatly excited in such a crisis, but his cheerful self-control under circumstances the most trying is a better evidence of his courage even than his composure while lying wounded at South Mountain.

As the day for the meeting of Congress approached, it was evident that the election would involve the country in a most serious dispute. Not only were the electoral votes of South Carolina, Louisiana and Florida at issue, but one from Oregon as well. In the Pacific State one of the Hayes electors was a postmaster and thus ineligible under the law. The Democratic governor of Oregon gave a certificate of election to the highest Tilden elector. The matter was purely technical, as Hayes had carried Oregon, and yet the Democrats had almost a better legal case here than in Louisiana and Florida, where the existing canvassing boards decided against them. They might possibly have done better to rest their cause on the single Oregon elector, who would have given Tilden the election, and refused to budge. There would have been no justice in their contention, but there was no justice in the Republican claim to Florida. As it was, the Democrats claimed the one Oregon elector, as well as the electors of the three Southern States. In the end they lost all the electors and the election.

When Congress met in December, the Republicans were

able to make out a claim to all the disputed electoral votes and thus to go before the country as legally entitled to the election. The Democrats put in contesting claims and refused to accede to the Republican contention. The election was disputed, and there was no court in the country competent to decide the question. It was a novel and dangerous situation.

Nothing better calculated to excite uncertainty and strife has ever been devised than the wretched machinery of our Constitution for electing President and Vice-President. It was a triumph of indirection and ambiguity. It had led to serious trouble in 1801 and was now again precipitating a crisis in 1876.

The Constitution gives the president of the Senate the power to count the electoral votes. What did this mean? Did it carry with it the right to decide which of two election returns was true? The Republicans contended that it did because the president of the Senate was a Republican; Hayes was of this opinion. But it seems certain that the framers of the Constitution did not intend to make the president of the Senate the arbiter of presidential elections, since that would make him the supreme elector. If neither set of returns was accepted, neither candidate would have a majority, and then the election would be thrown into the House of Representatives, which was Democratic. This was the danger the Republicans had to guard against—the throwing of the election into the House. In that event Tilden would surely be the winner. In 1801, when neither Jefferson nor Burr was elected, the House of Representatives had chosen Jefferson after a long contest. In 1825, John Quincy Adams was elected in the same way. It was the precedent for such a situation as that of 1876, but naturally the Republicans declined to submit to a procedure that would be fatal to their claims. The Senate declared that Hayes had been elected; the House of Representatives asserted just as positively that Tilden had carried the day. It was a deadlock.

Two attempts had been made by Congress to provide for the counting of electoral votes. In 1800 a bill had been offered for an electoral council consisting of six senators, six representatives and the chief justice, but this failed. In 1875, Oliver P. Morton attempted to have passed a law regulating the count but did not succeed. The question was left open.

Hitherto the only procedure regulating elections had been the Twenty-Second Joint Rule, passed in 1865. This provided that in case objection was made to the vote of any State, the two houses of Congress should decide, separately, whether the vote was to be received; no vote was to be counted except by consent of both houses. This rule was intended to prevent the electors from the States reconstructed by Lincoln, Louisiana and Tennessee, from having their votes counted on February 8, 1865. The Senate, in January, 1876, refused to readopt this rule because the House of Representatives was now Democratic. No law whatever remained to apply to the situation.

When Congress met, the House of Representatives appointed committees to investigate the election in Louisiana, Florida and South Carolina. The Senate retaliated by directing the Committee on Privileges and Elections to look into the election in South Carolina, Georgia, Florida, Alabama, Louisiana and Mississippi as well as Oregon. This procedure was dangerous to the South, as it threatened the reëstablishment of the Fifteenth Amendment in those States that had escaped from it. The horrors of Reconstruction once more loomed on the horizon.

The committees in most instances went to the States to be investigated. In nearly every case, the committees brought in majority and minority reports. The majority reports of the House committees declared that the electoral vote of Louisiana, Florida and South Carolina belonged to Tilden; the minority reports that Hayes had carried those States. The reverse was true of the Senate committees: with them, the majority favored Hayes; the minority, Tilden. In every instance partizanship was the rule.

Day after day the election was debated in Congress; neither party would abandon its claim. It was a deadlock of the two houses, and Grant's attitude became more and more threatening as time passed without a decision. Troops moved back and forth in ominous fashion. Indeed, the President's attitude was so partizan that some of the Democratic newspapers proposed that he be impeached; but Grant was perhaps driven on by the feeling of the ex-soldiers, who were resolutely opposed to the seating of Tilden.

It was evident that the country was drifting toward war. In fact, the only thing that prevented war was the war that had ended a decade before. The memory of that awful struggle made any other solution of the dilemma preferable. Especially were the Southern members of Congress against any thought of armed arbitrament. When the Northern Democrats, enraged at the prospect of having the election that they so firmly believed they had won taken from them, made threats of violence, the Southern Democrats mocked at them. The Southerners had had enough of war. They were for peace at any price.

What was the remedy for this situation in which the party in power, though beaten in the election, refused to surrender the reins of government? Was the dispute to end in the rule of naked force? That was the problem that faced American politicians as the year 1876 ended without either candidate having been declared elected.

As the days passed the outlook became more and more ominous. Undoubtedly, Grant began to make military preparations to repel an outbreak, and other measures were considered
that were not taken. It was proposed to remove General Winfield S. Hancock, commander of the Department of the East,
a strong Democrat, in favor of Philip Sheridan, a partizan Republican. New York City, that oasis of independence in an
overawed country, was to be kept in order by troops and war-
ships.

Some Democrats were unquestionably ready for violence in
the passion of the hour. The Democratic Veteran Soldiers Association, a body of Union veterans, seems to have been particularly belligerent, but could not have done much in view
of the fact that by far the greater number of Union soldiers
were Republicans. Henry Watterson, in Kentucky, threatened
to come to Washington with a hundred thousand men to in-
augurate Tilden, but this was merely the fulmination of a
journalist.

The Republicans made fewer threats but clung stubbornly
to their claim of the election. Since the electoral colleges had
met and voted, they were inclined to take the stand that Hayes
was certainly elected. Hayes himself was persuaded of his
right. "I fully expect to be inaugurated," he said. To the end
of his life he had qualms, but he believed he had been elected.
His friends told him so; the party leaders told him so; the
Republican newspapers shouted it. Enough to convince anybody.

But the time had passed for rule by assertion. The Democrats refused to submit to their opponents. On December 13, 1876, National Chairman Abram Hewitt announced the election of Tilden and Hendricks. Zach Chandler replied with a sardonic denial. Both parties stuck to their guns. If the Southern Democrats had been as heated as the Northern Democrats, war would have occurred; but Tilden's Northern followers, first and last, obtained little comfort from the Southerners, who plainly showed that they preferred peace to attempts to seat the Democratic candidate. Indeed the Southerners felt greater interest in getting control of the local governments of South Carolina, Louisiana and Florida than of the national administration. Home rule meant much more to them than Federal patronage.

And now the sober sense of the nation made itself felt. Petitions flowed into Congress asking for some adjustment of the dispute. On December 7, George W. McCrary, a Republican member of the House of Representatives from Iowa, introduced a resolution providing for the selection of committees from the House and Senate to establish a tribunal to decide the election. Later he was rewarded for this move by being made Secretary of War. Grant himself favored a compromise and approached the Democratic national chairman, Hewitt, who acceded to the proposal. Tilden himself did not like it, since he was acute enough to know that it was a device to jockey him out of the election. He preferred to make no compromise. Hayes desired no compromise, feeling that he had been elected, and reluctantly listened to Schurz. Many Republicans thought the same way. However, the imperative necessity of finding a way out of the dilemma prevailed. The resolution for the appointment of the two committees passed both houses of Congress.

On December 21, the president of the Senate appointed the

Senate committee, consisting of Edmunds, of Vermont; Morton, of Indiana; Frelinghuysen, of New Jersey; Logan, of Illinois—Republicans: and Thurman, of Ohio; Bayard, of Delaware; Ransom, of North Carolina—Democrats. Logan declined and was replaced by Roscoe Conkling. Speaker Randall selected the committee from the House of Representatives: Henry S. Payne, of Ohio; Eppa Hunton, of Virginia; Abram S. Hewitt, of New York; William S. Springer, of Illinois—Democrats: and George W. McCrary, of Iowa: George F. Hoar, of Massachusetts; and George Willard, of Michigan—Republicans.

The committee did not begin to function until after the beginning of the new year, but its very appointment indicated that some compromise would be secured that would obviate the danger of war. The intense excitement of the country began to subside. George William Curtis said in a speech in New York:

The vote of New England, I believe, going to the Capitol, would be this, that neither is the Republican Senate to insist on its exclusive partizan way, nor is the Democratic House to insist on its exclusive partizan way; but the Senate and House, representing the American people and the American people only, in the light of the Constitution and by the authority of law, are to provide a way over which a President, be he Republican or be he Democrat, shall pass unchallenged to the chair.

The two parties did not at once abandon their menacing attitude. Senator Ferry, the president of the Senate, whom Republicans thought entitled to "count"—that is, determine—the electoral vote, declared that he would "shirk no responsibility." Governor Lucius Robinson, of New York, in his inaugural address asserted the right of the House of Representatives to elect in case of a deadlock, undoubtedly expressing Tilden's view, which gave the best constitutional precedent. On January 8, 1877, conventions of Democrats were held in various places, in which violent speeches were indulged in. Some military organizations seem to have been formed. Still more dangerous was the condition in South Carolina and Louisiana, in which there were rival governors and rival legislatures. Only the presence of United States troops in those States prevented the outbreak of war, for the white population, exasperated to the limit of endurance, was determined to put an end to carpet-bag and scalawag government at any cost. On the other hand, many Republicans favored the maintenance of such governments in South Carolina and Louisiana and their reëstablishment in other Southern States by force. It was a situation in which the firing of a spark might have resulted in a national explosion.

Meanwhile the committees of the Senate and House of Representatives were wrestling with the great problem. Finally McCrary, the proposer of the committee plan, brought into the House committee the scheme of the Electoral Commission somewhat as it was finally adopted. This provided for a tribunal composed of the Chief Justice and a number of associate justices of the Supreme Court whose decision was to be final unless overruled by a vote of both houses of Congress. Meanwhile the Senate committee had evolved a similar plan, providing for a commission of thirteen, composed of nine members of Congress and four justices of the Supreme Court. In choosing the nine congressmen, each house was to choose five and then one member was to be eliminated by lot. It was thought that the lottery feature was injurious to Tilden's chances, and Tilden himself still resisted compromise. He stood for the right of the House of Representatives to choose the President in case no candidate was elected, and his position was a strong one if constitutional law were anything. He either did not understand, or understood too well, the real purpose of the Electoral Commission, which was to find some way of seating Hayes that would satisfy the body of the people and end the chance of war.

"Why surrender now?" asked Tilden. "You can always surrender."

In regard to the lottery, he said, "I may lose the presidency, but I will not raffle for it."

Hayes, for his part, was quite as much opposed to compromise. At first he had not been certain that he had carried Louisiana, since it was evident that only very strenuous work had secured the State for the Republicans. In fact, he was always just a little uncertain about Louisiana. This uncertainty was admitted by William Henry Smith, Hayes's intimate, in a letter of April 19, 1877:

A good deal of uneasiness has been observable among our friends for some days. The gentlemen I induced to go to New Orleans after the election to witness the count have waited on me, and while they have been kindly in their manner, they have manifested a good deal of feeling. They were the first to arrive at that city and there is not the least doubt that promises Farwell made to Kellogg and Packard determined the course adopted.[1]

The letter was written to Hayes when it became evident that he would abandon Packard, the Republican candidate for governor, and allow Nicholls, the Democratic candidate, to hold office.

Grant himself was disturbed by Louisiana. On January 25, 1877, H. V. Boynton wrote to Hayes:

[1] Hayes Papers. Many of these letters have been published, but thousands of them, mostly trivial, remain unpublished in Hayes's home, Spiegel Grove, Fremont, Ohio.

There is one sign that is troubling me a little. The statement which you have seen that Grant has expressed some doubt about carrying Louisiana is true. . . . That is not the kind of news to help. Just how far he went I could not learn, but it was to the extent of expressing a doubt—for just this thing from so many Republicans [causes] all our uncertainty today.[1]

If Hayes was troubled over the question of his election, his misgivings were laid to rest by his friends. On December 6, 1876, he wrote to Schurz:

. . . I am overwhelmed with callers congratulating me on the results declared in Florida and Louisiana. I have no doubt that we are justly and legally entitled to the Presidency.

My conversations with Sherman, Garfield, Stoughton and others settled the question in my mind as to Louisiana.

His conviction that he was properly elected did not incline Hayes to compromise any more than Tilden's intense belief in the justice of his cause made the idea of a tribunal acceptable to him. Hayes desired to stand on the returns issued by the canvassing boards of the three Southern States and on Senator Ferry's right as president of the Senate to "count" the electoral vote. This was not a sound contention when it came to the matter of deciding which of two conflicting returns was to be counted; certainly the Democrats would not have consented to Ferry's becoming the determining factor in the election.

For a time there was danger of war, or if not of actual war, of riots and bloodshed. If war had come it would not have been such a contest as the Secession War but a true civil war between parties instead of between sections. Almost every State would have been the scene of fighting, and the final result would have been incalculable. If the war between North and South impaired American liberties, it is probable that freedom

[1] Hayes Papers.

would have perished in a struggle between parties for the control of the government. In such a conflict the Republicans must have won, and the governmental measures that would have followed would have been even worse than those of Reconstruction.

Hayes was brought to agree to compromise by the influence of Carl Schurz, who always had great weight with him. On January 12, 1877, Schurz wrote him a long letter on the subject of the Electoral Commission:

. . . There has been a rumor in the papers that some friends of yours assuming more or less to represent your views had expressed a hope that no such agreement would be arrived at, but that the counting of the votes and the decision of all disputed points by the President of the Senate would be insisted upon. . . .

I send you an article taken from the last number of *Harper's Weekly*, undoubtedly written by Mr. Curtis . . . what he says about the doings of the Returning Board [in Louisiana], and the impression produced by those doings upon a very large number of conscientious Republicans, is unfortunately correct. It is certainly true that there are grave doubts in the minds of that class of citizens. Those doubts were not produced by "Democratic brag and bluster," to which no sensible man would yield; but they originated in the proceedings of the Returning Board itself, and, considering the well-known antecedent of that Board, and the suspicious circumstances surrounding its action in the present case, those doubts are not unnatural.[1]

Schurz urged, with great effect, his objections to having the count made by Senator Ferry; and Hayes, perhaps reluctantly, let himself be persuaded. He withdrew his opposition to the Electoral Commission.

[1] Hayes Papers.

Congress, resolutely grappling with the menace to the peace and dignity of the nation, was a picturesque institution then. Nothing has lost more in the mechanization and standardization of American life than Congress. Now it is a tiresome legislative body in which the differences between the members from the several sections are small. It is conventional, dreary. But in the seventies one looking from the galleries could pick the members by their appearance. There were the smooth, dapper, side-whiskered financiers from New York and other Eastern cities; farmers from the West, bushy-bearded, tanned, uncomfortable in their black Sunday clothes, proclaimed their closeness to the soil; gaunt, thin-whiskered men who chewed incessantly let the observer know that they came from the recently submerged but resurrecting South. Most of them had been soldiers, and the thin, erect senator with a Gallic air was the noted Confederate general, John B. Gordon. Oliver P. Morton, old and worn out but still ripe for strife, was there, as were Roscoe Conkling, most silent in the electoral debates— it was whispered because he believed that Tilden had been elected; John Sherman, the bloodless, unpopular thinking machine from Ohio; the warm, virile Thurman, also from Ohio; Logan, of Illinois, owner of the largest moustache in the United States; Bayard, the noted aristocrat from Delaware; James A. Garfield, past master of intrigue; and many others. In the last days of the session, when the count of the election neared the end and when the members of the House of Representatives almost came to blows, Congress was an inspiring and edifying sight indeed. The country is not likely again to witness such scenes.

The schemes at first proposed in Congress were killed by Tilden's resistance, but at length a plan was found acceptable to both committees. It was proposed to select five senior associate justices of the Supreme Court, two of them Republicans,

two Democrats, and the fifth, David Davis, a neutral. Lincoln
had placed Davis on the Supreme Court, but he was curiously
colorless in political preferences. The Republicans refused to
accept Davis and they had a reason for doing so, for they knew
the weakness of their case in Florida and had no desire to present it to an unprejudiced judge; they wished Davis to be
classed as a Democrat. Finally, the Senate committee proposed
to take four associate justices and let them select a fifth, which
was somewhat the same thing as the abandonment of the
Democratic claim, since the other justices, except Davis, were
Republicans. The House committee agreed to this, but Oliver
P. Morton objected to one feature: he feared, with reason,
that the commission would go behind the returns. If it did so
in Florida, Hayes's case would probably be lost. The Republicans now took an extreme States' rights position, which was
to their advantage. The three canvassing boards of South Carolina, Louisiana and Florida had declared for their candidate;
all the Republicans desired the Electoral Commission to do
was to confirm the findings of the canvassing boards on the plea
that the commission had no power to go into the election itself.
The Democrats just as naturally wished the commission not to
be bound by the findings of the canvassing boards. Morton's
position was the one taken by the Republican members of the
Electoral Commission.

The bill for the Electoral Commission fully provided for
the counting of the vote. Congress was to meet in joint session
the first Thursday in February. Joint sessions were to be presided over by the president of the Senate. If objections were
made to the vote of a State from which there was but one return, the two houses should vote on the question; no vote was
to be excluded except by the concurrent action of both houses.
In cases where more than one return came from a State, the
returns were to be read and referred to a commission of fifteen,

consisting of five senators, five representatives, and five justices. Provision was made for filling a vacancy in the tribunal. The decision of the commission was to stand unless an objection was sustained by the separate vote of both houses. The joint session was not to be dissolved until the count had been completed.

The bill was hailed with relief by the country at large. The Democrats, for the most part, favored it, as it gave them a scintilla of hope of gaining their cause. The Republicans, preferring to stand on the decision of the canvassing boards, generally disapproved of it. Determined to secure the election in any event, they did not wish to submit their case to a court that might possibly decide against them. With the President of the United States a Republican and the president of the Senate a Republican, and with the army back of them, they had every advantage and felt that all they need do was to stand firm; the Democrats would surely capitulate. But for once the Democrats had abandoned the rôle of humble resignation. It was understood that if the two houses did not come to an agreement, Senator Ferry would count the votes for Hayes, who would be inaugurated under the protection of President Grant. Consequently, the only chance the Democrats seemed to have was the Electoral Commission.

Tilden, with his keen insight, knew that the chance was illusory and preferred, if he must lose the election, to have the Republicans take it by usurpation, which might have been the case without the Electoral Commission. To him the commission appeared to be a mere graceful surrender, and yet there was a bare possibility that it would be a real court. The debate in the Senate was spirited. Edmunds began with a lively appeal for the passage of the bill. The grim Morton arose in opposition, declaring that Hayes was elected and thus there was no occasion for a commission. The iron man would not concede an inch to the Democrats. Cameron put in a plea for "purity" of elections that moved the house to laughter. Conkling spoke for the bill. It passed the Senate by a vote of 47 to 17—21 Republicans and 26 Democrats for it, and 16 Republicans and 1 Democrat opposed. It passed the House of Representatives by a vote of 191 to 86; 158 Democrats and 33 Republicans voted aye; 68 Republicans and 18 Democrats, no.

The Electoral Commission was a Democratic measure; it gave the Democrats their sole possible chance to win. It was not much of a chance, but still it was a chance. The reason the Democrats supported it was that they believed the four justices would select Davis as the fifth justice and the fifteenth and deciding member of the Electoral Commission.

There was a danger that this would be done. If Davis had become a member of the Electoral Commission, it is likely that he would have decided in favor of Tilden, since he was that *rara avis*, a public man with an unprejudiced judgment and a sensitive conscience, and since Tilden's claim was the better. In that case a majority vote of the commission would have given Florida to Tilden, to whom it belonged by right. The Electoral Commission would then have declared Tilden elected. In all probability, in the intense passion of the hour, the Republicans would have refused to accept the findings of the court. The danger of war would have been imminent. *Indeed, the great peril was that the Electoral Commission might declare for Tilden.* The Democrats, accustomed to oppression, would submit if the decision went against them; they would be angry but they would yield. The Republicans, used to covering violence and illegality with the cloak of necessity, would probably not surrender if the verdict went against them. The whole virtue of the commission lay in finding a way to clothe the determination of the Republicans not to relinquish the election with the pretense of legality. It was one of the strangest crises in American history, but it was a real crisis.

The situation was saved by the shrewdness of the Republican leaders. In some unexplained way they seem to have induced the Democrats of the Illinois legislature to fuse with a few independents in that body and elect David Davis senator. Logan was up for reëlection; the balance of power in the Illinois legislature was held by the independents, and Davis was elected. The one unprejudiced justice of the Supreme Court was thus made more or less ineligible for the Electoral Commission. The remarkable coincidence of his election at the most opportune time for Hayes would certainly seem to indicate that the Republicans in Congress engineered the matter. Tilden's one chance was now gone, but the danger of war was also gone. The country would submit; things would go on as usual.

The Electoral Commission was presently appointed. The House of Representatives chose Payne, of Ohio; Hunton, of Virginia; Abbott, of Massachusetts—Democrats: Hoar, of Massachusetts, and Garfield, of Ohio—Republicans. The Senate members were Edmunds, of Vermont; Frelinghuysen, of New Jersey; Morton, of Indiana—Republicans: Thurman, of Ohio, and Bayard, of Delaware—Democrats. Conkling was not selected, and the reason reported was that the New Yorker thought that Tilden had been elected.

The four associate justices of the Supreme Court—Clifford and Field, Democrats; Stone and Miller, Republicans—are said to have offered the fifth place to Davis. If so, the latter declined on the ground that he had just been elected to the Senate. No doubt Davis did not wish to take the responsibility of naming the President-elect, for that was what his selection implied. Wisely and fortunately, he declined. At that late date no decision could have made Tilden President. The Republicans would not have had it so, and they had back of them the army and hundreds of thousands of veterans. Justice Bradley was finally selected as the least objectionable remaining member of the Supreme Court. The Democrats had some hope that he would not be a partizan. Fortunately for the country, he proved to be entirely partizan. He paid for what was really a patriotic service by abuse that embittered the remainder of his life.

The Electoral Commission was now prepared to accomplish what the selection of Bradley meant—the surrender of the Democrats. It was a surrender; but it was a dignified surrender, without threat of force, and the farce of a court was played out to the end. There could be no question as to the decision that would be rendered, since there were eight Republicans and seven Democrats. The commission was, in reality, no tribunal at all. It existed simply for the purpose of confirming the electoral vote as that vote was counted by Ferry, the president of the Senate. Still the game had to go on as if there were something at issue, and no doubt many people thought that there was actually something at issue.

The count began on February 1, 1877. At one o'clock the Senate filed into the Hall of the House of Representatives, where the drama was played. Hall and galleries were packed. Senator Ferry took the Speaker's chair and called the joint session to order. Tellers were appointed, two for each house. Republicans objected when the two tellers of the House of Representatives were seen to be stalwart Southerners. Their fears of a fight were quieted. Ferry produced a wooden box containing the returns. Opening it, he produced the Alabama return and handed it to the tellers, who counted it for Tilden without objection. California and Colorado were, in the same manner, counted for Hayes. Then came Connecticut and Dela-

ware, which were recorded for Tilden. But when the vote of
Delaware had been counted, a hush fell on the hall, for now
came the crucial moment of the whole contention. Florida was
called.

There were three returns from Florida. The first read by
Ferry was that of the Hayes electors and was certified by Governor Stearns and the secretary of state. A second was of the
Tilden electors and was certified by the attorney-general. A
third, which had arrived that morning, was of the latter electors and was certified by the new Democratic governor, Drew.
Objections were raised against each of these certificates; the
Democrats filed another objection against one of the Hayes
electors on the ground that he was a Federal office-holder.

This was the occasion for which the Electoral Commission
had been created, and the Florida returns were now sent to that
body for adjudication. The commission had already organized
with Justice Clifford as president. The sessions were held in
the Supreme Court chamber, a place sadly inadequate for the
throng that came to look on. The fifteen judges resembled
sardines in a box. This was perhaps as well, for the Electoral
Commission was a comedy and there should be something ris-
ible in comedies. As it was, the solemn performance was played
out in the dull, dreary manner of a real trial, though the Republican leaders knew well enough what the outcome would
be. The gullible Democrats still cherished the illusion of hope.

On February 2, the Electoral Commission began its hearing
on Florida. Charles O'Conor was chief counsel for the Democrats but was too feeble to be of much value. David Dudley
Field, the real Democratic manager, made a poor speech of
some length and was succeeded by John Randolph Tucker, of
Virginia, who did not greatly distinguish himself. They both
contended that the court should go behind the return in
Florida and determine who had really been elected. John

Kasson and McCrary replied for the Republicans, stating that it was out of the question for a Federal tribunal to go behind the properly certified return of an election. They were more convincing than the Democratic speakers.

The next day, February 3, however, Richard T. Merrick made for the Democrats the best argument of the whole Electoral Commission proceedings. He claimed that a Federal court had the right to go behind the return of a State election when the State itself had invalidated the election certificate, thus creating the need of a Federal decision. This was the case in Florida, where Governor Drew had issued a return nullifying the earlier Hayes return and giving the vote of the State to Tilden. Unquestionably Merrick was right if there is any logic in legal proceedings, for the Electoral Commission had been expressly appointed to consider just such points as this; and it ceased to be a court and became a mere recording instrument when it refused to go behind the first return and determine which of the returns, both in proper legal form, was the right one. The decision was made by a strict party vote of eight to seven. When Congress was again convened, the vote of Florida was announced for Hayes. After that, discerning Democrats had no further hope, for if the strongest case was decided against Tilden, what chance had he in the doubtful States of South Carolina and Louisiana? Objections were made to the commission's decision, which was then referred to the two houses of Congress separately. The Senate sustained the decision; the House of Representatives voted to reject. As the law provided that a decision should stand unless rejected by both houses, the vote of Florida was finally counted for Hayes. The question at issue was now decided, but the pageant had to go on to the end.

The count was continued until Louisiana was reached. The same farce was reënacted; the vote of the State, after a long

discussion, was counted for Hayes. Again the Democrats sought
to go behind the return and bring proof of the frauds committed in manufacturing a majority for the Hayes electors;
again the Republicans stood squarely on the certificate of the
canvassing board and upheld the principle of States' rights. And
this admission of States' rights was the good accomplished by
the Electoral Commission. In after years the Republicans desired to go behind election returns in Southern States and force
the application of the Fifteenth Amendment, but the precedent
of the Electoral Commission was against them. It was not possible again to treat a State as a conquered province and have its
elections determined by the President of the United States or
by Congress. Behind the Electoral Commission the Southerners were able to reëstablish civilized government in their
wasted section.

When the decision on the Louisiana case was debated in the
Senate, the Republicans practically admitted the frauds of the
canvassing board but claimed that it was a case of fighting the
devil with fire.

"Mr. President," John Sherman said, "a good deal is said
about fraud, fraud, fraud—fraud and perjury, and wrong.
Why, sir, if you go behind the returns in Louisiana, the case is
stronger for the Republicans than upon the face of the returns.
What do you find there? Crime, murder, violence, that is what
you find. . . . I say now, as I said two months ago, that while
there may have been irregularities, while there may have been
a non-observance of some directory laws, yet the substantial
right was arrived at by the action of the returning board."

Again the House of Representatives rejected the decision,
but as the Senate accepted it the vote of Louisiana was counted
for Hayes. The count then continued until Michigan was
reached, when a slight objection was raised but not sustained.
Nevada was counted, and then came Oregon, a bone of con-

tention. Two sets of returns came from Oregon: the Democratic, certified by the governor; the Republican, not so certified. If logic counts for anything, it would seem that the Democratic return was in the same class as the accepted returns for Florida and Louisiana; but since the loss of the one challenged elector would mean the defeat of the Republicans, the Electoral Commission accepted the uncertified return and cast the vote of Oregon for Hayes.

By this time a group of Democratic members of the House of Representatives, disgusted at being tricked and unwilling to accede to the bargain they themselves had made, wished to delay the count. This was a dangerous stand. It was now late in February, and the Constitution requires the presidential term to begin on March 4. If no President were elected by that date, there would be an interregnum fraught with infinite possibilities of mischief. War would be a not impossible outcome, since Grant, if he continued to act as President, would be a plain usurper, and the president of the Senate would have no better title. The passions of the Democrats were more thoroughly aroused than at any previous time, for they felt profoundly that they had suffered injustice and wrong. By accepting the Electoral Commission they had merely enabled the Republicans to commit an act of usurpation under the forms of legal procedure and, while this was a gain to the country, it was a deep humiliation to the politicians who had been so outwitted.

There were two groups of Democratic insurgents in the House of Representatives. One was led by Blackburn, of Kentucky; Springer, of Illinois; Mills, of Texas; O'Brien, of Maryland; Cox, of New York. Convinced that the proceedings were fraudulent and that the Electoral Commission was actuated only by the basest partizanship, these men wished to hold out against Hayes's election to the end. Another group, Southerners, took a very different position. They were willing to abandon Tilden's cause, since they saw that it was hopeless, but they wished to save their own States. Indeed they were infinitely more concerned in bringing about the end of misgovernment in the three still reconstructed States and secure decent rule than they were in the election of a President, in either case a Northerner. What they had most desired from Tilden's election was the reëstablishment of home rule in these States, and they now saw the opportunity to gain from Hayes what was no longer to be hoped from Tilden. Negotiations began between these Southerners and Hayes's representatives immediately after the Louisiana decision showed that there was no chance for the Democrats to secure the election.

Hayes had already held out the olive branch to the Southerners. Charles Foster, member of the House of Representatives from Hayes's own Cincinnati district, in a speech on February 23 declared that it would be Hayes's policy to wipe out sectional lines and conciliate the South. Conferences began as early as the night of February 16, just after the Louisiana decision. Stanley Matthews talked with Major E. A. Burke, special agent for Louisiana. Bishop Wilmer, of Louisiana, saw Grant in Washington and then went to Columbus to confer with Hayes. From that place he telegraphed, "Peace not to be disturbed in Louisiana."

On February 26, three conversations took place. At one of these, held in the room of the House committee, Charles Foster, Representative John Young Brown, of Kentucky, and Senator John B. Gordon, of Georgia, who was a moving spirit throughout the negotiations, were present. A second meeting, in a Senate committee room, brought together Major E. A. Burke, John Sherman, Stanley Matthews and ex-Governor Dennison, of Ohio. The third and most important talk took place that night at Wormley's Hotel between Burke, E. J. Ellis and W. M. Levy, Democratic representatives from

Louisiana, Henry Watterson, Stanley Matthews, James A. Garfield, Dennison and Sherman. Matthews asked Ellis what the people of South Carolina and Louisiana wanted. Ellis replied that they were determined to put in Hampton and Nicholls as governors, fearing that Hayes would use troops to install Chamberlain and Packard. For that reason the Southern Democrats were prepared to filibuster, thus delaying the electoral count. Matthews, declining to commit Hayes absolutely, agreed to have Nicholls recognized as governor of Louisiana. At length the Southerners accepted his assurances.

These conferences bore fruit in an agreement known as "The Bargain." It was nothing less than a bargain, though it was not venal, being dictated by strong public interests on both sides. Both had much to gain. In spite of the Electoral Commission, the House of Representatives might refuse to recognize Hayes's title or, at least, might filibuster until after the fourth of March, thus bringing a crisis on the country. The Southern element in Congress was strong enough to terminate the filibuster and bring about the peaceful admission of Hayes's election. On the other hand, Hayes's good will meant everything to three suffering Southern States. By recognizing the Democratic candidates for governor, he would end the Reconstruction and the conditions that were destroying the Lower South.

The Republican members of the conferences agreed in Hayes's name not to interfere in South Carolina, Florida and Louisiana, and to withdraw the troops from those States. That meant the reëstablishment of Caucasian government. The Democrats promised to use their offices to prevent filibustering and guaranteed the protection of the law to whites and blacks alike.

Foster gave John Young Brown the following unsigned letter, which practically pledged Hayes:

GENTLEMEN: Referring to the conversation had with you yesterday in which Governor Hayes's policy as to the status of certain Southern States was discussed, we desire to say in reply that we can assure you in the strongest possible manner of our great desire to have adopted such a policy as will give to the people of the States of South Carolina and Louisiana the right to control their own affairs in their own way; and to say further that we feel authorized, from an acquaintance with and knowledge of Governor Hayes and his views on this question, to pledge ourselves to you that such will be his policy.[1]

Brown was not satisfied with this assurance. Foster conferred with Matthews and brought another letter signed by himself and Matthews, which Brown accepted. Thus the South abandoned the thought of resistance to Hayes, and Hayes terminated the Republican government of South Carolina, Florida and Louisiana. On one hand, Tilden was sold by the Southerners; on the other, the negro was sold by Hayes's representatives. But the causes of both Tilden and the negro were hopeless, so that no actual injustice was perpetrated by the swap which abandoned opposition to Hayes in return for the surrender of the state governments to the Democrats.

William E. Chandler gave a racy account of "The Bargain" in a letter to the New Hampshire Republicans of December 26, 1877:

. . . Certain Democrats in the House of Representatives, seeing Hayes certain for President, thought they would save something from the wreck. They had therefore threatened by dilatory motions and proceedings to break up the count and then opened negotiations with such timid or too eagerly expectant Republicans as they could find ready. They had succeeded beyond their most sanguine expectations. Senator Sherman had visited Ohio and consulted Governor Hayes. Mr. Henry Watterson, a Democratic member and a nephew of Mr.

[1] Haworth, 271.

Stanley Matthews, had acted as a go-between; and on the one side Messrs. Matthews, Charles Foster, John Sherman, James A. Garfield, and on the other L. Q. C. Lamar, John B. Gordon, E. J. Ellis, Randall Gibson, E. A. Burke and John Young Brown had agreed (1) that the count should not be broken up in the House, but that Hayes should be declared and inaugurated President. (2) That upon Hayes' accession the troops should be withdrawn from protecting Governors Chamberlain and Packard, and that the new administration should recognize the governments of Wade Hampton in S. C., and F. H. Nicholls in La. By certain general and indefinite letters since given to the public, by a secret writing now in the hands of E. A. Burke, and in other ways, the agreement was authenticated and President Grant was immediately requested by Governor Hayes's council on no account to recognize Packard or Chamberlain, but to leave the ultimate decision as to their fate to the incoming President. . . .

Before the actual declaration of his election and to secure the same, a deliberate written bargain was made in his behalf by the same Senator Sherman and his associates, by which it was agreed with Gen. Gordon and other Southern rebel Democrats that when he should be President no attempt should be made to enforce the above principles of his party but that the South should be allowed to manage its own affairs in its own way, and in particular that he would abandon the lawful State governments of La. and S. C. and recognize in their stead the mob governments of Wade Hampton and F. H. Nicholls.

John Young Brown contributed his version of the conferences of February 26 in a newspaper interview:

I had come to request of him [Chas. Foster] written assurances that if Gov. Hayes was inaugurated he would restore home rule in the States of La. and S. C. and that the people of these States should control their own affairs in their own way, as free from any intervention of the Federal authority as the

State of Ohio. He agreed to give me the desired letter and said he would also request Stanley Matthews to sign it.

He came about midnight and said he had that evening procured a meeting of some gentlemen from La. and S. C. at Wormley's Hotel, at which also the Hon. Henry Watterson was present.

Next day he gave the letters . . . told me that President Grant would, as soon as the count was completed, issue a certain order to Gen. Augur in La. . . . The order was issued by Gen. Grant, the Hon. Chas. Foster secured the inauguration of the President. Except for this letter the result would never have been reached.

Feeling that there is some obloquy in such a trade, many writers have denied that Hayes was an actual party to it, as if his representatives could have bound him without his sanction. However, Hayes's papers show beyond a doubt that he was a party to the bargain and that the Republican conferees did not act on their own authority alone. He was informed of every step in the proceedings.

As early as December 15, 1876, Dennison had written to Hayes urging him to attempt to come to an understanding with the Southern Democrats. Even at that date that consummate practical politician, James A. Garfield, was flirting with the Southerners, and Dennison reported his conclusions. He added:

I said to Garfield that if he would paranthetically in a speech refer to your letter of acceptance and other utterances, if any, but not commit you, good might come of it. . . . Garfield's information on the subject is reliable. I mean of the friendly disposition of some of the Southern members.

On December 12, Garfield had written to Hayes:

Several of our most thoughtful Republicans there have said to me during the last three days that they believed it possible to make an inroad into the Democratic camp, which should at least divide them on their policy of violence and resistance. . . . Just what sort of assurances the South wants is not quite so clear, for they are a little vague in their expressions, but I have no doubt it would be possible to adopt a line of conduct which would be of great help to them. . . . It would be a great help if in some discreet way these Southern men, who are dissatisfied with Tilden and his violent followers, could know that the South is going to be treated with kind consideration by you.[1]

Even before this, Murat Halstead had informed Hayes that L. Q. C. Lamar and other Southerners seemed anxious to avoid trouble and suggested some sort of guarantee. Wilson J. Vance wrote to Halstead:

The Southerners are rather getting over the idea that they can help Hayes more than he can benefit them—but it has taken time, patience and argument to beat it into them. Garfield has been visited confidentially by a number of them of late and is disposed to take stock in the thing.

In the latter part of December, Noyes told Hayes that the tendency of the Southerners to surrender the contention was attracting the attention of Northern Democrats and advised Hayes to be very cautious in his conduct.

That Hayes gave at least verbal assurances is proved by a letter to him from L. Q. C. Lamar of March 22, 1877:

. . . It was understood that you meant to withdraw the troops from South Carolina and Louisiana. All that was required was an order to withdraw the troops from the States where they were a positive interference with the popular will, and in which the conditions produced by their presence was a daily violation of your own sense of constitutional right and

[1] Hayes Papers.

threatened further and still more mischievous complications.

Upon that subject we thought you had made up your mind, and *indeed you so declared to me.*

The Packard and Chamberlain governments . . . exist in those States *only so long as they are supported by you.* . . . More than that the country recognized the fact and the justice of the spirit in which you proposed to deal with it. . . . Your declaration of what you would do prevented a fearful crisis at the South but the tension is too severe. If you would achieve what you have begun you must *do* as you *said* you would do.[1]

Albert D. Shaw wrote to Hayes on December 22, 1876:

. . . I have taken occasion to explain your views of the status of the South and other questions of state policy. I believe it will result in great good in many ways. My opinion is, however, that for your sake and the vast interests you represent the time has come when more than a general outline of your policy should be unfolded to two or three discreet and leading men here. [2]

John Sherman wrote him on January 5, 1877:

As to the Southern matter, that I shall pursue on my own responsibility.

Sherman wrote again on February 17, 1877:

. . . I have not quoted you directly and did not think it wise to do so. You have gained largely by your silence and caution since the election, and I do not wish to impair this by quoting you. To those who wish to be convinced I give ample assurance.

Hayes was committed to the bargain by agents with whom he was in close touch, though he was too cautious to give pledges in writing. That he was fully informed of all that went

[1] Hayes Papers.
[2] Hayes Papers.

on and approved of it is shown by a letter of Charles Foster to him of February 21, 1877:

On Monday the Southern people who had agreed to stand by us in carrying out the electoral law in good faith were seized with a fright if not a panic. Randall made a violent speech in caucus declaring that your policy would be of such a character as to overwhelm any Southern man in view who aided in carrying out their agreement in good faith. . . . In the emergency I was called upon late at night by several of the gentlemen from the South and urged by them to say about what I did say. I consulted with my Ohio friends, among them Matthews and Garfield, also with Evarts, who all agreed as to the propriety of my making the little speech. Matthews thought I ought to go further. I was elected first because Garfield is our probable candidate for Speaker. And secondly, he is handicapped just now as a member of the commission. I hesitated because I would not under any circumstances say a word or do a thing that would embarrass you in the least, but it seemed that emergency demanded that I should take the responsibility I did. What I said has been very kindly viewed by gentlemen from the South and has been severely criticized by the Democratic malcontents of the North.[1]

From this statement, it would seem that Garfield began the negotiations with the Southerners, who, becoming uncertain after Randall's speech that they had received definite pledges, demanded further promises and obtained them from Foster and Matthews—pledges sufficiently positive to satisfy them.

On November 8, Hayes, thinking himself defeated, declared, "I do not care for myself; but I do care for the poor colored man in the South." Now in February, he was abandoning the colored man of the South to make certain his election. Yet it cannot be said that he acted wrongly and he certainly acted wisely. "The poor colored man" was not much more than a vague sentiment with Hayes, who was eminently a practical

[1] Hayes Papers.

person. After all was said and done, negro rule had failed in the South and could do nothing more than go on failing. So Hayes abandoned the Fifteenth Amendment, though he had no idea whatever of injuring the negroes, concerning whom pledges were taken from the negotiating Southerners. Hayes hoped, indeed, to have negro suffrage accepted by the South, but his withdrawal of the troops made negro suffrage ineffective. He did not expect this result.

The bargain was never popular with Republicans, some of whom thought (and did not hesitate to say) that Hayes had betrayed the Republican party of the South in entering into his agreement with the Southerners. Hayes himself would never admit that he was an actual party to the bargain, probably because of the ill feeling it had brought him from fellow-Republicans. In a conversation on August 8, 1890, reminiscing, he said: "On another occasion General Comly received a dispatch which he did not communicate to me and which he answered on his own responsibility. This was better than showing me the dispatch. His reply was correct undoubtedly. In the same way Foster and Matthews took upon themselves the responsibility of giving assurances without consulting me, but always inferentially from the knowledge of my views and temperament. I had written to Foster commending a short speech he made and he may have assumed that I approved all that he said. Foster showed good judgment and was generally correct in his expressions of opinion as to my course. He did not say that he was authorized to speak as he was, but from what he knew he inferred what I could do."

On January 22, 1877, H. V. Boynton had given Hayes a pretty correct account of the situation:

You know by this time that many of the Southern men care nothing for Tilden, that many of them distrust the Northern

Democrats. This was early affirmed here and the knowledge of it has proved of great consequence. In fact, my conviction is that such factional use had been quietly made of the knowledge that if the House Democrats had undertaken to push through any revolutionary resolution that they would have found themselves effectually resisted from within their own party. . . . But the matters to which I refer and which you know were not such as to be trusted outside of a narrow circle. . . . If we could get Bradley, all would go right, I believe.[1]

The Southerners saw their chance and seized it; the disputed election was their golden opportunity. They got more from Hayes than they could have obtained from Tilden, for the latter could have withdrawn the troops from the three States only with the greatest difficulty. By agreeing to Hayes's election and promising to break up the threatened filibuster in the House of Representatives, the Southerners secured what they wanted above all things. Indeed here, as a dozen times before and after, Northern and Southern Democrats pursued different purposes. The Northern Democrats, in 1876, were bent on obtaining control of the national administration; their aims were general. The Southerners, on the other hand, were concerned in having the troops removed from South Carolina, Florida and Louisiana; and if this were done, they did not greatly care who was President, since they expected little Federal patronage in any event. It cannot be said that the Southerners acted with generosity; they repaid the efforts of the Northern Democrats in their behalf with something much like ingratitude; for they had not saved themselves; they had been saved by the Northern Democrats—Tammany congressmen among them—who time and again prevented the Republicans from passing force bills that would have destroyed the Lower South. But the Southerners were practical men playing a game

[1] Hayes Papers

for large stakes and they played it with few scruples. The bargain with Hayes was one of the most important events in American history. It ended the Reconstruction and started the South on the road to prosperity and power. It closed a period —the period of Republican hatred of the South and concerted measures of President and Congress to oppress the South. If Tilden was sacrificed to make this Southern holiday—well, what chance did Tilden have anyway?

Of almost greater importance to the South even than the withdrawal of the troops was the acknowledgment of States' rights made by the Republicans in the arguments before the Electoral Commission. It was imperative for the Republicans, weak as their case was in Florida and shaky as it was in Louisiana, not to have the Electoral Commission or Congress go behind the state canvassing boards.

The logic of the situation was turned against themselves when the Democrats, finally in control in South Carolina, Florida and Louisiana, sent in returns in later elections electing Democrats. Much as the crusading spirits in the Republican party would have liked to go behind these returns, they were prevented by the precedent of the Electoral Commission. Potential negro majorities there might be—great majorities—but so long as white returns came certified to Congress, nothing could be done about it. Thus was the negro sacrificed for expediency, but it was a sacrifice no one need regret, the negro least of all. Predominance built on mere numerical majority, against knowledge, virtue, property, has no enduring base.

The end came rather quickly after the alliance between Hayes and the Southern Democrats was completed. It meant that now the Republicans had something like an actual majority in the House of Representatives as well as in the Senate. The Northern Democrats, tricked by the Republicans and betrayed by their associates, naturally desired to resist, would have resisted if that had been possible, since never in American history have men so labored under a sense of wrong (and with reason) as did the Democratic representatives of the North and West.

That the situation would have been dangerous if the Southerners had stood by their Northern colleagues is evident from what happened. A bill actually passed the House of Representatives providing that, in case of failure to elect a President, the line of succession should be the president of the Senate, the Speaker of the House, and the Secretary of State. The Senate, however, defeated a measure which would probably have made Thomas W. Ferry President if passed.

On February 28, the decision in the South Carolina case was read before Congress in joint session. The houses separated to consider it. The House of Representatives rejected the decision, after it had been accepted by the Senate, but under the law the vote of South Carolina was counted for Hayes.

When Vermont was reached in the count, Abram S. Hewitt, Democratic national chairman, arose and offered a return sent by a minority elector on the ground that one of the Republican electors was ineligible because a postmaster. A scene of wild confusion followed. The two houses separated to consider the Vermont return. The Senate unanimously accepted the Republican return, but the House of Representatives adjourned. The session of the following day was one of the most violent ever witnessed in Congress; even the slavery debates before the Civil War aroused less passion. The deluded Democrats were desperately seeking some escape from the net so inexorably closing about them.

If the Democratic Speaker Randall had sided with the protesting faction, the count of the Vermont vote might have been held up indefinitely, precipitating the interregnum. Randall, however, ruled that the two hours' debate on the return, as provided for in the Electoral Commission law, should proceed. The filibusterers would not surrender. Demands were made for a recess; a crowd of milling, wretched congressmen sought to get the floor. Motion after motion was made, but Randall refused to submit them. The galleries, packed to the limits, applauded the disorder; Randall resolutely faced the mob of protesting, reproachful fellow-Democrats and finally put down the revolt.

Levy, of Louisiana, faithful to the compact with Hayes, declared that he would put no obstacle in the way of the completion of the count. He said:

The people of Louisiana have solemn, earnest, and I believe truthful assurances from prominent members of the Republican party, high in the confidence of Mr. Hayes, that, in the event of his election to the presidency, he will be guided by a policy of conciliation toward the Southern States, that he will not use the Federal authority or the army to force upon those States governments not of their choice, but in the case of these States will leave their own people to settle the matter peaceably, of themselves.

Levy called on his fellow Southerners to aid him in opposing the filibusters, and the refusal of the Southern Democrats to join in the demonstration caused its failure.

A resolution had been offered by Proctor Knott to receive the second certificate from Vermont and then refer both certificates to the Electoral Commission. This would mean delay and probably an interregnum. But the example of the Southerners had not been without its effect; Hewitt was won over, and the resolution was defeated. The regular return for Vermont was accepted.

Virginia was then counted; then West Virginia. An effort was made to hold up the count of the Wisconsin vote; it appeared that one of the electors might be ineligible. The two houses separated to consider. The Senate voted to accept the disputed elector. In the House of Representatives, Mills of Texas, one of the few recalcitrant Southerners, offered a resolution for the House of Representatives to proceed to elect a President of the United States. The debate on the Wisconsin return began.

At twelve o'clock on the morning of March 1, 1877, Blackburn, of Kentucky, closed the historic case in the House of Representatives. "Today," he said, "is Friday. Upon that day the Savior of the world suffered crucifixion between two thieves. On this Friday constitutional government, justice, honesty, fair dealing, manhood, and decency suffer crucifixion amid a number of thieves."

Speaker Randall received a telegram from Tilden sanctioning the completion of the count. At four o'clock in the morning of March 2, the Senate filed into the hall of the House of Representatives for the closing scene. The vote of Wisconsin was counted; then the list of all the votes was read. After that the president of the Senate, Ferry, arose and said: "Wherefore, I do declare: That Rutherford B. Hayes, of Ohio, having received a majority of the whole number of electoral votes, is duly elected President of the United States for four years, commencing on the 4th day of March, 1877. And that William A. Wheeler, of New York, having received a majority of the whole number of electoral votes, is duly elected Vice-President of the United States for four years, commencing on the 4th day of March, 1877."

In this way was consummated the most spectacular act of injustice in American history. A majority of the American people believed that the decision was wrong; the country has not to this day been convinced that it was right. Even now the term "stolen election" is sometimes heard. Even now, after the great interval of time, indignation moves the unpartizan reader who examines the evidence. "The Crime of '76" is still occasionally used as a designation of the performance.

If elections were usually fair this judgment would be right enough. But because the function of the Electoral Commission was a public trial, made before the whole world, because the injustice was patent, because the election was really decided by the veiled threat of force, we blind ourselves to the larger lessons of the forever-memorable crisis of 1876.

As a matter of fact, our attitude is hypocritical. We delude ourselves; we think that the election of 1876 was something exceptional, that the injustice committed was unique, a bad link in a sound political chain.

Rutherford B. Hayes was as much entitled to his seat as some other Presidents. In the first place the election was close. Hayes carried a majority of the Northern States, and the Southern States were hardly a part of the Union again. Then our elections, especially our presidential elections, are all too often a triumph of bribery and fraud. How many men have been kept out of the White House by unfair devices? How many elections have been turned by the use of money or of means to overawe the voting masses into something not their will?

The election of 1844 was corrupt and Clay may have been elected instead of Polk. In 1880, the Republicans, taught by the squeeze of 1876, raised a great campaign fund and purchased, as President Arthur admitted, the doubtful state of Indiana. Garfield's title to the presidency may indeed be considered better than that of Hayes since it was bought and paid for. Blaine always thought that he was cheated out of the vote of New York and thus of the presidency in 1884, and this may be true. The same thing may be said of Cleveland's defeat in 1888. McKinley was elected in 1896 only by bribery and intimidation unparalleled in American history. Who was really elected in 1916? Possibly Hughes.

Blaine was prevented in 1884 from opening a similar contest to the Hayes-Tilden dispute by motives honorable to him. He said to General Russell A. Alger, who questioned him on this point:

I was a witness to all that occurred before and after the seating of President Hayes, and I made up my mind that another contest of that character, no matter what its merits might be, was likely to precipitate insurrection of possibly fatal character. I then determined that should I ever become a candidate for President and suffer defeat by a narrow margin I would under no circumstances imperil national peace by bringing into question the announced result. Public opinion may be trusted to correct an error or crime of that nature, and it is better that the individual should suffer than that the country should be thrown into turmoil.

But it was the return to true civil government consummated by Hayes that brought to an end efforts by a defeated party in power to snatch victory from successful opponents.

In some ways we have improved little since 1876. Writers still hold up their hands in horror over the frauds committed by both sides in South Carolina and Louisiana, in that epic struggle of Anglo-Saxons against savagery. Yet the corruption of that election was less, not more, than the corruption in Pennsylvania at almost every election. The seating of Hayes over Tilden was not worse than other transactions in American history; but it was a dangerous precedent because it was based on the possibility of the use of force. Republican institutions better endure fraud than open flouting of the people's will, for the employment of force in elections speedily ends in a military dictatorship under the forms of a republic. For this reason it is supremely fortunate that none of the force bills introduced in Congress since the first reconstructive measures has passed. It would be impossible to have elections decided by bayonets in one section of the country and have them free and fair elsewhere. The will of the people may still, if with difficulty, assert itself.

Notwithstanding the manner in which it was done, the seating of Rutherford B. Hayes was fortunate. It was high time to heal the Southern sore. Yet if it had been ended by any other than a Republican President, the matter would have been invested with the gravest danger. The ex-soldiers had been taught to believe that the election of Tilden would mean not only the freeing of the South but its reëstablishment in power as the dominant section of the United States. The results of 1865, they thought, would be thrown away. Inspired by this propaganda, civil war would not improbably have followed if Tilden had actually been allowed to take his seat and govern, for he must have withdrawn the troops from the South. Hayes was bitterly blamed for doing this, and Hayes was a Republican and a Union soldier. There was no taint of "treason" about him. If this was true, it may well be judged what would have happened when the "Confederate" Tilden brought the Reconstruction to an end and left the Southern states to the mercy of their civilized inhabitants. Even if war had not come, a political struggle of unexampled bitterness would have ensued, which would have been followed in case of Republican success by the renewed persecution of the South. From all these dangers the country was saved by the accession of Hayes.

Tilden was one of the greatest of Americans—a great administrator, a great reformer, a great party leader. Since the days of Jefferson the Democratic party has had no chief of larger calibre; he towers over Cleveland like a colossus over an ordinary mortal. Yet his very ability, his justice, his broad nationalism brought him the dislike of millions of Americans. As the leader and restorer of the Democratic party he was more bitterly hated by the Republicans than anyone except Jefferson Davis. His presidency would have been a struggle against fanaticism and malevolence such as might have tasked the powers of any man. It would probably have brought him speedy death.

The fear and hatred felt for Tilden by the Republicans is evidenced by their unworthy treatment of him. It is the darkest blot on the administration of Hayes that an indictment was brought against Tilden on the campaign charge that he had failed to pay his full income tax in 1862. It was a political persecution of an ill and injured man. It dragged on for years and, although the government was never able to produce the slightest evidence, was not permitted to drop until it was apparent that Tilden was out of politics. Then this victim of the political passions of the seventies was at last permitted to rest.

THE controversy had stretched to a taut point by March 2, but at that moment tardily arranged terms prevented its being snapped on the fourth. At four o'clock in the morning of March 2, a furious company of defeated Democrats, an exultant body of victorious Republicans, trudged to their yawning beds. News of the result reached Hayes when it awakened his party at Harrisburg on their way to Washington. Of course he was embarrassed; no President before him, even Lincoln, had found the White House latchet so reluctant.

There had been humiliating and terrifying threats against Hayes's life. Anonymous letters tumbled about the ears of the incoming President informing him that if he clung stubbornly to his rights he would never be inaugurated, warning him to remember Lincoln, cautioning him that Watterson had said that if he were seated one hundred thousand men would know the reason why.

Somebody had even toyed with assassination. While the Hayes family was at supper one night, the clatter of knives and forks was suddenly silenced by the crash of glass as a bullet bit into the parlor window, the partly lowered shade of which masked the would-be murderer. The ball passed through two parlors and an open door to burrow in the library wall. The harassed household was sworn to secrecy; it would never do for the world to know. After that Webb Hayes went along with his revolver as an amateur secret service man when his father strolled out each evening to his niece Laura Mitchell's home, but nothing further happened.

There was sufficient apprehension to necessitate the planning of the Washington trip as secretly as a nuptial journey. Stanley Matthews, one of Hayes's counsel before the Electoral Commission and soon to be rewarded with a seat in the Senate, wrote him from Washington on February 19, 1877:

An arrangement will be made as I am informed by the Secretary of War for a private car *via* Harrisburg and Baltimore and you had better come twenty-four hours in advance of any knowledge of the fact.

A Baltimore friend considered the hospitality of that city too hazardous to be proffered. Yet the placid Colonel L. C. Weir, who was in charge of arrangements for the Washington journey, declared that he "took just enough stock in it [danger] to watch for it and no more."

Hayes had thought that no invitation from Washington would move him from Columbus until the result of the election was declared; but as inauguration day approached two private cars were attached to the regular afternoon train on the Pennsylvania Railroad. That was on Thursday, March 1. On Wednesday evening the good people of Columbus had fêted the governor and his wife with a brilliant reception at the state house. Throngs of friends accompanied by college cadets gulped down Hayes's last message as he spoke from the rear platform of his car. He was encompassed by his immediate family, Laura Mitchell, the inevitable William Henry Smith and a few other devoted friends.

Of the affection of the nation Hayes was not so sure and he approached Washington with a slight timidity quite natural under the circumstances. He thought it best that the inauguration festivities should be trimmed to their simplest instead of the usual tremendous parade followed in the evening by the universal spree, the manner in which Americans paid respect to a new President in those days. He wished to be installed in the

White House with the minimum of pyrotechnics. On account of his embarrassment he had declined Grant's invitation for that of his old friend, John Sherman. Met at the station by the senator and his greater brother, the general, the Hayeses were driven immediately to the Sherman residence. After breakfast Hayes called on Grant and drove with him to the Capitol. Outgoer and incomer conversed casually, neither one exhibiting his emotions of the occasion. At the Capitol Hayes was met by members of the cabinet and congressmen of both parties, finding the Southern Democrats cheerful and cordial as they awaited their pound of flesh. The rest of the day was spent in consultation with party leaders.

On Saturday evening, March 3, President Grant gave a state dinner in Hayes's honor, a great banquet of thirty-six covers that included Vice-President Wheeler, the Chief Justice, members of the cabinet, John Sherman, and wives. It was the last splurge of the old order: sherry with the first course, then white wine, red wine, all kinds of wine. Just before dinner a little group isolated itself from the other guests in the Red Room. Ulysses S. Grant, his son, Chief Justice Waite and Hayes were there. It would be unorthodox to swear in a President on Sunday, March 4, unorderly to be without one. To take care of the first difficulty the public inauguration had been postponed until Monday; to take care of the second, a private ceremony Saturday night before dinner prevented an interregnum. That night until twelve o'clock the United States had two Presidents.

Monday at noon the performance was duly repeated before thirty thousand visitors. In spite of the threatening political weather there were decorations and shoutings as the procession streamed to the Capitol. Still sensitive, still suspicious of his welcome, Rutherford Hayes took comfort in this cheering, trusting that it expressed the feeling of the American people.

He especially noticed the warm acclaim of the negro cab drivers, who were not gifted with prophetic vision. Although the celebration lacked the usual afternoon parade and inaugural ball, a torchlight procession served to discharge the pent-up emotions of four months. An army, though not Watterson's, swept up Pennsylvania Avenue shrieking campaign songs. The paraders even invaded the White House grounds, exploding fireworks, until they got a curtain-call bow from their candidate at a front window. The reception at the Willard Hotel brushed away the last doubt of a haggard day. Hayes was securely seating in the White House with no ousting to fear.

He was President at last and the thrilling third act of the melodrama was over. The Electoral Commission had faded into history; the new President could bend his thoughts toward government. Indeed he had been thinking of government ever since the election decision in the Florida case had forewarned him what the result would be.

That delicate performance, the selection of a cabinet, had relieved the tedium of the Electoral Commission proceedings. It was anything but a simple affair in those days. The President did not then occupy the commanding position that is his today, and many forces clashed in cabinet making. The President, only a chief among rivals who hated him, had endured many sorrows since 1861. Lincoln had ruled, but with difficulty. Johnson had tried to rule and had failed. Out of the chaos of war a congressional oligarchy had arisen which defied Lincoln at times and which brazenly snatched the reins from Johnson.

So long as this oligarchy remained united the President was powerless against it. The oligarchs passed the Tenure of Office Act to prevent Johnson from dismissing cabinet members distasteful to him. When the President, unable longer to endure Stanton's insolence, removed him, impeachment proceedings were begun that failed only because a few conscientious Repub-

THE INAUGURATION OF PRESIDENT HAYES, MARCH 5, 1877

licans joined the Democrats in the Senate to prevent the outrage of ousting a President for executing his constitutional functions. The case brought against Johnson was a pretext. Drunk with power, the oligarchy sought to get rid of him and seat one of its members in his place. No outrage was beyond it; it regarded constitutional government with unrestrained contempt.

The oligarchy was led by Stevens and Morton, with Conkling as junior partner; Stevens was its great man and with his death its decline began. Among its minor lights were Logan, Wade, Sherman, Zach Chandler, William E. Chandler, Cameron, Jewell, Ferry, Boutwell, Bingham. Having almost overthrown Johnson and secured the election of Grant, the oligarchy was in a strong position until 1876. Conkling was the go-between who conveyed to Grant the wishes of his colleagues. If Grant had not had to deal with the oligarchy, he would have been a pretty good President; since he had to deal with it, he was a bad President. He was partly corrupted, partly overawed by it. Under its influence he renounced the large-minded nationalism that had led him to dictate generous terms at Appomattox and became a persecutor of the South. In almost every way the oligarchy was evil, and its tenure of power is one of the disgraces of American history.

If the oligarchy had lasted for many years, democratic government in the United States might have come to an end. Opposition would have been overwhelmed or howled down. The South would have been throttled and the States with negro majorities would have become private preserves of the oligarchs. The use of troops would not have been confined to the South; they would have been employed anywhere to help out a tight election. Force would have been the order of the day, the method of American government. To Grant's credit, it must be said that he did not fully carry out the will of the oligarchy. He sometimes rebelled and he had withdrawn

troops from most of the seceded States; Virginia, indeed, he
had even treated with indulgence. He was convinced that coercion in the South was a failure. The oligarchy did not agree
with him. It believed in violence, intimidation, illegality,
spoils.

The Liberal Republicans, organizing to oppose the congressional oligarchy rather than Grant, had been crushed in 1872;
Greeley had been offered up on their altar. Having long served
the oligarchy, the famous editor suffered the fate of apostates
when he turned against it. Blaine, seeking the presidential
nomination in 1876, courted it by flattering its well-known
antipathy for the South. If he could have won the oligarchs he
would have been nominated, despite the reformers. But Conkling and Morton both had ambitions of their own and
Conkling was an enemy not to be placated. The oligarchs,
weakened by the rise of a new generation indifferent to war
hatreds, had been obliged to accept Hayes in order to defeat
Blaine, but they had accepted the Ohioan most ungraciously.
Immediately after the nomination Conkling discovered that he
was suffering from malaria and so could not campaign and he
did not hesitate to express his opinion that Tilden was elected.
However, the other oligarchs had acted to seat Hayes. This
snatching of an election from the elected was characteristic of
their methods and their ethics. If they had continued in power,
every close election would have been settled in the same way.
In other words, the government of the United States would
have become frankly Mexican.

Hayes had now to reckon with this group, cynical, lawless,
resolute. It was one of the critical moments in American history. The new President was an obscure man, elevated because
of his obscurity, and he was called on to succeed where Grant
had failed with all his military prestige. Was Congress to continue to control the government or was the President to be the

real ruler of the nation? That was the question. And it is hardly too much to say that the future of the republic was vastly influenced by the decision reached. The oligarchy had reduced Johnson to a cipher; it had controlled Grant. If it had made a dupe and tool of Hayes, it is not improbable that the government of the United States would have become parliamentary with a figurehead for chief executive.

Fortunately for Hayes, Stevens was dead, Morton dying, Conkling declining. The political fanatics were not of their former strength. They had been attacked by the party organs; they had been exposed; they could no longer command the unthinking devotion of the multitude. Many and grave scandals had weakened the ascendency they had established over the country by their ability, audacity and lack of scruple. So far as the oligarchy still survived its many losses, it was now led by Blaine, who bravely sought to wear its mantle. Conkling, making a truce with Blaine, sided with his lifelong enemy against Hayes; and Conkling was still a power even if his defeat in the convention of 1876 had diminished him. But there was no man like Stevens to assail the President with ferocity and at the same time skill. The oligarchy had decayed in time to give Hayes a chance to defeat it, to overthrow congressional control of the executive.

The President had only one cabinet seat filled long in advance, and that was the treasury, which was to go to John Sherman. Gratitude not less than judgment dictated the choice of Sherman, who had done so much to nominate Hayes and was also the leading political financier of the country. Evarts was early thought of for the state portfolio, partly because Evarts was suggested by Schurz and partly because Evarts suggested himself, being almost the only man in the Republican party capable of filling the billet. Hayes requested Sherman to invite Evarts to become Secretary of State. A few days later the Department of the Interior was offered to Schurz, who accepted it. So far all was well.

Beyond this were difficulties. Hayes approached Justin S. Morrill of Vermont, whom he ardently desired for the cabinet, but the Vermonter wisely preferred the Senate seat that was his for life. Eugene Hale, son-in-law of the cynical but efficient Zach Chandler, could have had a portfolio as a reward for Chandler's services in raising a campaign fund and bringing the campaign to a victorious conclusion in spite of defeat. Chandler himself would not do, as he was too odoriferous for the sensitive nostrils of reformers. Hale declined. His proposed job, the attorney-generalship, was passed on to Charles Devens, a member of the Massachusetts supreme court.

Hayes wanted Benjamin Harrison and John M. Harlan, but here he ran counter to the will of Oliver P. Morton. The Indiana oligarch had had no small share in nominating Hayes and he was still a power even in the article of dissolution; his lieutenant, Richard W. Thompson, was made Secretary of the Navy. This was the only appointment dictated entirely by political considerations and it was the only bad one; but the American navy at that time, as at most times, was a negligible quantity. The esteem in which Thompson was held may be judged by the humorous story told of him, that on his first view of a ship he exclaimed in wonder, "Why, the durned thing's hollow!" McCrary became Secretary of War as a reward for suggesting the useful Electoral Commission.

Bristow, who was primarily responsible for Hayes's nomination—without whom Hayes would not have been nominated —was passed over. He had resigned his seat in Grant's cabinet after his momentous exposures; he was the head and front of the reformers. That was the trouble; he was much too much of a reformer. Schurz, true to his principles, urged Bristow for the Treasury, and Bristow would have liked to return to his old berth; but Hayes was too shrewd to appoint a man who would have been a red rag to the bull of the Republican rank and file. Bristow was hated by the practical politicians, who regarded him as one of the main reasons for the crisis of 1876. If he had only kept his mouth shut and let things be, the country would never have awakened to the outrageousness of the Whiskey Ring! The Kentuckian had done the unpardonable thing; he had cast party discipline to the winds and prosecuted Republican office-holders as if they had been Democrats. So he was thrown to the lions. Not without a certain flourish, however. In 1878, Hayes gave him a state dinner (without wine) and that was the only reward the gallant Bristow ever received for services that may fairly be called unique. He passed from the public stage and is now entirely forgotten. His fate points the moral of what happens to a reformer who is too uncompromising a reformer for the canons of practical politics.

Hayes had desired a Southerner for his cabinet and had meditated on Joseph E. Johnston, most noted surviving Confederate general. But W. T. Sherman, as cautious as a man as he was great as a soldier, had protested, and Hayes reluctantly renounced his dream of reconciliation. Instead, he picked a lesser Confederate, David M. Key, of Tennessee, who became Postmaster-general. For a Republican President to put in his cabinet a Democrat and ex-Confederate in the year 1877 was an act of temerity and virtue that we can hardly appreciate today. It was the final act of the war drama. Peace had come at last, made by Hayes not Grant.

All in all, it was an admirable cabinet that Hayes placed around his council table. No better men could have been found for their places than Evarts, Sherman and Schurz. Evarts, learned, brilliant, nonpartizan, was able to handle foreign affairs without humiliating the nation. Sherman, morally unstable, became an incomparable subordinate under Hayes's wise guidance. Schurz, the most picturesque and unbiased public man of the day, was an advertisement that the corruption of Grant's reign had come to an end, an earnest of better things. Devens, Key and McCrary were competent. Only Thompson was weak, but Thompson was Secretary of Nothing.

No sooner were the cabinet selections announced than friction followed. Conkling was, of course, outraged; he was always outraged unless he could dictate the governmental policy. For some reason he chose to look on Evarts's appointment as a slight to himself—probably because Evarts was from New York and Conkling thought it his sacred duty to pass judgment on the eligibility of all New Yorkers. He had asked for the Postoffice for Thomas C. Platt, his lieutenant, that perfect machine politician; and he had had ambitions himself for the Department of State. Neither he nor Platt went in, and so he became the bitter enemy of a President he had never desired and had only helped to make in order to unmake Blaine. Infuriated by his ill success against Hayes, Conkling made the supreme effort of his life in the Republican convention of 1880 to nominate Grant and, when he failed, turned against Garfield with the hatred that led, indirectly, to the latter's death. But already in 1877 he was beginning to fail, although he lasted for some years longer. It was not until some years later that the people discovered him for the imposing emptiness he was.

Another oligarch, Cameron of Pennsylvania, had demanded the retention of his son, Don Cameron, as Secretary of War. Hayes refused, and Cameron whetted his knife. Blaine also had his grievances. He could not expect much for himself but he urged William P. Frye for the cabinet, only to be ignored. Ben Butler once more disgraced the House of Representatives with his odious presence and was eager to make trouble for the new administration. These malcontents objected to Evarts (because he was disagreeable to Conkling), to Schurz

(because he was a reformer), to Key (because he was a Southerner and ex-Confederate), and were enthusiastic over nobody
except Sherman, who was a practical politician and thus one of
them. They planned to defeat the confirmation of the cabinet
and embarrass the hated interloper at the beginning of his
administration.

The special session of Congress began on March 5. The case
of the disputed Louisiana Senate seat was postponed until the
next day, as well as the consideration of the cabinet. On March
6, Blaine, who had been compensated for the loss of the presidency (so far as such a trifle could be compensation) by election
to the Senate, rose in his place and began a bitter attack on
Hayes, coupling the latter's election to the presidency with
Kellogg's election in Louisiana to the Senate. Blaine had been
a great bully in the House of Representatives, winning his way
by his quick wit and his browbeating, but such methods failed
in the upper house. "The stentorian voice and kimboed arms
had no terrors for the Senate," which in 1877 was a strong
body, including as it did James B. Beck of Kentucky, George
F. Hoar of Massachusetts, David Davis of Illinois, Isham G.
Harris of Tennessee, Stanley Matthews, Allen G. Thurman
and others. Blaine's attempt to prevent the confirmation of the
cabinet was a mistake, since it was impossible to keep out a
whole cabinet and since it displayed the animus of a defeated
office-seeker desiring revenge on a successful rival. Nevertheless, Hayes might have been greatly embarrassed if the Southern Democrats had not come to his aid. The cabinet was confirmed, and Blaine's jaundiced denunciations fell harmlessly
from the new President. Hayes had passed the first obstacle
and could now develop his policy.

The problem that pressed for immediate solution was the
Southern settlement. Grant had drifted, dreading to take the
necessary course that would antagonize the oligarchy and the

fanatics who were still bent on humiliating the South. Hayes was more courageous and more resolute than the conqueror. He took the plunge and, at great cost to himself, succeeded. He restored the oppressed provinces, and gave the South a place again in the nation, though the Southerners have erected no monuments to him who was a better friend to the South than all its soldiers and statesmen.

Hayes had the insight (though it needed no great insight) to realize that the Lower South could not remain in its anomalous condition; and the courage (for it needed great courage) to grapple with the situation. The Federal government had either to support the negroes by armed force and with sufficient energy to make the Africans absolutely predominant—a way of settling the problem that would have necessitated the abandonment of several States by their white inhabitants—or it had to remove the troops and allow the law of nature, which has put the white man over the black, to take its course. Hayes chose the latter way.

In its Southern policy the oligarchy had done its worst. The downfall of the Confederacy in 1865 had found the South ripe for wise and generous methods. It needed modernizing—roads, schools, manufactures. The war would soon have been forgotten if conciliation had been tried and if real benefits had been conferred on the Southern populace, for the South was weary of the leaders who had led it to the debacle and had turned its face to the future. But instead of bread it was given a stone. All constructive measures were overthrown in the effort to force negro rule on the South, which saw nothing come out of the North but demagogues, agitators, grafters and thieves. The policy of negro supremacy was pursued with incredible fatuousness and inconsistency, since the oligarchy, insisting on the equality of African savages with Anglo-Saxons— almost their superiority to Anglo-Saxons—utterly ignored the claims of the Indians to fair treatment and prepared to eject the Chinese from American shores as foul and dangerous intruders. Racial equality was meant only for the favored black race, not for the red or yellow. The consequence of this unbelievable folly and injustice was the creation of a bitterness that has not yet entirely passed away. In 1865 the South was singularly lacking in ill feeling; in 1876, the land was consumed with hatred; there was hatred of the South for the North, of the North for the South, of the black for the white, of the white for the black. Such was the net result of the great humanitarian scheme of healing the wrongs of the negro by placing him on the neck of the white man—that is, the Southern white man. The negro as a ruler would have been tolerated nowhere in the North.

Hayes had made his bargain with the Southerners to secure the peaceful acknowledgment of his sovereignty; but if the ex-Confederates had not shown the spirit of reconciliation they did, the President's course would have been much the same. Hayes was essentially a statesman, one of the sanest of American statesmen, and as such he was singularly lacking in personal prejudice. Few men have ever been more entirely actuated by general considerations. He recognized that Reconstruction was a failure, and if the Southerners had never entered into the bargain he would have withdrawn the troops just the same, for the reason that it was the thing to do. He had no intention, however, of betraying the negroes. He did not believe that they could be benefitted by holding power by bayonet rule and realized the intensity of hatred that repression was storing up in the South for the black men. He wished to build up a Republican party in the South that would not depend on negroes but that would include the best white men, and he was optimistic enough to think that such a thing was possible. He did not understand that race rivalry and race bitterness had gone too far to permit of a simple solution of the great problem. He did not realize that ordinary political issues meant nothing in the South, where men had come to divide solely on the race question, which overshadowed everything else, even the most important economic considerations. Consequently there was not the least chance that his kindly policy would meet with success, though by ending carpetbag government and permitting the three still Reconstructed States to set up white governments again he conferred on the South an inestimable benefit and did the whole nation a service. The condition of semi-civil, semi-military rule, with all its menace to free institutions, came to an end and the South began its long climb back to prosperity.

Hayes had no illusions as to the attitude of the Republicans toward his policy. He knew that it was the right course, but he also knew that the multitude is too shortsighted to see beyond the present. What the multitude saw was that the enfranchised freedmen were about to be deprived of their place of privilege and left to work out their own salvation. In April, 1877, the President said, "I know how sore a trial this business is to staunch antislavery veterans like you. I expect many to condemn. I shall not worry or scold if they do. I know they mean well. It will, I trust, turn out that I am right."

The Southern problem was now double instead of triple, for Florida, by virtue of the last election, was white again. The Republican administration fell of its own weight, and the Democratic governor from New England entered office without resistance. Forced for a moment into the Republican column to give Hayes the necessary majority, the State was now safely Democratic and might count on the recovery of peace and order. But tough nuts remained to be cracked in South Carolina and Louisiana.

It is difficult to say who had been elected governor in these States. Probably Chamberlain carried South Carolina and possibly Packard was elected in Louisiana. In the former State the Republican canvassing board declared all the Republican candidates for state offices elected except the governor and lieutenant-governor, who were canvassed by the legislature. The legislature as determined by the canvassers had a small Republican majority. It appeared that the Republican administration of the State would continue, since the Republican legislature would certainly declare Chamberlain elected.

When the legislature met, on November 28, 1876, troops occupied the capitol and excluded from their seats in the house of representatives certain Democratic candidates who claimed to have been elected but who were not so acknowledged by the Republican canvassers. The Democrats of the house thereupon withdrew to the hall of a rifle club and organized separately. The Republicans, remaining in the capitol, formed a house of representatives of their own. The senate, however, organized without much difficulty, though several Democratic members were excluded.

The Democrats, determined to gain control, secured from General Auger, commanding the troops in South Carolina, assurances that he would not interfere in the organization of the house of representatives. The early bird catches the worm. On the morning of November 30, the Democrats, reaching the capitol before the slothful Republicans were out of bed, proceeded to take possession of the hall of the house of representatives and organize, admitting three of their fellows excluded by the Republicans. The doorkeepers, attempting to prevent the proceeding, were overpowered. Then the tardy Republicans appeared on the scene and a battle would probably have followed but for the troops, whose principal function was to keep the legislators from cutting each others' throats.

The sequence was comical. For four days rival houses of representatives occupied the same hall. There were rival speakers and officers. Sometimes debates were going on in both houses simultaneously, and the confusion and absurdity made a scene of joy for the humorous. Finally, the Democrats, learning that constables backed by troops were coming to eject the members excluded by the Republicans, withdrew again to the rifle club. On December 5 the Republicans, meeting in the capitol without opposition, proclaimed Chamberlain's election. By way of retort, the Democratic house of representatives canvassed the election returns to its own satisfaction and announced that Wade Hampton had been elected governor and William D. Simpson lieutenant-governor. On the same day they were formally inaugurated.

There were now two governments in South Carolina. Peace was kept only by the troops, and it was evident that the Republican administration could maintain itself only by the constant threat of armed intervention. Chamberlain's title was brought before a circuit judge, who decided that neither candidate had a legal right but that Chamberlain should hold office until a successor had been elected. Hampton's title was then brought into court, and a negro judge decided against him.

The State supreme court, however, granted an injunction forbidding banks acting as state depositories to pay out money except on court orders. This left the Republican government without funds, since the property owners were nearly all Democrats and paid taxes to the rival treasury. By March 4, 1877, Chamberlain's government had become so tenuous that he could not have remained in office a day but for the bayonets.

Hayes dealt very promptly with South Carolina. On March 4, 1877, Stanley Matthews wrote to Chamberlain asking him to arrange some compromise or come to an agreement that would obviate the need of troops. Matthews frankly announced that that state government would remain in power which proved best capable of continuing—the survival of the fittest. This amounted to an abandonment of Chamberlain, who indignantly declined to be the instrument of his own humiliation. His vexation was excusable; he had secured the electoral vote of South Carolina for Hayes and he was now being sacrificed on the altar of expediency. On March 23, Hayes invited both claimants to come to Washington; the case was thus before Cæsar.

Hampton's journey northward was an ovation. He was recognized as the representative of the Lower South going to the capital to obtain his rights, and the novel spectacle of a Southerner's attempting to assert any rights cheered the whole South. Crowds greeted the noted cavalry general at every station as he sped Washington-ward. Chamberlain traveled as a private person, not a conquering hero. He had a plan for submitting the election to a commission, but the Democrats had had a surfeit of commissions and declined. Chamberlain assured the President that the withdrawal of the troops from South Carolina would mean the end of Republican rule, and this was perfectly true. But Hayes still had hopes of an honest and respectable Republican party in the South. Hampton, speaking for the South Carolinians, urged the removal of the troops and pledged himself to respect the Fifteenth-Amendment privileges of the freedmen. Hayes brought the matter formally before his cabinet, which agreed with him that it was best to have the soldiers go. On April 3 the President informed Secretary of War McCrary that "domestic violence" did not exist in South Carolina. Thereupon McCrary directed General Sherman, who directed General Hancock, who directed General Auger to withdraw the troops. On April 10, 1877, they marched out of the state house, where they had held sway so long, amid the extravagant rejoicings of the populace. The next day Chamberlain, helpless without the blue-coats, surrendered his office. South Carolina once more came under the sway of its white people.

Louisiana gave more trouble. On January 1, 1877, the day of the convening of the legislature, the Republican boss, Kellogg, had the capitol garrisoned by his police and negro militia; no persons were admitted to the legislative halls unless they bore certificates of election from the Republican canvassing board. Thereupon the Democrats withdrew to another building and organized apart, admitting such members as had been pronounced elected by the Democratic canvassing board. The Republican legislature declared, on January 2, that Packard and Antoine had been elected governor and lieutenant-governor respectively. On the same day the Democratic legislature proclaimed the election of their candidates, Nicholls and Wiltz. Both sets of governors and lieutenant-governors were inaugurated, and war loomed on the horizon.

The White Leaguers now attempted a *coup d'état*, overawing the negro militia and gaining possession of the government buildings. The Packard government would have been sent packing but for the soldiers, who alone maintained the carpetbag rule and possibly protected the carpetbag governor from mob violence. Grant, waiting for Hayes to take the reins, refused to acknowledge either of the Louisiana administrations. They both continued to exist, but, as in South Carolina, the Republicans were without money while the Democrats were supplied by taxpayers with the sinews of war. Packard beyond a doubt would have to go unless some other general declared him the rightful governor and upheld his gubernatorial chair with bayonets.

The situation in Louisiana was embarrassing to Hayes. In South Carolina the Hayes electors had been returned and no awkward questions were raised by permitting Hampton to take the office of governor, to which he might or might not have been elected. In Louisiana, on the other hand, the Tilden electors had received a large majority, which was reversed only by throwing out the vote of whole parishes. According to the final canvassing, Packard, the Republican candidate for governor, had received a much larger vote than some of the Hayes electors and was, consequently, considerably more elected than they were. In other words, if Packard was not elected governor, Hayes had not carried the State. It was a difficult procedure to unseat Packard in favor of the Democratic claimant and yet maintain that the Hayes electors had been chosen.

But consistency means nothing in politics. Hayes was safely installed as President and, while many persons disputed his title, nobody had taken up arms against him. In Louisiana, however, the whole white population was only restrained by fear of the United States army from attacking the Republican administration and forcibly ejecting it from the capitol. The citizens were armed and waiting; even the presence of the troops might not restrain them long. Thus, while the people of the United States accepted the government of Hayes, the people of Louisiana—except negroes—violently objected to the government of Packard. And this was a slight practical difficulty that led to the fall of Packard.

Yet it was necessary to let the carpetbagger down gently. Otherwise all of the apostles of freedom in the North would have vented their wrath on Hayes. The latter appointed a commission, intended like the Electoral Commission to work the reversal of an election—only this time in favor of the Democrats. Against this commission William E. Chandler bitterly railed, knowing only too well why commissions are. He had the temerity to declare that the President had betrayed Packard. And indeed but for Packard's efforts Louisiana would probably have gone into the Tilden column. Yet Packard could not justly claim ill treatment, for if he was relieved of the governorship of Louisiana (which he could only have kept at the price of a small war), he was richly compensated by a Federal berth in which he could sleep in peace without White League nightmares.

The commission, reaching New Orleans on April 5, was aided in every way by the Democrats, who well knew that the commissioners had come to aid them. The Democratic legislature was making strong efforts to do away with the rival body by offering inducements to the enemy. The members of the Packard legislature actually elected (according to the Democratic returns) were cordially invited to join the Nicholls legislature and receive back pay. This procedure would leave many Republicans in their seats but would ensure a safe Democratic majority. To the negro legislators of a bankrupt government the offer of pay was irresistible, since they were penniless and had a natural desire for food and shelter. Most of those urged to the feast accepted, and the Packard legislature melted away until it ceased to exist by reason of the fact that all the African members were now to be found in the Democratic assembly. Packard then threw up the sponge. All opposition to Nicholls was abandoned. On April 24, 1877, the troops filed out of New Orleans to the music of clanging bells and thundering cannon announcing the rebirth of a Southern commonwealth. As in South Carolina, Hayes had merely let gravity act; but if he had, like his predecessor, interfered with nature, the consequences to Louisiana and the whole South might have been incalculable.

Hayes had indeed only done what any wise and strong man might have done, but in our silly world there are few strong and wise men. Most politicians play politics, and a mere politician would not have withdrawn the troops from Louisiana, knowing what intense opposition the act would arouse. It did arouse intense and long-lasting opposition on the part of a majority of the Republicans.

The withdrawal of the troops was thus an act of some heroism. It was, also, decisive of the future. Since 1877 only fanatics have applauded the idea of holding the States of the Lower South in subjection to African majorities, though at times the fanatics have given trouble. But they have never succeeded in coming again into control, as they were from 1867 to 1877. The present political system of the South is not ideal, but it is practical; it works. Indeed, the Southern States are better governed than the Northern; the Southern politicians are, generally, more honest. Southern politicians would prefer to have negroes participate in politics if that participation could take some other shape than a horrible race struggle. Since they believe that the general admission of the negro race to suffrage would renew the conflict of the two races for supremacy, they prefer not to have the negro take part. Much is to be said for their side of the case. Why should peace and prosperity, and perhaps civilization itself, be sacrificed in order to give the blacks a chance to overthrow white rule and reëstablish on its ruins the empire of color? That the South in 1877 once more became definitely Anglo-Saxon is due to Rutherford B. Hayes and to no one else. After all is said and done, he was the greatest Southerner of the day, even if he hailed from the north side of the Ohio River.

Republicans who had striven for the negro in politics or fought for him in war could not reconcile themselves to the practical nullification of the recently-enacted Fifteenth Amendment, which they clearly and rightly saw would follow Hayes's action. William E. Chandler, who had done as much as any other man to make Hayes President, now turned against the sovereign he had throned. Boutwell, Ben Butler, old Ben Wade, Blaine, still sour over his failure to win the great prize, all joined in the chorus of condemnation. To them what Hayes had done seemed the betrayal of the Republican party instead of what it really was, the salvation of the party. For the President's policy, vital to the South and beneficial to the nation, was necessary to the Republican party. The Northern people were thoroughly weary of the Southern problem, sick of tales of outrage and desirous of leaving the Southerners to manage their own affairs. If the same disturbances had continued through Hayes's administration that had disgraced Grant's, it is practically certain that the people would have arisen against the Republicans in 1880 and put Hancock in the White House. But by that time the issue which the Democrats had used with such effect from 1873 to 1876 was settled; the South had home rule again and had subsided into peace and order; other questions claimed attention. Hayes has received no more gratitude from the Republican party, which he saved from crushing defeat, than he has from the South. Virtue, too often, is its only reward.

His action was not only wise; it was necessary. The Republican cause in the South was lost because it was an attempt to invert nature. Hayes merely recognized facts, a habit he had. If the wounds of the Civil War had not been healed, the consequences to the nation would indeed have been serious, would have been permanent. In 1877 these wounds were not only not healing, they were becoming more inflamed. If the conditions of 1876 had continued to exist in the South, generations would have passed before the sections would have been reconciled. The South would have been merely another Poland, not the less oppressed because the oppressors spoke the language of democracy. Hayes brought the North and South together.

The ejected Southern Republicans wore martyrs' crowns that were a little tarnished. Packard, crying out to the world his wrongs, permitted himself to be reimbursed by the peaceful and lucrative office of consul at Liverpool, where he received fees amounting to more than President Hayes's salary. Stearns, defeated for governor of Florida in the same election that saw the Hayes electors "elected," relapsed into a snug Federal berth. Kellogg, who had been chosen senator from Louisiana by the Packard legislature before it dispersed, went at once to Washington and succeeded in inducing the Republican Senate to seat him, though his claim was disputed by another senator elected by the Causasian legislature.

The "visiting statesmen," who had guided the canvassing boards of the three disputed States into the Hayes harbor, were well rewarded for their invaluable services. Noyes became minister to France; E. W. Stoughton, minister to Russia; John A. Kasson, minister to Austria. Stanley Matthews was promoted to Sherman's vacated place in the Senate. Lew Wallace governed New Mexico and wrote religious novels. Everybody received something.

These appointments were proper enough if gratitude be esteemed a virtue, but Hayes went pretty far in that direction. The electoral vote of the three States had not been secured without a vast deal of manipulation and bargaining; numberless promises had been made, and the President now proceeded to keep them. All the members of the Louisiana canvassing board or relatives were granted Federal jobs. Forty-seven members of the disrupted negro legislature of Louisiana were taken care of, mostly in the Treasury, which Sherman made a house of refuge for discarded Republican politicians. Yet, all in all, a cheap price was paid for the ending of an intolerable state of affairs, a condition menacing the security of the nation.

Some other politicians who had done nothing for Hayes obtained favors. Logan, ousted to make room for David Davis and thus prepare the way for the electoral decision, was slated for the post of collector of the port of Chicago; but he was so malodorous that a popular protest arose against his appointment. Fred Douglass, representative of what the negro might become by self-education and imitation of white politicians, was made marshal of the District of Columbia as a sort of vicarious atonement for the abandonment of the Fifteenth Amendment. Babcock, the corruptionist who had nearly involved Grant in his disgrace, was given a lighthouse to keep but considerately spared the administration further embarrassment by getting drowned in a storm. Some other places were given to rather degraded men. Hayes was blamed for this, but he only did the unavoidable. He accomplished much for the reason that he never forgot he was dealing not with high idealists but with small and corrupt politicians, and he trimmed his sails to the wind.

The indignation of the Republican oligarchs at Hayes's Southern policy shows what a storm they would have raised if Tilden had essayed to do what he did. The oligarchs had nominated Hayes and forced him on a reluctant country, but now they repudiated him. Wade cried aloud that he had been "deceived, betrayed and humiliated." Wendell Phillips, speaking for the fanatics, declared that he preferred Tilden to Hayes, and William Lloyd Garrison uttered unutterable things. To these abolitionists, who had devoted their lives to freeing the slaves and raising them above the Southern whites, Hayes was Iscariot himself. They could not remotely comprehend the motives that move statesmen. The President wrote in his diary, on October 27, 1877, "The pacification of the South is a total departure from the principles, traditions and wishes of the Republican party." That was true enough. The true-blue Republicans desired nothing so much as the lasting ruin of the seceded States.

There was something fine in Hayes's indifference to hostile criticism when he felt that he was right; indeed, he had moral courage in a higher degree than any other American public man of his time. He had not only freed the three enslaved Southern States; he set the seal on his liberal policy by visiting the desolated section in person, the first President to do so since Lincoln entered Richmond as a conqueror. Hayes went as a conciliator, a peace bringer. The tour began in Louisville on September 17, 1877. Lucy Hayes, femininely curious, went along. Secretary Evarts brought with him wife and children. Schurz, Key, McCrary and the governors of Rhode Island and West Virginia were of the happy party. Wade Hampton, joining, made the pilgrimage a love feast indeed. The jaunt included Nashville, Knoxville, Atlanta, Lynchburg and Charlottesville. The South was greatly pleased at witnessing its hero traveling with the President in a comradely spirit.

Hayes soon followed this journey by a visit to Richmond. The former capital of the Confederacy was now a forlorn place, ruined, half-deserted. But Virginians were courageous and the people of Richmond were able to bear the blows of adverse fortune with a tolerable philosophy. They even had a State fair, to which Hayes had been invited; to everyone's intense surprise he accepted the invitation. Late in October, the party, consisting of Hayes and Lucy Hayes, Evarts, Sherman, Thompson, Devens and Senator Morgan, landed in Richmond and paraded to the fair grounds under the escort of the local militia. Most of the members of the party made speeches extolling the bird of peace. Hayes was pleased; the crowd was charmed, flattered. If it had not been for the disputed election and the performances of the Electoral Commission, Hayes would have been widely popular in the South; but circumstances denied him. The fact that he was a Republican, more than the manner of his election, alienated the South; his broad and liberal policy displeased the North. From first to last he was a lonely figure, but what a splendid loneliness it was!

Yet in spite of the fact that he was a Republican and most dubiously elected, Hayes might have enjoyed a certain measure of popularity in the South if his somewhat rigid ideas had not prevented. Although he had made the existing Federal election laws of no account by withdrawing the troops, he obstinately refused his consent to the repeal of those laws. The South demanded, needed their repeal, for there could be no lasting security for it so long as they stayed on the statute books. There were acts providing for the supervision of polls by United States marshals in order to ensure "purity of elections," though the boards that canvassed those elections were state boards. The laws had been passed for the purpose of maintaining negro majorities in power in the Lower South and teeth had been put in them by patrolling the polls with troops. So long as they continued in force, the South could not be sure that Reconstruction would not be acted over again.

The matter was more than local; it was national. If the states are to enjoy any measure of sovereignty they must have control of the elections held within them. If elections are nationally controlled, a party in power can secure any results it desires. Hayes's own election was an apt illustration of the way in which the Federal election laws worked, permitting as they did any degree of manipulation on the part of the party in control in Washington. Many officials who carried out these laws were persons of dubious character. The laws, moreover, had been used in the interests of the Republican party, and in Florida they had aided a gross perversion of right and justice. Nothing could be said for them but that they assisted the election of ignorant and venal negroes to offices for which they were incompetent. This last was a virtue in the eyes of the fanatics.

The Democrats, having a majority in both houses of Congress at the beginning of 1879, were in a position to repeal

PRESIDENT HAYES AND CABINET

At the President's right, William M. Evarts, George W. McCrary, David M. Key. At his left, John Sherman, Richard W. Thompson, Charles Devens, and Carl Schurz.

these obnoxious Reconstruction acts, designed solely to keep
the Republican party in power in the South regardless of the
interests of the white inhabitants. All that was needed was
Hayes's consent, but unfortunately he balked. Inconsistently
enough, he insisted on retaining laws that he himself had made
of no effect and that continued only as a menace to tranquility.

A deadlock followed. Congress tacked on to appropriation
bills riders repealing the act authorizing the use of Federal
troops in elections, but Hayes resolutely vetoed them. He exclaimed in his diary:

I must resist it to the last extremity. . . . No precedent
shall be established with my consent to a measure which is
tantamount to coercion of the executive. . . . Experience has
shown that the protection and conduct of national elections cannot be safely left to the States. . . . If national military force
is not allowed to keep the peace at the polls, civil authority
should be provided for that purpose.

Strong in this virtuous ignorance, Hayes continued to veto
the bills. His position puzzled the Southerners, who could not
understand why he declined to allow the repeal of acts sanctioning the use of troops in the South after withdrawing the
troops. By his persistent vetoes of bills passed by the Democrats
for repealing the election laws, Hayes won the first measure
of popularity he enjoyed with the Republicans, who witnessed
with delight his feud with the Southerners. As a last act of
resistance, Congress held up the pay of the United States
marshals after finally passing appropriations for the army and
the navy.

The net result of a struggle in which the Democrats wasted
their strength and began to go downhill was the actual ending
of Federal interference in elections but the failure to establish
this principle definitely. As the question remained open, the

Republicans made a determined effort in 1890 to restore Federal supervision of elections in the Southern States, with military coercion. This was the famous "Force Bill," designed to insure Republican success in the approaching presidential election of 1892 by bringing some of the Southern States once more under negro domination. A few Republicans had the virtue and courage to vote with the Democrats against the re-opening of the wrongs of Reconstruction, and the bill, fili-bustered against vigorously, failed to pass. Yet, in 1879, a President who would have surrendered the principle of coerc-ing States would have been looked on as recreant indeed, and perhaps Hayes felt that he would be going too far in permit-ting the overthrow of the election laws, evil as they were. As a consequence of his vetoes the Democrats continued to control elections in the South by practices highly injurious to the com-munity; not until State laws practically disfranchising negroes were approved by the Supreme Court did politicians feel at ease in regard to national elections. Then, and only then, were bribery—the regular price for a negro's vote was two dollars—and the throwing out of ballots abandoned. But by that time infinite harm had been done and Southern politics had been immeasurably lowered.

At last Hayes had time to think of reform. "In my anxiety to complete the great work of pacification," he said, "I have neglected to give attention to the civil service—to the appoint-ments and removals." But the South was pacified, and the task of cleansing the Augean Stable called the American government came next.

Hayes was to attempt to do what Tilden had promised. No matter with what high ideals the Republicans may have come into power in 1861, those ideals were frayed and ragged by 1877. From being on the outside looking in, the Republicans had changed to insiders, with the usual change of view consequent on that transformation. The Civil War, too, had been a breeding bed of rottenness; dishonest contractors, multiple enlisters, crooked politicians, every noxious human weed had flourished in the neglected garden of the republic. Adventurers, drifters, soldiers gifted with a dislike of work, all attached themselves to the Republican party as the fountain of benefits.

The Republicans could not well afford to scrutinize these recruits because in the sixties a majority of the American people actually belonged to the opposition; the masses did not hate the South and would have welcomed a compromise that would have saved the Union and, at the same time, saved the seceding section. The Republicans had had a rough work to do in preserving the Union and could not regard a Constitution which would have fatally handicapped them if scrupulously observed. Faced by an urgent condition and not by a theory, they trampled on the Constitution and the laws but saved the Union thereby. In order to do this work of revolution unscrupulous agents were needed, who could not be discarded the moment the crisis was past. Continuing in the Republican party, they became its danger and embarrassment; they supported the oligarchy in its worst excesses and seemed not to understand that a new era was opening. The time had now come to dismiss these corruptionists, as Hayes realized. It was his great glory that he brought the infamous condition of the government to an end, not at once, because that was beyond the power of any man, but eventually.

The crying need of reform had long been present in the consciousness of the people, but many men had despaired of ever seeing it. In response to the demand for better things a Civil Service Commission had been created under an act of 1871, and the eminent if somewhat impractical George William Curtis had been chosen chairman. Never was failure more dismal. The politicians in Congress had not the slightest desire to see taken from them the jobs they peddled out to henchmen and they defeated the purpose of the commission by refusing it money. Thus it sorely languished and became a subject for jokes. It was this corpse that Hayes proposed to endow with life. He did this deliberately, fully understanding the risk he was taking. "The only thing," he said, "that makes real trouble is the purpose to take the Federal offices out of party and personal political management."

Grant might have done something if he had not been so thoroughly intimidated by the congressional oligarchy. He was no friend of corruption but he was ignorant and timid, the most poorly prepared man that was ever President of the United States. Hayes was not ignorant and anything but timid—indeed, he was one of the bravest souls that ever held power in America. So he prepared to grapple with the prevailing graft, an idea that sent cold chills down the spine of every ordinary politician. For seldom has graft been more strongly entrenched than in the United States of 1877—not even in Russia or Turkey.

Coolly, methodically, without any heroics whatever, Hayes faced the problem. How was he to break up a system begun in the Civil War and firmly fastened on the country after fifteen years? Even a moderate pruning would involve the pruner in endless difficulties. How was an army of idle office-holders who looked on the government as a private inheritance to be got rid of? That loafing, pimpled army had to go; Hayes had resolved on that, and he was resolute. He knew what was coming—a storm of indignation among the politicians such as we cannot understand today when the theory, at least, of honest government obtains. At that time corruption had been elevated by the sanction of use into a kind of virtue.

Hayes preached what was then a novel doctrine—the crying

of a new prophet—when he announced that efficient service should be the test of office-holding. No such heresy had been openly aired by one in power since the inauguration of the spoils system under Andrew Jackson. Hayes did not permit himself to be besieged and overwhelmed by a hungry mob of ward heelers. Applicants for clerkships were referred to the heads of departments, who were, for the first time, made responsible for the selection of their subordinates.

Schurz, for instance, had preached reform for years; he now had a chance to practice it. At the very first cabinet meeting he and Evarts were chosen to draft rules to govern appointments. The Secretary of the Interior devised admirable regulations, letting it be known that sound work would be required of all members of his department and that no man would hold his place merely as a reward for party services. Other cabinet officers followed his example. The notable exception was Sherman, who rather mournfully witnessed the inauguration of methods that were anything but agreeable to his political soul.

Schurz had the hardest task of all; the Indian Bureau was under him and that agency of government was notorious. That the bureau was rotten through and through had long been known. The government was paying $6,000,000 a year in the effort to solve the Indian problem without obtaining any results whatever except scandals and small wars. Determined to achieve honesty, Schurz appointed a board, in June, 1877, to investigate the Indian Bureau.

The board soon uncovered every sort of inefficiency and irregularity in the conduct of Indian affairs. The Indian commissioner had set up as a petty tzar and awarded contracts and purchased supplies with a disregard of business principles and common honesty so utter as to be almost sublime. Manipulation and fraud were everywhere. Contractors ruled the Indian

Bureau and supplied what they pleased. Indian agents put relatives on the payroll as teachers, physicians, farmers, millers, carpenters, in every sort of capacity; and, in nearly all cases, the appointees were wholly ignorant of their duties. Rotten provisions were bought for the Indians at high prices; the wretched aborigines starved while contractors and agents divided profits. The investigating board reported that the Indian agency was "simply a license to cheat and swindle the Indians in the name of the United States of America." Office-holders on small salaries performed the miracle of becoming rich. The redskins, who, not being negroes, had no vote and received no consideration from humanitarians, suffered this ill treatment without hope of redress. Cheated by government agents and ousted from their lands by squatters, who were protected by United States soldiers if the outraged Indians attacked them, the miserable savages—the victims of injustice tenfold worse than slavery—lacked the power to invoke the sympathy of romanticists and only too often gratified their resentment and sense of injury by indulging in violence. Miners and cowboys invading Indian territory were sometimes murdered; and if ever murder was justified it was in the case of these trespassers and robbers, who despised the redskins and denied their claim to the elemental rights of humanity. In this way most of our Indian wars originated. In the summer of the election, 1876, a long series of injustices culminated in a rebellion of the Sioux. In suppressing these brave and determined savages, General Custer and a portion of his command were cut off in an engagement styled the Custer Massacre.

Schurz dismissed the Indian commissioner, the chief clerk and the worst of the subordinates, completely reorganizing the Indian Bureau. The result of his reform was evident in the decline of Indian disturbances and in a vastly improved method of dealing with those who were, to a far greater extent than the negroes, the "wards of the nation." The discharged corruptionists, however, began a war on Schurz that led in the end to his retirement from active politics. Few men have done more for the cause of honest government in America.

Back of the disregard for the Indian's rights was hunger for the Indian's land. The fact that gold had been found in the Black Hills sounded the death knell of the Sioux nation; it was the main cause of the war. The gold did not pan out, but thousands of acres held by the Indians or by the government were coveted by cowboys, farmers and lumbermen. It was the classic age of land piracy. The magnificent forests of the Far West were plundered on an epic scale as the lumbermen, with cynical dishonesty, carried their sawmills into Indian reservations or government tracts without the least pretense of payment. Schurz attempted to check the suicidal policy of denuding the forest areas of the West for no better purpose than to make fortunes for scoundrels. Indeed, it might almost be said that our policy of forest conservation began with this statesman.

So much for the thieves who preyed on the Indians and the open spaces of the Far West. Hayes grappled with mightier foes than these when he threw down the gauntlet to Conkling over the question of civil service reform. This was the bravest act of his whole life. If he had ever entertained the dream of a second term, he now relinquished it, for no man might confidently hope to win the Republican nomination who had gained the enmity of the New York boss. Blaine's fate, though other factors had helped to defeat Blaine, was an example.

The New York custom house had long been a scandal and a disgrace. It is the best tribute to Hayes to say that no such conditions would be tolerated in the United States today; nowhere now are governmental agencies openly and brazenly prostituted to graft and partizan politics. But that was done in the New York custom house in the seventies. In after years Chester A. Arthur made an acceptable President, but when Hayes attained power he was collector of customs in New York and, together with A. B. Cornell, naval officer, represented the most vicious traditions of the spoils system. Cornell was an ordinary grafting politician, but Arthur was different. He was a fat, dapper, side-whiskered man of the world who had become an important person in New York. He was able and preferred honest courses, though honesty was not possible under Conkling. As the custom-house service everywhere was notorious, John Sherman appointed—perhaps reluctantly—a commission headed by John Jay to investigate New York, and similar committees for Philadelphia, San Francisco and New Orleans. New York, being the largest place, smelled the worst.[1]

The Jay commission made the interesting discovery that two hundred small politicians were supported by the New York custom house without performing any public services whatever; they were Conkling's ward heelers, paid for party work with sinecures. Ignorant politicians held positions demanding technical training. The New York custom officers undervalued imports landed in New York in order to force importers to come to that place in preference to other ports. And almost every other imaginable abuse flourished. The salaries of all employees were relentlessly levied on for party purposes.

Reading the commission's findings, Hayes ordered that useless men be discharged and that salaries be no longer taxed for campaign funds. He further demanded that the system of rewarding ward heelers for dubious services by berths in the custom house be discontinued, commenting scathingly on Ar-

[1] Venila Lorina Shores, *The Hayes-Conkling Controversy* (Smith College Studies), 228–237.

thur's method of conducting his office. Thus forced to reform, Arthur effected many improvements and loudly claimed credit for them. Clerks were dismissed to make way for efficient workers, and the atmosphere of privilege and plunder disappeared.

Thus courageously Hayes put his finger on the sorest spot in American public service. The New York custom house was Conkling's pet preserve, his source of power, the paradise that rewarded his faithful disciples. It had never occurred to him that the President of the United States had jurisdiction of any sort in New York; everything there pertaining to the Federal government was his personal affair. He looked on Hayes's attempt to end a notorious graft as an attack on himself, a violation of his prerogatives as senator and leader of the New York Republican machine. Probably never in American history has a politician been more wholly overcome with indignation —righteous or otherwise—than was Roscoe Conkling at Hayes's attack on the New York custom house. Each small boss in every small center of corruption felt the same disturbance. New York was not the only cesspool; in a dozen other cities similar conditions existed; but New York was much the most important and, in striking at New York, Hayes attacked the system of corruption that was eating at the heart of the American civil administration.

The stage was set for one of the greatest controversies in our history, albeit the occasion was only the purification of a custom house. The real issue was the question of the control of Federal appointments—whether these were to be under the senators of the various States or under the President. It was the fight with the oligarchy again. Was the President to rule or a congressional group? Was the government of the United States to be monarchical, as provided for in the Constitution, or was it to be parliamentary?

For a short time the conflict was deferred. Conkling sailed

for Europe in June, 1877, to recover his health, which was somewhat infirm, and his self-esteem, which was much jarred. He could not help seeing that he was no longer a great national figure. He had succeeded neither in becoming President nor Secretary of State; he remained a senator who would never get any higher. Indeed, he had fallen on evil days and worse were to follow. The hand of sacrilege was laid on him; his claim to the ownership of New York was denied and by no less a person than the President he had helped to nominate— whose nomination, he reflected with anguish, he could have prevented. Blaine would have been better than Hayes. Unquestionably Conkling needed a holiday in Europe, amid quiet scenes.

In August the oligarch returned to New York, which still stood by him, to the accompaniment of steam whistles, cannon, and brass bands. He was welcomed precisely as the crude New York of that period would have welcomed some monarch; and indeed Conkling was a monarch, if a somewhat unstable and discredited one. On his way to Utica, which took pride in being his home city, the curly-haired giant spoke to crowds from the platform of his car just as if he were the President himself, though he was now perfectly aware that he would never gain the prize.

Conkling struck his first blow at Hayes at the New York Republican State convention, which met at Rochester on September 26, 1877. Here he embraced his prized lieutenant, Thomas C. Platt, and his assailed henchman, Alonzo B. Cornell. Platt was chosen temporary chairman and, when Conkling declined the permanent chairmanship, he was elected to this, too. George William Curtis, that excellent if simple-minded *litterateur*, was there to defend the administration, of which he was the champion; by this time he had become convinced that Hayes had been elected and it rankled in his mind to hear Republicans everywhere doubting or denying it. So he presented a well-meant resolution that "the lawful title of Rutherford B. Hayes to the Presidency is as clear and perfect as that of George Washington." But Conkling was in a bad humor and Conkling never hesitated to express his opinion that Tilden had been elected; the result was that Curtis's whitewashing resolution was overwhelmingly voted down. It was a delicious ·comedy. The Republican convention in the largest State flatly refused to go on record as expressing its belief in Hayes's election. According to the almost outspoken opinion of the convention, Tilden was the rightful President of the United States. This was not the extent of the insult that Conkling heaped on Hayes that day; he denounced the President for a whole hour in the bitterest terms. Pouring out his sarcasm, he declared, "When Doctor Johnson said that patriotism was the last refuge of a scoundrel, he ignored the enormous possibilities of the word *refawr-rm*." Poor Conkling! Brought up in a school where any abuse or corruption was condoned, and indeed praised, if declared necessary for the preservation of the Union, he could not understand that men were no longer willing to accept evil simply for the sake of sounding phrases. He had outlived his time.

This Rochester convention led to a division in the Republican party that was long in healing and gave the State and the presidency to Grover Cleveland in 1884. In other States politicians exhibited their deep discontent with the President's policy of reform. Conventions in Maine and Iowa declined to commend him. Democratic victories in 1878 illustrated Republican chagrin. Ohio went Democratic by 20,000, a jolt that Hayes must have felt. Even Pennsylvania turned against the Republicans. The House of Representatives continued Democratic, though by a reduced majority.

Hayes was now to be left without party support. The Republican majority in the Senate, which had made his seating possible, was at the vanishing point. Morton died and was succeeded by a Democrat, which was, no doubt, Morton's way of going to hell. In December, 1877, there were in the Senate thirty-eight Republicans and thirty-seven Democrats. David Davis, the great neutral, actually held the balance of power. With the Stalwarts, as the sturdy Republicans who scorned reform now came to be called, in bitter humor, it was evident that both houses of Congress were lost to Hayes. The Democrats, indeed, recognized the merits of his administration, claiming with some truth that he was conducting the government on Democratic principles; but they were, of course, debarred from giving him the support they had afforded Johnson by the manner of his election. Some of the Southern congressmen went so far as to back him in the beginning, and Hayes dreamed of uniting them with moderate Republicans in a party devoted to the cause of reform; but the Southerners refused to abandon their own organization for a rather tenuous combination, and Hayes's broad-minded effort to build up a party on non-sectional lines failed. It is none the less to his credit that he tried.

The sentiment among Republicans in favor of Arthur and Cornell was so strong that Sherman urged the President to keep them in office. But he had made up his mind to oust them, be the consequences what they might. And this was a decision of supreme virtue, for Hayes was no enthusiast, no dreamer lost to reality, but a highly practical man who understood much of the art of politics. Apparently he had everything to lose and nothing to gain by ejecting two popular and powerful politicians, and yet he did it. He did it because of his patriotism, his determination to do his best for the country. When in that mood, Hayes permitted no personal considerations to move him.

Unperturbed by the signs of storm everywhere on the horizon, the President, in September, 1877, requested Arthur and Cornell to resign their custom-house offices,[1] offering the former the consulship at Paris as a consolation prize. Both spoilsmen refused. Hayes, in return, late in October nominated Theodore Roosevelt, father of the famous statesman of that name, as collector of customs, L. Bradford Prince as naval officer, and E. A. Merritt as surveyor.

The issue was now fairly joined. The names of the nominees were at once sent to the committee on commerce of the Senate, of which Conkling was chairman. His ownership of this committee was so absolute that a snicker ran through the Senate when Hayes's nominations were read. The Senate Republicans, meeting in caucus, considered turning the President out of the party. Conkling strutted and raved, as was his wont. The committee on commerce procrastinated until at length, on November 14, Conkling blankly called on Secretary of the Treasury Sherman for the reasons for the removal of Arthur and Cornell. The delay continued, and the extra session expired, on December 3, 1877, without the three names having come before the Senate for confirmation.

Early in the regular session, New York politicians made a determined effort in Conkling's behalf; fifteen of the seventeen New York Republican members of the House of Representatives signed a petition for the retention of Arthur and Cornell. Hayes tartly replied in his annual message that when he wished the advice of congressmen he would ask for it. Still when the New York delegation called on him, he received the members with that kindly, somewhat Middle-West urbanity that was his own and sent them on their way, baffled but not angry. On the same day he returned his nominations to the Senate.

[1] Venila Lorina Shores, *The Hayes-Conkling Controversy*, 238.

Once more the names were referred to Conkling's own committee. Delay could not be eternal, and on December 11 the committee on commerce reported unfavorably on the confirmation of Roosevelt and Price but favorably on that of Merritt. The next day the Senate went into executive session. It was a stormy sitting, for the thoroughly angry Conkling strode up and down the aisles and declaimed, as was his way when excited. He pointed out the reforms instituted by Arthur and declared that the business men of New York unanimously supported him. Hayes's action, he asserted, was part of a plot engineered by the wicked intriguer, Evarts, to gain control of the New York Republican machine and wear his mantle. Hayes aimed at debasing the senators and centering all power in himself. Conkling's cause, Conkling cried out, was the cause of every senator of both parties. His defeat would be a defeat for the Senate.

Edmunds and Teller supported Conkling, along with most of the other Republicans. The Democrats were largely on the President's side, for Hayes was putting into effect the reforms they had vainly promised. John B. Gordon led the fight for confirmation; Bayard, with Kernan of New York, backed him, as did the faithful Stanley Matthews, although perhaps at great cost to himself, for Stanley Matthews felt that in fighting regular Republicans he was opposing God. Conkling triumphed for the time. The nominations of Roosevelt and Prince were rejected by a vote of 25 to 31. Merritt was unanimously approved.

Conkling had won, but the newspapers the country over, with the exception of the most violent Republican organs, condemned the Senate's action. Arthur and Cornell remained at their posts, insulting all reformers with their presence; it seemed that the right to make Federal appointments remained with the Senate, that the President's power was practically limited to the District of Columbia. But on December 13, 1877, Hayes wrote in his invaluable diary:

In the language of the press, "Senator Conkling has won a great victory over the administration." My New York nominations were rejected 31 to 25. But the end is not yet. I am right and shall not give up the contest.

Yet Hayes did not immediately renew the conflict by sending the rejected names back to the Senate or by selecting new ones to substitute for them. He permitted Congress to adjourn and the country to believe that Conkling had won and that civil service reform had suffered a catastrophe in its first tilt with the spoils system. Reformers everywhere were discouraged; they thought that Hayes lacked tenacity.

Conkling, however, had not won, for it is hardly possible for a congressman to win over a determined President. When Congress adjourned Conkling was helpless, while the President was always in session. Hayes knew this and acted on it. On July 11, 1878, he abruptly removed Arthur and Cornell by appointing E. A. Merritt and Silas W. Burt collector and naval officer respectively. Roosevelt had died in the meantime. The two new officers took up their duties on July 20, and Arthur and Cornell moved out.

No charges were made in removing them, a fact that reformers criticized. Hayes acted simply on the ground that the good of the service demanded a change. Reformers thought that he should have stated specifically that the spoilsmen went because they were spoilsmen. They did not have the vision to see what Hayes had done, that he had defied the oligarchy to do its worst. He had struck a vital blow at Conkling and the whole parliamentary super-government that had grown up in the United States.

When Congress opened the regular session on December 2, 1878, the names of Merritt and Burt came before the Senate for confirmation and were referred to Conkling's committee. The senator postponed action on them for two weeks.

On January 15, 1879, the Senate in executive session heard read a statement from John Sherman of the reasons for the removal of Arthur and Cornell. The charges against Arthur were that he neglected his duties, permitted a deputy to run the office, and conducted it in an expensive and inefficient manner, keeping on the payroll a number of politicians who did no work. Cornell was accused of spending his whole time in playing politics, thus giving the government nothing in return for his salary. When it was proposed to make this letter public, Conkling rose in opposition, attacking Hayes with the utmost venom.

The committee on commerce, on January 24, 1879, voted to report adversely on the nominations of Merritt and Burt. All the Republicans were against; the Democrats did not vote. In the executive session, three days later, Conkling reported the action of the committee as well as Arthur's and Cornell's answer to the charges against them. The Democrats now made the mistake of not supporting the President. Again the Senate, on January 29, considered the matter. Sherman asked for more time to answer Arthur's and Cornell's letters. Stanley Matthews supported him, but Conkling objected. Two days later a message from the President, accompanied by Sherman's reply to Arthur and Cornell, was laid before the Senate. Hayes's message repeated firmly and clearly that the former customhouse officials had used their offices for purely partizan political purposes.

Conkling spoke at length in Arthur's defense. Matthews asked for a postponement to consider new evidence, and his motion carried by 35 to 26. It was the first time that Conkling had lost and was a precursor of the end. This came after an executive session of seven hours. Conkling stormed and raged, but the Democrats had veered and now supported the President. Conkling outdid all former performances in his vehemence and, in his bitterness, went to the length of reading notes from members of the administration asking for the appointment of friends to the custom house. He declared that the President's whole purpose in the matter was to build up a political machine of his own and plaintively demanded of the senators if they would sit tamely by and see the power of the government turned against innocent men. For once the Senate wearied of his oratory and before he had finished senators were calling for the question. The vote was taken and the nominations were confirmed, Merritt by 35 to 24, and Burt by 31 to 18.

The strongest speaker for confirmation was Bayard of Delaware. Dawes and Beck also spoke in favor of it. Edmunds held that the Tenure of Office Act protected Arthur and Cornell, but the Tenure of Office Act was slipping into oblivion. On party lines, twenty-five Democrats and fifteen Republicans favored confirmation, while seven Democrats and twenty-three Republicans opposed. The Democrats who voted against confirmation were Tilden's friends. Nothing could induce them to side with the usurper. Sherman had much to do with the result, winning over to Hayes's side several Republicans.

Conkling's defeat was complete. Hayes's triumph was more than a personal victory over odds. The long domination of the executive by Congress was at an end; the issue was settled that the appointive power rests in the President. There was not much longer to be any doubt as to who ruled the nation. The struggle was not quite over; it was destined to be renewed when Garfield became President and to be settled by his martyr's death. That event put an end to the toppling system of congressional control of the executive and made the President really a President.

The revolution that was effected in American government by the administration of Rutherford Hayes should not be forgotten. From 1865 to 1877, the American people looked to Congress as the main cog in the governmental wheel; Congress was the initiator and determiner of policies, and when the President came in conflict with Congress, it attempted to put him out of office. Grant was never, in any real sense, the head of the government, the leader of the nation. He was completely controlled by the predominant party in Congress, which did not hesitate to use him for foul purposes and in such a way as to cloud his glorious reputation. In Grant the President of the United States sank to be the tool and mouthpiece of the worst group of corruptionists in American history.

On the contrary, Hayes, from the first hour of assuming office, made himself the champion of the people. In doing so he defied the most powerful politicians of his time and attacked entrenched machines. As he said in the New York customhouse controversy, "unaided by public opinion," he had fought for what was right and, largely unaided by public opinion, he had brought the conflict to a victorious close.

He was not able to secure the measure of civil service reform he desired. Not having the command of a majority in Congress, he did not obtain the needed legislation. But he had paved the way, and his good works did not die with him. In 1883, civil service legislation was finally passed, and under Grover Cleveland the government was definitely reformed. But it was Hayes who took the initiative, who bore the heat and burden of the day, but for whom the government might never have been reformed and would have continued to be, as Carl Schurz said, a reproach in the eyes of Europe to republican institutions. Why has Rutherford B. Hayes never received the credit, and indeed the lasting fame, that should be his? Simply because the man had no dramatic possibilities. He was a drab business man going about the affairs of the United States honestly and efficiently, just as he might have gone about the affairs of some corporation. And nothing leaves a lasting impression on the human mind but dramatics. Lincoln has become a gigantic figure because his life was a play and his death the perfect close of a great tragedy. But it was not Hayes's good fortune to be brought down by the bullet of some excited partizan of Roscoe Conkling, and it was Garfield's ill fate to be slain in the first act of his presidential drama, leaving the play in other hands. Lincoln's great deeds are not too much remembered; but Hayes is not remembered nearly enough.

Conkling never forgave Hayes for his overthrow in the custom-house case. Indeed, he pursued the President with incredible malignity to the last hour of the administration. In 1878, he and Ben Butler, who was making another political summersault, instigated the Democrats to reopen the electoral question. The Potter Commission was appointed by the House of Representatives to investigate anew what had been settled once and what could only be reversed with grave danger to the nation. A sensational interview with Hayes was published in the newspapers, in which he was made to say that he would have Tilden shot if the latter attempted to take the presidency from him. The interview was false, and the Potter Commission came to naught when Conkling failed to make the sensational exposures he had promised. Perhaps he had nothing to expose; perhaps some remnant of prudence kept him from revelations that might have wrecked his party. The former hypothesis is decidedly the more probable.

"Poor man," Hayes said of Conkling, "he will never forgive me for having beaten him in the Cincinnati convention."

And indeed gnawing envy more than anything else was at the bottom of the New Yorker's hatred for the President. Fate was relentlessly bringing out the littleness of Roscoe Conkling. He was a striking figure in a group of rancorous and corrupt politicians controlling Grant, but the moment he could no longer use Grant as a cover and a shield he became a failure. His brazen, cheap, flamboyant methods alienated good men everywhere; he was only the hero of touts and ward heelers, the becurled, perfumed grandee gazed at by gallery gapers in the Senate. If he had possessed courage he would have obtained a place on the Electoral Commission and voted to seat Tilden. That would have been a classic revenge indeed, but the machine politician was not brave enough for that. Now in 1878 he was egging on the Democrats to attempt to unseat Hayes, trying to keep behind the curtain as much as possible, seeking to shoot from ambush.

In 1879, the Democrats had control of both houses of Congress and might have reopened the question of Hayes's title with some prospect of success. But to have attempted to eject a President who had held office for two years would have meant a revolution and could not have accomplished any good. Besides, Hayes had done so many excellent things that many of the Democratic members admired him and some of them supported him. The Southerners, who formed a majority on the Democratic side, had no reason whatever to expel a President who had saved the South; any real attack on Hayes would have met their decisive opposition. So poor Conkling ground his teeth in rage, seeing the materials for revenge at hand but finding himself unable to use them. And he was further mortified to learn that public sentiment was with the President, for in 1879, for the first time since 1873, the elections went in favor of the Republicans. Hayes had not wrecked his party, as had been so widely declared; he had saved it. Even if the party repudiated him, it profited by his policy. The Democrats, not being able to decide on any definite policy, drifted and suffered for doing so. The political balance was shifting again.

The Democrats brought about Conkling's defeat by their support of Hayes; if they had held off, Hayes's appointees never would have been confirmed and the Republican party would have been divided into factions. Indeed, the Democrats went too far or not far enough. They were right, in principle, in supporting Hayes even if they were wrong in policy. Possibly they would have done better if they had rallied squarely behind the President, adopted his measures as their own and offered him their presidential nomination in 1880. It would have been the greatest vindication ever given a man in public life, but it was not to be. It is difficult for commonplace men to act otherwise than commonplacely.

If the Democrats had offered Hayes full support they would have been carrying out the principles of their party, for they were pledged to restore honest government in the United States and the President had just turned out of office two of the men who impeded honest government. Hayes was not to be nominated by the Democrats, as he should have been; it was his fortune to be the John the Baptist to Grover Cleveland. The latter carried to a successful conclusion what Hayes attempted and when he laid down his office in 1889 the United States again had a government worthy of a civilized nation.

Hayes had already divided the Republican party, or, rather, the Republican party had divided itself. The old oligarchical party, the radicals who had sought to destroy the South, the corruptionists who resisted all reform had come to be called Stalwarts, a name that was to assume mournful significance when borne by Garfield's assassin. Early in Hayes's administration the Stalwarts showed their hand; all through his reign they fought him tooth and nail. Always he had to reckon on their enmity.

In addition to this he was from time to time assailed by Blaine, though later on the Maine statesman subsided into sullen opposition. But in 1877 Blaine was in an ugly mood and lost no opportunity to assert that Hayes was in corrupt collusion with the Democrats. Moved by his rage of disappointment at not obtaining the presidential office (which probably would have been his if he had been nominated, since a majority against him could have been reversed just as well as a majority against Hayes), he rose in the Senate, on July 4, 1877, and announced his suspicion that the President had entered into a conspiracy with the Democrats to annex Mexico. The reason for this remarkable statement was an intimation that had been put out that Hayes would like to secure Mexico in order to enlarge the power of the South. It is curious how the myth that the Slave Power was forever attempting the conquest of territory in order to hold its sway over the nation survived the Civil War and found its last victim in the person of a Republican President who had fought valiantly for four years against the South. But myths die hard.

Blaine's speech was prompted by one of those revolutions in Mexico which seem as regular and inevitable as the movements of the stars. In 1876, Porfirio Diaz was just rising to the mastery of the congery of half-civilized Indian tribes that makes up the Mexican nation. However, the redoubtable Diaz was not sufficiently entrenched then to exercise the benevolent despotism that carried Mexico some distance along the path of civilization, and Mexican revolutionists were indulging in their favorite pastime of raiding across the border into the United States. American troops were ordered by Secretary of War McCrary to follow Mexican marauders on their return across the boundary line and seek to recover stolen property. Diaz vigorously protested against this order as a violation of international law. John W. Foster, minister to Mexico, ably upheld his government, and American troops continued to patrol the border. Finally, Diaz, having been recognized by the United States, put down lawlessness with a strong hand and restored order. For many years Mexico continued to wear the mask of civilization, but finally Diaz was overthrown and the carnival of robbery and murder that Mexicans call freedom was renewed. The intensity of Blaine's hate defeated him a second time, and Hayes emerged from the Mexican embroglio with undiminished prestige, only to find a new conflict. There is no rest for the wicked; there is less for the virtuous. Hayes was destined to meet one of the chief issues of the time, that of the currency, in one of the most dramatic trials of strength between executive and legislature. This time he was not to win, but his course adds luster to his name today, for today all men acknowledge that he was right.

FEW Presidents of the United States have been called to face questions of more importance than was Hayes, and no President has ever faced them with less of the spirit of playing politics and with a purer determination to settle them for the public welfare. For this reason he ran counter to both the contending parties and lacked almost from the first any regular support in Congress. He stood alone; and, after all, that is his greatest glory—that he stood alone when most men were mistaken and when most minds were clouded by the passions of the day. In the matter of civil service reform he may be said to have succeeded; but in the struggle over the currency he failed, with disastrous ultimate consequences to the country. If his rational view of one of the most disturbing issues raised in American politics had been accepted, the nation would have been saved some of its worst experiences and some of its devastating emotional crises.

In 1876, for the first time since the Civil War, a conflict arose in Congress that cut across the lines of both parties and could not be solved by traditions or precedents. In 1876, the currency question became acute after disturbing the country for some years. It blew out of the West and had the East aghast as its possibilities for mischief unfolded.

The business expansion of the Civil War was followed by deflation instead of by such an increase in foreign commerce as succeeded the World War and saved the national finances from shipwreck. To meet the war needs of the sixties a large issue of fiat money had been put out—$450,000,000 of the famous greenbacks. The output was so large for that small age and the result of the war so uncertain that by the summer of 1864 a gold dollar was worth about two dollars and a half in fiat money. Although the victory of 1865 raised the value of greenbacks, it seemed at that time that generations would pass before the paper currency could be redeemed in metal. The fluctuations of paper money in relation to gold led to the most dishonest and demoralizing gambling the country has ever witnessed, culminating in Black Friday of 1869, when gold, after being manipulated to dizzy heights by the notorious Jay Gould, suddenly broke in price and precipitated a panic. No later disaster staged on the calamitous New York stock exchange ever surpassed Black Friday in tragic interest.

It was evident to financiers that the currency must be put on a metal basis if the injurious fluctuations of gold and paper money were to cease; their continuance damaged American trade in every part of the world. Besides, the need of attracting European capital to American enterprizes demanded a redeemable currency. The panic of 1873 was caused, in part, by the difficulty of securing money for railroad expansion; Jay Cooke could not sell his Northern Pacific stock and the crash came. The panic emphasized the necessity for a reform of the money system and in January, 1875, Congress passed an act providing for the resumption of specie payments on January 1, 1879.

Almost immediately a large part of the country rose in protest. In spite of the fact that the money of the nation was irredeemable paper currency, there was not enough of it; farm products were low and the West and South were in the grip of financial stringency. Consequently this proposal to reduce the amount of money in circulation aroused consternation and passionate opposition. Sound money is certainly the best money; but most people prefer unsound money to no money at all, and in the middle seventies money was rising in value, as falling commodity prices showed. The easy remedy for falling farm-product prices was the emission of more money, and the Greenback Party contested elections on a platform calling for a vast emission of paper money based on the country's credit but on nothing else. More greenbacks. Greenbacks enough for everybody! The Golden Age had not solved the problem of poverty; the Greenback Age would. But the United States was then a debtor nation, and an immense issue of irresponsible paper currency would have ruined American credit in the money marts, a small objection the Greenbackers overlooked. Politicians were thus faced by a puzzling dilemma: if the currency was restricted or not increased, prices would continue to fall and politicians would lose jobs. If the currency was not put on a metal basis or if it was increased by further issues of paper, credit would decline and the nation's business would suffer. The situation was serious.

As a matter of fact, the situation had been brought about by the economic revolution of the Civil War period. The rule of the planters had been overthrown; the country was now governed by manufacturers and financiers. The protective tariff had increased the cost of manufactured articles, while the vast production of raw materials following the opening of the West and the invention of the grain reaper had lowered the price of farm products. The farmers everywhere were beginning to feel the consequences of their folly in putting the industrialists in power without in the least understanding the cause of their distress. They believed that an insufficiency of money was the root of the evil and that all would be made right by an emission of cheap money, a cure that would have aggravated, not lessened, the disorder.

The agitation over paper currency had its beginning in the conflict over the redemption of bonds. The United States government was forced to issue in the Civil War period bonds to a vast amount, yielding for the most part an excessively high rate of interest. Only in this way, in addition to the green-backs, did the government secure sufficient means to finance the war to a successful conclusion.

The end of the war found depreciated paper currency and appreciated bonds, held largely by Eastern business men and Europeans. Immediately an agitation arose to accomplish what was, in effect, a scaling down of the debt. It was not nominated in the bonds in what kind of money they were to be redeemed, but they were bought from the government for gold and it was assumed that they were to be paid in the same coin. But the Greenback Party disputed this and desired, in addition, im-mense issues of paper money. If the Greenbackers had had their way, the public debt of the United States would have been largely repudiated by the convenient process of redeem-ing bonds paid for in gold by fiat currency. This scheme came to be known as the "Ohio Idea," and was dubbed by the sound-money men the "Rag Baby." It was warmly supported by both Republicans and Democrats in the Middle West and was not entirely objectionable to such a financial authority as John Sherman. That is, Sherman for a time proposed to use the doubt expressed by many people as to the necessity of redeem-ing the bonds in gold as an inducement to the holders of the bonds to convert them into securities bearing a lower rate of interest, but specifically payable in coin. Hayes himself sternly rejected the plan as dishonest and partly won his reputation as an opponent of it. Indeed, he owed his support from the East in the nominating convention to his general soundness on the money question.

To the farmers and laborers of the seventies, suffering from an acute money shortage, the Eastern and foreign bondholders who insisted on being repaid in gold were veritable Shylocks demanding many pounds of flesh. It never occurred to the inflationists that the financiers who had invested in United States bonds in 1861–70 had taken a considerable risk and that they were thus entitled to a profit. The interest on the bonds was burdensome; the conversion of the bonds at a lower rate of interest, 4.50 and 4 per cent, was a difficult operation and one not wholly successful. The credit of the government, even in the seventies, was not so good in Europe that much money could be obtained at less than 5 per cent interest. This was one of the reasons for the financial crisis of 1873. The fact should have been patent to all intelligent persons that the United States could not continue to borrow money in Europe without meeting its obligations in full, but it was not. The effort persisted to redeem bonds in paper money and was a part of the agitation to defeat specie resumption. Had not Hayes stood so resolutely for honest redemption it is possible that legislation would have passed Congress providing for the payment of bonds in paper and thus destroying, at one blow, American credit. The movement failed but its proponents did not abandon the hope of redeeming bonds in some less costly medium than gold. Not only was silver to take the place of fiat paper in the new financial scheme, but it was to take the place of gold in the redemption of bonds. Indeed, what the silverites indirectly, and doubtless unknowingly, aimed at was to put the United States on the single silver standard along with Mexico and China. It was from this fate that the financiers of the seventies, eighties and nineties saved us.

There were no party lines whatever on the currency issue. Democrats generally favored increasing the amount of money rather than decreasing it, and so did a majority of Republicans. Hayes, from the first, took a resolute stand for sound money and never altered it; he was elected governor of Ohio in 1875 on a sound-money platform, though probably his record for securing pensions for needy or weary veterans had more to do with his victory than the financial question. When he became President in 1877, the Resumption Act was on the statute books, but few people believed that it would be put in effect. It was Hayes's task, and no small one, to see that it was carried out and not repealed, amended, mutilated into nothingness. He succeeded, and it was a great victory.

John Sherman, that genius cursed with the desire to be President, really squared the circle of the resumption problem. The popular conception of resumption was that of a run on a bank; people imagined that so soon as the government paid out gold for greenbacks, there would be a general rush for the yellow metal, thus necessitating the redemption of the entire paper currency at once. Sherman, however, knew well that the value of money depends on the credit of the government that issues it; but he knew, moreover, what the fiat-money advocates did not, that a government must show its ability to redeem in order to enjoy sound credit.

The result was precisely what he foresaw. By selling $140,-000,000 of bonds for gold—that is, about 40 per cent of the outstanding greenbacks—he secured ample coin for all needs. In spite of protests and orations, Congress did not repeal the Resumption Act and January 1, 1879 approached while the world looked on with interest. Would the great Western republic be able to keep its pledges? Europe, sceptical, waited. On the first day of the new year windows opened in the appointed places for exchanging good gold for worn-out paper; but the expected did not happen. There was no general rush of persons desiring to witness the miracle of paper turning into metal; there was no rush at all. Satisfied that they could get gold if they so desired, people preferred paper as more convenient. From New York that evening came the significant report: "$135,000 of notes presented for gold; $400,000 of gold for notes." The famous phrase, "The way to resume is to resume," was justified. The trick had been turned and with ridiculous ease; American credit was on the heights again after all the immense expenditure of the Civil War era. The glory belongs mainly to Sherman, but also, in part, to Hayes, who supported the brilliant Secretary of the Treasury fully and resisted the tremendous pressure against redemption.

Resumption, however, could not be expected immediately to cure the curse of falling prices and wages which so sorely disturbed farmers and laborers in the seventies. There was ever a demand for more money—much more money. Greenbackism had failed; but if the people could not obtain indefinite issues of fiat money they might be able to get large emissions of better money. Silver—Free Silver—now stalked on the American stage. For just twenty years it was destined to disturb the country, upsetting business and bringing on one of the most furious presidential campaigns the country has ever known. Bimettalism became an issue in Hayes's administration; it continued to be an issue because his wise views were not followed.

The silver agitation was a variant of the Greenback movement. Foiled in their efforts to secure money based on nothing, the advocates of a cheap currency turned to the cheapening metal, silver, now available in enormous quantities. But for the sudden fall in the price of silver, its use as money along with gold would never have been suggested.

At the time of the Civil War the actual ratio between silver and gold was less than sixteen to one, which was the coinage ratio. That is, the silver coined in a dollar was worth a trifle more than the gold in a gold dollar. The result was that silver tended to disappear from currency, since it was more valuable as bullion than as coin. For many years silver dollars were practically unknown in the United States. So scarce had they become, of so little use in the monetary scheme, that they were dropped from the list of coins in the reorganization of the currency in 1873. The passing of the silver dollar was un-noted and unlamented at the time, because at the time the price of silver was high and the foreign demand large.

Almost immediately afterward, however, the value of silver began to decline because of the enormous amount being mined in the United States and because of international happenings, the most important of which was the adoption of the gold standard by the German Empire; it not only bought no more silver but went into the market as a seller. The gold standard had come into favor in Europe, partly as a result of the large increase in the world's supply of gold due to the California Gold Rush of 1849 and the discovery of gold in Australia. Gold mining in California had soon played out and had been superseded in America by silver mining on a scale unknown in the world before.

Mark Twain, who was in the Far West in the sixties, has left a graphic description of the silver mining in Nevada and Montana. From such deposits as the great Comstock Lode came vast quantities of the frosty metal. The stage coaches that plunged over the mountains to San Francisco, running the gauntlet of Indians and road agents, were laden with bars of silver; Nevada produced $25,000,000 of bullion in 1863, and the silver production in Montana later exceeded this. Mark Twain thus speaks of Virginia City in *Roughing It:*

I spoke of the underground Virginia as a city. The Gould and Curry is only one single mine under there, among a great many others; yet the Gould and Curry's streets of dismal drifts and tunnels were five miles in extent, altogether, and its popu-lation five hundred miners. Taken as a whole, the underground city had some thirty miles of streets and a population of five or six thousand. In this present day some of those populations are

at work twelve to sixteen hundred feet under Virginia. . . .
When you reach the bottom, you take a candle and tramp
through drifts and tunnels where throngs of men are digging
and blasting; you watch them send up tubs full of great lumps
of stone—silver ore. . . . Arrived at the top, you find a busy
crowd of men receiving the ascending cars and tubs and dump-
ing the ore from an elevation into long rows of bins capable of
holding half a dozen tons each.

The silver industry had indeed assumed large proportions,
with a vast capital investment and thousands of workers. As
might have been foreseen, but was not, the increased production of silver, coinciding with the abandonment of the
double standard of currency in Europe, caused a falling market
for silver and a market that held no hope of improvement.
At once the American silver miners looked to the remonitization of silver as their salvation; if silver were coined in unlimited quantities at a certain ratio to gold, the problem would
be solved, for the government itself would take all the silver
mined off the hands of the miners at a fixed price. Then, and
then only, was "The Crime of '73," the omission of the silver
dollar from the currency, denounced. Protests against the "de-
monitization" of silver began to come from all the West and
from the South as well. There was not enough money in circulation; here was a way to secure abundance, a money having
considerable intrinsic value, too. Hayes, having succeeded in
defeating the agitation for fiat money, had now to face the
full tide of the first enthusiasm for free silver.

On the subject of free silver, Democrats and Republicans
from the West and South were in accord; Republicans and
Democrats from the East were in opposition. Thus was seen
that realignment in Congress of the West and South that was
destined later almost to bring about the victory of silver.
It was in this hour that Richard P. Bland, of Missouri,

Democrat, rose to the leadership of the silver forces. He was to be the accredited prophet of the cheap-money movement until 1896, when William Jennings Bryan in the Democratic convention of that year displaced him and obtained the presidential nomination that should have been his. William B. Allison, of Iowa, Republican, was the silver leader in the Senate.

Bland, on July 25, 1876, introduced a bill in the House of Representatives providing for the free coinage of silver brought to the mints in the same way as gold was coined. This bill was warmly debated in the house but at length, on November 5, 1877, passed by a vote of 165 to 34, showing the overwhelming sentiment in favor of free silver in the lower branch of Congress. The bill then went to the Senate, on December 6, 1877 and came into the hands of the committee on finance under the direction of Allison of Iowa.

Allison was more cautious than the silverites of the House of Representatives but he shared their delusion. Speaking in the Senate, he said, "Legislation gives value to the precious metals, and the commercial value simply records the condition of legislation with references to the precious metals." Thurman thought that the remonitization of silver by the United States would lead Europe to take the same step. L. Q. C. Lamar, in spite of the silver sentiment of the South, opposed the bill, and Bayard, of Delaware, was perhaps the leading figure in the fight against it. Controverting the thesis that laborers belonged to the debtor class and would, therefore, profit by inflation, Bayard said truly enough, "It cannot be said that the laboring class is the debtor class. On the contrary, as I say, there is not a day in the year when the sun goes down when they are not the creditors of capital for the amount of their wages for that day." [1] Blaine made an absurdly sophistical speech in favor of silver.

[1] J. L. Laughlin, *The History of Bimetallism*, 198.

The conservatism of the Senate showed in its treatment of the bill. Although a majority of the senators favored silver, the free-coinage clause, the all-important feature of the measure, was tamed down into a compromise. Silver might not be brought to the mints to be turned into money, but the Secretary of the Treasury was directed to purchase silver bullion at the market price, to the amount of not less than $2,000,000 and not more than $4,000,000 each month, and coin it in dollars.

This amendment, which gave the silverites only a crumb when they had expected a feast, was received with rage and chagrin by the leaders in the House of Representatives. But the Senate seemed resolute, and the silverites, perhaps mistakenly, thought that they had obtained all that was possible at the time.

"Silver Dick" Bland gave in to the amendment, on February 21, 1878, in a bitter speech that illustrated the feeling of the Middle West against capitalists. "I do not like this bill," he declared. "It is not what the country expects. But I am in favor of taking this now as making one step in the right direction. But I give notice here and now that this war shall never cease so long as I have a voice in this Congress until the rights of the people are fully restored and the silver dollar shall take its place alongside the gold dollar. Meanwhile, let us take what we have and supplement it immediately in appropriation bills; *and if we cannot do that I am in favor of issuing paper money enough to stuff down the bond-holders until they are sick.* (Applause) I say I protest against this bill while I vote for it under protest. . . . It is not what the country expects or desires; but we vote for it now to secure what we can at this time, intending to continue the necessary legislation hereafter. . . . I say pass the bill, and let us then get up a free-coinage bill and pass that also."

The amended bill passed the House of Representatives and went to Hayes for approval or rejection. The cabinet met in anxious consultation over it. Thompson, in sympathy with silver, did not think the President had the right to veto a bill incorporating no unconstitutional features. Sherman rather sided with him, for the Ohio statesman, though aware of the fallacy of the free-silver panacea, was prepared to bow to the gale blowing out of the West and threatening ruin to conservative politicians. McCrary likewise deprecated a veto. On the other hand, Evarts, Key, Devens and Schurz sided with Hayes in favoring a veto.

Hayes returned the bill with his veto message on February 28. It is a noble state paper and interesting even at this distant day. His position was that the government had no right to make a legal-tender dollar that was of less value than the gold dollar expected by all creditors of the government. He wrote as follows:

The bill provides for the coinage of silver dollars of the weight of 412½ grains each, of standard silver, to be a legal tender at their nominal value for all debts and dues, public and private, except where otherwise stipulated in the contract. It is well known that the market value of that number of grains of standard silver during the past year has been from ninety to ninety-two cents as compared with the standard gold dollar. Thus the silver dollar authorized by this bill is worth eight to ten per cent less than it purports to be worth, and is made a legal tender for debts contracted when the law did not recognize such coins as lawful money. . . .

In view of these facts it will be justly regarded as a grave breach of the public faith to undertake to pay these bonds, principal or interest, in silver coin worth in the market less than the coin received for them. . . . The standard of value should not be changed without the consent of both parties to the contract. National promises should be kept with unflinching fidelity.

There is no power to compel a nation to pay its debts. Its credit depends on its honor.

The pressure put on Hayes at this time was great, but he stood firm. Murat Halstead had written him, "On the side of silver are the laws, the morals, and the interests of the nation." Everywhere except in a few Eastern cities there was a strong tendency to look on the free coinage of silver as the cure of all financial ills, since all financial ills were believed to be due to an insufficient supply of money. Congress rose in its wrath and passed the Bland-Allison act over Hayes's veto on the same day, February 28, 1878.

The measure was a weak substitute and thus destined to failure from the beginning, though Sherman honestly carried it out. The government purchases of silver had some effect in keeping metal prices up but not very much. The government was, month by month, a buyer of silver in a falling market, which meant that at the end of some years it was greatly a loser by its enforced purchases. The price of silver, artificially buoyed up by this measure, continued to trend downward as less of it was used in Europe. Silver producers had to look to backward countries such as Mexico, China and India for their principal market.

The act of 1878, not proving satisfactory, was superseded by another measure in 1890, which provided for the purchase of a certain number of ounces of silver each month. This act was no improvement, and the country gradually drifted into the panic of 1893, brought on in some part by the uncertain currency position. In 1893, Congress again took action on silver. Bland made desperate efforts to secure free coinage, offering successive measures for coinage at the ratio of 17 to 1, 18 to 1, 19 to 1, and 20 to 1. They were all defeated, and the purchase of silver by the treasury was suspended. This had the effect of bringing the whole silver question acutely into politics. The United States from 1894 to 1896 was financially depressed, and the remedy for low prices of wheat, corn and cattle was believed by millions to lie in the free coinage of silver. Both parties were affected alike, there being Silver Republicans and Silver Democrats. But as the South was wholly Democratic and had gone over to free silver, the silver sentiment came to prevail in the Democratic party to a greater extent than in the Republican. The Democratic President, Grover Cleveland, was practically repudiated by his own party for refusing to enter the silver camp. In its national convention at Chicago, in 1896, the Democratic party came out squarely for free silver and nominated William Jennings Bryan for President. The Republican convention declared rather lamely for gold, holding out hopes for bimetallism. Free silver now became the single issue of one of the most hotly contested campaigns in American history, in which William McKinley was returned the winner.

The country had definitely decided in favor of the gold standard and a few years later the effort to maintain, as a double standard of value, two metals constantly fluctuating was abandoned. The United States joined England, Germany and France as a single-standard country.

Hayes's part in this historic controversy is often forgotten. In reality, his position was determinative. If he had favored the free coinage of silver, or if he had not resolutely opposed it, it is almost certain that Congress would have passed Bland's bill, unamended, in 1878. Hayes's resistance had much to do with toning down the measure to comparative harmlessness even if he could not defeat it entirely. The United States on the eve of specie resumption was thus saved the drop from the status of a leading country of the world into the single-silver standard group, with all of its backwardness. The issue was deferred to a later time—a time when it had lost some of the glamor it possessed in 1878 as the sudden heir of Greenbackism and the hope of debtors bent on frustrating the demands of creditors. In 1896, the sound-money people were strong enough to defeat silver by hook or crook—possibly largely by crook. The currency fight of 1878 was a real crisis and Hayes's stand was profoundly important for the future.

It was the fate of Rutherford Hayes to have to face almost every leading question that has appeared in American politics in the last two or three generations. His action brought to an end the Civil War and restored the Union to normal conditions. He opposed and frustrated free silver. He had also to contend with the first acute labor crisis in American history. Fortunately for the United States, it came under Hayes instead of Grant. Under Grant the United States was drifting down the stream of social revolution; under Hayes it began to move against the current toward the modern industrial system.

The world still remembers the Ku Klux Klan and its spectacular performances of the sixties and seventies; it has forgotten the much more dangerous Molly Maguires of that period. The Civil War had been more of a revolution than an improvement. The slaveholders were out in the cold now; they were slaveholders no longer but weak and poor, yet, singularly enough, the promised millenium of the abolitionists had not come. All that had been accomplished was the exchange of one set of masters for another. The industrialists, far more cruel and relentless than the planters had ever been, now ruled the country and ruled it like hereditary lords.

The United States had made an immense industrial advance in the Civil War period but the condition of the toilers was little bettered. Great factories, in which herds of "hands" labored much harder than slaves toiled, had taken the place of the small establishments of primitive America in which owner worked side by side with his men. The steamships brought throngs of helots from Europe to the now strongly protected American factories and mills; and when the panic of 1873 halted industry and commerce, the distress of the workers was acute indeed. The starving laborers everywhere were ripe for mischief.

The anti-Southern state of Pennsylvania was the scene of the worst exploitation of labor. The "coal barons" of that day were the most overbearing group of men in America. Because of their unsympathetic attitude, conditions mainly due to the economic depression were attributed to them. The underpaid coal miners of Pennsylvania revolted and brought about a state of affairs dangerous to the public peace.

In the early seventies conditions in the anthracite region were worse than they had ever been in the blackest South; but since the miners were called free men instead of slaves, the altruists were not aroused to attempt betterment. Everything is in a name. Wages were very low and strikes common. In this time of distress men could be found to work for any wage, and strike breakers were introduced. The miners, organizing in the Molly Maguires, retaliated by bringing a reign of terror on the community. Murder was commoner than in the South in the midst of the Reconstruction agitation. Anonymous threats and warnings, followed by violence, were the constantly employed weapons of the disaffected. Nonunion workmen—"scabs" as they then came to be called—were treated with every indignity and many of them were beaten or killed. The Molly Maguires controlled elections and, thus, local officials; the anthracite region at this time was as lawless as the mining camps of the Far West. Gradually the forces of law and order prevailed, but only after a long and terrible struggle that left scars for years.

Even more dangerous was the great railroad strike of the seventies. The crisis came in 1877, just as Hayes took the helm of state. It was the first great American railroad strike and it shook the whole country. Three million men were out of work in the summer of 1877. Nearly all the railway lines between the seaboard and the Mississippi River were in the control of the strikers. In Pittsburgh hundreds of freight cars were burned by rioters. Militia called out to restore order were besieged in a round house, and fierce fighting took place in which a number of men were killed and wounded. There were also terrible disturbances in Chicago, just rising from the ruins of the great fire. The blacklist was invented at this time as a punishment for the leaders of the strike; the strikers retaliated with the "boycott," a word just then coming into use. Trains on the Reading Railroad were preceded by tenders bearing armed posses, and every locomotive engineer carried his pistol within handy reach. The loss in life was considerable; the property loss was very great.

Hayes was destined to break the back of the strike. The conditions grew so bad that the governors of Pennsylvania, Maryland and West Virginia at length called on the President for troops to restore quiet. If he had been a politician thinking of place, Hayes might well have hesitated. The sending of troops in a time of peace to put down riotous workmen would certainly leave an aftermath of bitterness that might well be reflected in elections. What would be the effect on his own fortunes? What on those of his party? Hayes could not tell but must have felt that strong action would be hazardous.

All the same he acted, and promptly. The soldiers, entering the disturbed area, speedily brought the disorder to an end. It was one thing to attack nonunion workmen, quite another to do mischief to regular troops. By the end of the year the great strike was over, and industrial and transportation conditions were becoming somewhat normal again; but the bitterness of this period has never entirely died out. The Knights of Labor, soon to be powerful, had opened their career with the effort to secure better wages and better conditions for the laborers of every trade. The great age of labor disturbances had begun.

It was also Hayes's ill fortune to be cursed by the Chinese exclusion agitation, which became acute in the seventies. In the early years of the settlement of California the Chinese were welcomed, since they provided a desired labor supply. The Union Pacific Railroad, too, needed their industry and patience, and thousands of them worked in the mountains and plains in bringing to completion the great railway construction which united the East with the Pacific slope. But as time passed and laborers poured into the West from the Eastern cities and Europe, it was suddenly discovered that the Mongolians constituted a deadly menace to "American labor," three-fourths of which had been recently drawn from across the Atlantic.

Then it was that the picturesque agitator, Dennis Kearney, made the rounds of the San Francisco "sand lots," denouncing the unfortunate Chinamen in unmeasured terms and ending each of his inflammatory harangues with the Catoesque formula, "The Chinese must go!" In other words, the Orientals were called on to pay the penalty of being able to work better and live cheaper than Europeans. There followed the most detestable persecution in American history. These unhappy strangers on our shores, come to do the hard work of empire building and generally peaceful and law-abiding, were attacked by mobs in twenty Western towns. Pelted with mud and stones, set upon and beaten and killed for the crime of competing as laborers with white men, the wretched Chinamen endured without attempting retaliation and their effete government could give them no protection.

The Chinese persecution put the seal on the hypocrisy of the sixties and seventies. The Indians had been driven from their lands and shot down by United States troops when they resisted the invasions of squatters and land robbers; the Chinese were assaulted and murdered because they came in competition with roustabouts and ditch diggers. For neither red nor yellow was there mercy or ordinary human consideration in a country that lamented the wrong done the black race in not permitting it to destroy the civilization of the South. Some of those who stoned unoffending Chinamen had wept their eyes out over *Uncle Tom's Cabin*. But the Chinese, like the Indians, had never been a *casus belli*, never served as the occasion for the attack of one section on another and, consequently, like the Indians, they were sacrificed to political necessities. A hysterical agitation arose for the exclusion of the members of this race of ancient culture and many virtues from the United States.

It should be noted to the honor of William Lloyd Garrison and Henry Ward Beecher that both of them championed the cause of the Chinese, pleading for toleration and holding that America should not be closed to settlers of any race or color. They, at least, were true to their principles. But it was altogether otherwise with a majority of the politicians; many of those foremost in demanding the protection of the rights of negroes favored the shutting out of Mongolians. The laborers of the Pacific slope were numerous enough to make Congress, that cringer to every propaganda, bow to their will. Republicans and Democrats vied in passing an exclusion bill, bidding against each other for the support of the Pacific States in coming elections.

Nothing is more to Hayes's credit than that he vetoed this bill. He vetoed it on the ground that it violated the treaty made by the United States with China, by which the latter's nationals were permitted to enter American territory. After the veto, the government negotiated a new treaty with China which arranged for the exclusion of Chinese immigrants. Congress was now able to provide against the contamination of American nationality—white and black—by the admission of yellow. Thus was the great principle of Racial Equality assassinated in the house of its friends.

Another of Hayes's thousand embarrassments was the Panama Canal. The restless De Lesseps, who had attained world fame by the Suez Canal, built for France but promptly gobbled up by England, snatched at the evident opportunity for opening a waterway across the narrow Isthmus of Panama. France went wild with enthusiasm over the scheme. The building company was French; the international questions raised were delicate. It had been only a few years since the French had sought to make Mexico a French protectorate, and here they were interfering again in this quarter of the world. Consequently, the American public looked on the project with distinct disfavor. It was felt that if any country built a canal at Panama, the United States should be that power. The Monroe Doctrine was being violated in an indirect way.

Hayes was strongly opposed to the canal but did not care to make it an issue with the French government. The canal company strove to gain American favor by buying American politicians. In most cases it failed but it succeeded with Secretary of the Navy Thompson. This absurdity became an employee of the canal company and thought that it would be no bar to his remaining in the cabinet. Hayes dealt with him swiftly, sending him a note to the effect that his resignation (unoffered) had been accepted. Thus the weakest member of the official family stepped out. It was a good riddance.

The government was spared the need of active intervention by the utter failure of the canal. Yellow fever and mismanagement made havoc with it, and after some thousands of Chinamen and others had died in the then pestilential Panama, the project was abandoned. The debacle ruined De Lesseps, who was held personally responsible for a catastrophe that was probably beyond his power to avoid. It was thus left for the United States many years later, in the administrations of McKinley and Roosevelt, to take up the venture anew and bring it to a successful conclusion.

The last year of Hayes's administration was not without its compensations. The President had gained the respect of the nation, if not its love. The government, progressing in the painful process of shedding its skin of graft and corruption, was once more on the road to health. The Republican party, too, thanks to Hayes, had regained the confidence of the country, for it had been proved that a Republican administration was not, necessarily, a carnival of theft. This rehabilitation of the Republican party was no small feat. When the Electoral Commission had finished its partizan labors, fair-minded men in the country generally regarded the Republican organization with abhorrence, and if a presidential election had been held in 1877 the Democrats would have swept the country. But as the year 1880 and the next presidential election approached, matters were very different. The dreary tales of Southern outrages, which had filled the Northern newspapers from 1867 to 1877, were a thing of the past since satisfactory State governments had been set up in the conquered provinces. For this relief from Southern tangles the people were grateful as they turned their attention elsewhere. It was evident, too, to business men that Hayes had done the country a great service in defeating the unlimited issue of paper money and the unlimited issue of silver coinage. Owing in part to his sound administration, the nation was beginning to recover from the prostration that had followed the panic of 1873 and prosperity was once more in sight. Hayes had made the President the real as well as the titular head of the government. He had put down the efforts of senators to control offices and had progressed far on the road to reform. Consequently, the executive branch of the government had risen greatly in the public esteem. On the other hand, Congress, in which the Democrats had now a majority in both houses, had lost in popular favor, and the Democratic party was suffering thereby. Put in possession of both houses, it had accomplished nothing and had not been able to formulate any policy for the future. For this the silver fallacy was in no small part to blame. At all events, as Hayes's term drew toward its close, the Republican party began to revive. For the first time in six years, the elections of 1879 showed a marked trend toward it. Beyond a doubt the presidential contest of 1880 would be close, but the Republicans, because of Hayes, were in a far stronger position than in 1876. They would not have to rake up war hatreds and sectional prejudices in order to avoid paying the penalty of their misdeeds as they had in the Centennial Year.

When the time came for the Republican convention of 1880 to assemble, Hayes was not a candidate. He made a formal announcement to that effect, which was eagerly accepted by the politicians of his party. They were glad enough to profit by his admirable administration but they wanted no more of the reformer. They hopefully awaited a return to the spoils system so dear to their hearts. Hayes was not disappointed that nobody took up his cause. He had earned the hatred of Blaine and Conkling and so had no reason to hope for a second nomination; besides he had said that one term was enough. He had said that before he had had one term, but he had said it. The politicians agreed that one term was enough for a President who desired honest work from office-holders. He was too wise to come before the nominating convention; if he had done so, Conkling would have avenged himself for the custom-house humiliation.

There can be little doubt that Hayes would have liked a second term; every President desires it. The Democratic party might have done better to name him than Hancock, though Hayes would hardly have accepted a nomination from the Democrats if they had offered it. But they could not, of course, forget the Electoral Commission and thus had no thought of offering the nomination to the man who best represented the principles of their party.

With Hayes's administration closing Conkling came to life again. His importance had vastly diminished but when he declared for a third term for Grant it revived. The New Yorker had few illusions left; he knew that he had no chance for the nomination himself but he might be able to get it for his great and good friend, the general. Grant was more in favor with the public than he had been since 1872. The scandals of his administration were stale, and his trip around the world had been a huge success. Plain Americans thought that the American who had been so fêted by European royalty must be a great man indeed. The movement for Grant assumed strength.

The antagonism between Conkling and Blaine remained, however, and blazed up anew in the convention. Blaine, unlike Conkling, was a candidate and had much support. The contest lay really between Blaine and Conkling, masking himself behind the victor of Appomattox. Grant overshadowed Blaine, and it is possible that but for Hayes's administration the great soldier would have been nominated once more. But Hayes had taught the public the value of good government, and men remembered that the government of Grant had been bad. The reformers, dissatisfied as they were with Hayes because he had not accomplished the impossible, realized the vast difference between him and Grant. The veterans were shouting for Grant, the small politicians were clamoring for a return of the good old times; but sober citizens preferred another President to the great historical figure who had failed before.

Hayes's candidate, so far as he had one at all, was John Sherman, who made a formidable bid for the nomination. Sherman ardently desired the prize and had fairly merited it by his services to the country; but in spite of the fact that he was a practical politician, he was never able to get the nomination. His brother, General Sherman, could have had it for the asking, but John Sherman was denied. Probably his rejection by nominating conventions was due to his cold, unmagnetic nature; unpopular with politicians, he might not have made an appeal to the country. Yet the fishlike Benjamin Harrison was nominated, while the brilliant, magnetic Blaine only won a nomination after three efforts and then was defeated in the election. Political currents are difficult to fathom.

Hayes's good wishes availed Sherman little in view of the hatred with which the President was regarded by the rank and file of Republican politicians; it was one case when administration support was more of a liability than an asset. Indeed, the President himself was quite disregarded. He waited in Washington for the result of the convention, conscious that he was unable to influence the decision in the least. With his term now drawing to a close, he was almost forgotten by the politicians, eager to acclaim the succeeding sovereign.

The politicians, generally, would have preferred to nominate Grant, knowing that Grant meant unlimited plunder. But they were afraid to name him because the scandals of his administration would be revived by the Democrats and might beat him. There were scandals, too, about Blaine, and Conkling still opposed him. Since both Grant and Blaine were impossible, there had to be a dark horse. Who? Curiously enough, the convention turned to Sherman's manager. Again the Middle West had the choice of the candidate, for Indiana and Ohio were potent and still doubtful States. If the Democrats carried them, they would win. Once more the Ohio politicians were in the saddle. They could not nominate Sherman, and indeed they did not wish to nominate him. But Garfield was a man after their hearts, one of the suavest, trickiest politicians of his age, the perfect political representative of the Middle West. He had made a great speech in presenting Sherman's name before the convention, but he was not without hope that the lightning would strike him. When Grant and Blaine both began to decline in the balloting, his name became prominent and he finally received the nomination. Not without show of reason, he was accused of treachery to Sherman, who, however, bore the injury in silence.

Garfield had trimmed his sails well. He had supported Hayes in the Senate and had, therefore, earned the President's good will, but he was not so much identified with the administration as to have incurred any of its unpopularity. He was not hated by reformers, but he was not looked on as a reformer, for, if he had been, he would never have been nominated. He was nominated because the Middle West was bent on keeping the presidency and because neither Conkling nor Blaine would give way to the other. Blaine lost a second time to a lesser light. The Maine statesman must have reflected on the rewards of politics, which are seldom for those who bear the heat and burden of the day but usually are the baits of expediency. In the same way Bland was shoved aside by Bryan; Clark and Underwood for Wilson; Lowden and Wood for Harding. Compared with politics, the dizziest gamble in the world is a safe and rational pursuit.

Garfield's nomination pleased Hayes. He preferred Garfield to Sherman, whom he respected but did not particularly like. Nobody ever liked John Sherman, who was incapable of drawing men to him and holding them. Thus, by keeping his hands off absolutely, Hayes had accomplished more than he could possibly have done if he had played any part in the convention. If he had appeared as a candidate, Blaine would probably have been nominated by way of rebuking him; certainly no friend of his would have been chosen. As it was, Hayes was satisfied.

The President took no part in the campaign of 1880. Garfield was elected, partly because the Democratic party had no program to offer and had declined in the public esteem, partly because of the extensive bribery practiced by the Republicans. Great scandals attended the contribution of funds to the Republican Treasury, and the use of these funds in some close States. Garfield at the end had an insignificant plurality of the popular vote over Hancock, and much less than a majority of the total vote. To make sure of the election in advance by an ample use of money was much safer than to reverse the election result later by the Electoral Commission.[1]

Hayes surrendered the reins to his friend Garfield on March 4, 1881, no doubt with some secret reluctance. In spite of the labor and strain of his administration, he was in excellent health and ready and capable for four years more of it. But the politicians had had four years too much of him. Garfield was wildly acclaimed; good times for politicians were returning. It was Hayes, however, who had made the return of such good times impossible, and civil service legislation came in 1883. The good times never did fully come back until Warren G. Harding was inaugurated, and then not for long.

The importance of Rutherford B. Hayes has been as much underestimated as some other things—slavery, for instance—

[1] Cf. Edward Stanwood, *A History of the Presidency*, 1928 Edition, I, 418.

have been overestimated. Indeed, it is unfortunate that American history is not written in a realistic way; but it is our custom to have realism in fiction and romance in history. Consequently, there has yet appeared perhaps only one really adequate account, from beginning to end, of the career of the American people.

The great significance of Hayes lies in the fact that he came to the presidency at one of the most critical moments of our history and thus had much to do in shaping the future. The republic was founded by the Southern planters and Northern farmers, who after 1789 conducted it until the Civil War. It was an honest and efficient government. Unfortunately, however, the rule of agriculture had become an anachronism in an industrial world, and the planters stood in the way of the economic development of the manufacturing States. For this reason among others they were overthrown, and the anti-slavery cause offered to selfish interests a perfect cover for the attack. It is ever by raising slogans, by inaugurating self-sacrificing causes that the astute secure the action of the masses in the desired direction.

Freedom triumphed, and the South was forced back into the Union it had been driven into leaving. But the expected did not happen. In place of the excellent government of the agriculturists, the republic had fallen into the hands of exploiters and from 1865 to 1877 our history is one long scandal. The victory of industrialism seemed to have been purchased at the expense of morality. The United States was on the downward path; nothing showed this more than the election of Hayes himself, when, for the first time in American history, a presidential election was snatched from the victors by the party in power. Paradoxically enough, it was Hayes himself who made a second Hayes-Tilden contest impossible. For in his administration he showed that the industrial North could give as honest and efficient government as the agricultural South, and the lesson has never been entirely forgotten. The election of 1884 was as close as that of 1876, but despite the fact that the Republicans were still in power there was no thought of another Electoral Commission. The Democrats were allowed to have their narrow victory. That this was so was due to Hayes, whose great mission it was to be the restorer of constitutional government in the United States.

The life of Hayes should teach us optimism and hope for the future of the republic. In spite of the moral devastation wrought by some phases of industrialism, Americans are still sound. Hayes was not a great man. He was only one of a thousand brigadier-generals of volunteers in 1865. But he was a good man of the true New England strain, and that strain, partially weakened as it has been by wealth and luxury, is yet splendid. Grant was one of the great figures of the nineteenth century, and nevertheless he had been a calamity as a President. Was it to be expected that a lesser one would do better? A plain, shrewd, capable, honest business man did much better—did so well that the country was put on the right path again. That should teach us not to be disheartened by the failures of brilliancy, but to put our destiny in coming crises in the hands of other plain men—American business men, who blend practical ability with idealism just as Hayes did. Hayes was, in a way, an average man, but what an average it was! The future of the nation is safe if it continues to breed men like Rutherford B. Hayes.

HAYES might be the head of the nation; Lucy Webb Hayes was surely ruler of the White House. There were unkind critics who claimed that she was both head of the nation and mistress of the White House. Did not newspapers comment on a trip Lucy made to the West, saying that, "in the absence of his wife, Mr. Hayes is acting President"?

Mrs. Grant, when she went away, with her usual lavish hospitality provided the White House with a day's provisions, welcomed the new custodians, presided over a luncheon for the official family, and got into the carriage with her husband with a sigh of relief. As they drove off, Hayes, sportive on the crest of his sudden apparent popularity, bantered them: "General, if I had a slipper, I'd throw it after you."

Verily, the old order had changed. The reign of Lucy had begun. The White House was aired of cigar smoke, exotic perfumes, the scent of champagne. "It was not long after the new President arrived in the White House that every one felt a new atmosphere," wrote Colonel W. H. Crook, the disbursing officer. Rutherford Birchard Hayes had resolved to live down his dubious title to the presidency. He did it to such an extent that he was termed "just the poultice the country needed," and his term was smoothed to such dullness that those most anxious for improvement were afraid that its very normality might lull the country into a long nap. Rutherford and Lucy Hayes had set out to be the revered religious parents of a nation for which Victoria and Albert of England had set the terrible example. Virtue was at last fashionable.

People liked Hayes. He was, declared Colonel Crook, one of the most lovable men, "one of the best-natured men who ever lived in the White House, of a rather humorous, light-hearted temperament, of a disposition that was truly happy." He was distinctly not formal like Washington, not moody like Lincoln, not imaginative like Wilson. His friend, Judge William Johnston, said, "It may be asked whether this man of destiny has any marked peculiarities. I answer none whatever. Neither his body nor his mind runs into rickety proportions." A farmer had once spoken of him in all admiration as "such a common man."

At that Hayes guarded his health solicitously. Having trained himself to free his mind of worry, he slept easily. Besides taking gymnastic exercises on rising, he made it a daily duty to walk a certain distance in the hall after each meal and that deliberately. He restricted himself to one cup of coffee at breakfast, to one of tea at lunch, and indulged himself neither with tobacco nor stimulants. After breakfast he wrote letters until eleven o'clock; cabinet meetings or official visitors took up his time until lunch. After looking over his mail, he went out driving at three-thirty, returning for a short nap before dinner; then he received guests until bed time. He was less rugged than his wife, more sensitive of public opinion. She was the first college graduate to be a first lady of the land. She "entered official life at a time when the female lobby was at its height, when scandal had the nation in its slimy coils and when ideals and principles were hibernating." She was an American Victoria, a handsome, matronly woman, kind-hearted, strong-willed, disciplining her family and putting it on a pedestal as a model for the nation. She was accordingly revered as "the noblest of women" or ridiculed as "Lemonade Lucy." Mary Clemson gossiped about Mrs. Hayes to her lady readers:

She has a singularly gentle and winning face. It looks out from the bands of smooth dark hair with that tender light in the eyes which we have come to associate always with the Madonna. I have never seen such a face reign in the White House. I wonder what the world of Vanity Fair will do with it? Will it frizz with hair-powder that face?—draw the sweet fine lines away with pride?—hide John Wesley's discipline out of sight, as it poses and minces before the first lady of the land?

She was pitilessly pelted with ridicule, mimicked behind fans, but she never swerved from her ideals. There was a pioneer sturdiness about her.

Although Lucy usually steered clear of political matters, she once indulged in a sensible bit of lobbying. She wanted to have the portrait of Martha Washington, which had just been painted by Eliphalet Andrews, coming to Washington to found the Corcoran Art Gallery, hung opposite Washington's in the East Room. With shrewd feminine strategy, waiting until after dinner, when Speaker Randall emanated benignancy, Lucy led him to see how well the portrait looked there, how well it would be if a wise government chose to buy it. Randall thought the idea excellent but directed her to Senator Edmunds of Vermont, who was chairman of that committee. The picture remained. Before Lucy left the mansion, a portrait of herself hung there.

The W. C. T. U. desired some tangible evidence of her favor. They clung at first to the symbolic scheme of a fountain, of which Hayes disapproved. The fountain, he wrote Mrs. McDowell in August, 1880, would be expensive, or, if cheap, would be unsightly and dirty. Would it not be better to have Lucy's picture in every house? For historical analogy he cited the original Martha Washington in the White House. He was fond of allying his own name with those of his predecessors whenever the association pleased him. After a picture

HUNTINGTON PORTRAIT OF MRS. HAYES IN THE WHITE HOUSE

was completed (from which numerous copies could be taken), it might hang in the hall of Lucy Webb's former boarding school to show undergraduates the high estate to which modesty and temperance had been raised, or else, as finally happened, be placed in the White House. The portrait was painted by Daniel Huntington, and pictured Lucy in maroon velvet holding three cream roses.

Though she could be a "grand lady" at times, she revealed a naïve and suitable simplicity at others. When the British minister came in one afternoon to introduce distinguished foreign visitors to the mistress of the White House, he was shocked to find her sunk in a hedge of bristling skirts on the floor. She had not fainted—Victorian though she was—but was merely stooping to sew sergeant's straps on the trousers of an old veteran who wanted to have his picture taken in full dress. Sir Edward Thornton coughed fastidiously, but Lucy Webb Hayes was flushed only from exertion as she rose to greet her guests.

They had little trouble with servants. Colonel W. H. Crook says, "I never knew an employee or a servant to be reprimanded during the four years when Mr. and Mrs. Hayes were in the White House." There was a colored woman by the name of Winnie Monroe, who had come with the Hayeses from Ohio to enjoy life in Washington, but who refused to leave it later. When the family went back home she put down her black foot. "Law chile," she told one of her colleagues, "I carn't stay in no Ohio—not after I been the fu'st cullud lady in de land." When Winnie died her daughter sent to the President for help and was allowed to charge all funeral expenses to him. No doubt they were adequate. Hayes often dispensed bounty. An ex-newspaper man who had wielded a hostile pen in the seventies was later humiliated to see this white-haired philanthropist visiting the prison to which he had drifted and offering to get work of his published and to send the proceeds to his family.

The Hayes family were reasonably economical, and were, in fact, unjustly accused of parsimony in their temperance activities. It was a day of reckless extravagance. The wedding dress of Boss Tweed's daughter had cost four thousand dollars. The newspapers gushed with gorgeous details about the laces, diamonds and furs of ladies of state. At the dinner given the Hayeses by the Grants, Lucy appeared in cameo-tinted silk, with the high-necked collar that choked the ladies of the period but at least rewarded them with a color they would not have gained by simpler means. Her black hair was brushed smoothly back and fastened with a tortoise-shell comb.

That was also the day when children were "brought up," scolded, spanked, disciplined. Those in the White House were taught the waste of money spent for tobacco and the danger of alcoholic beverages. Every night after dinner they were marshalled to the Red Room to sing a succession of Stephen Foster songs, old ballads and hymns. The daily routine led thence to the Blue Room for family prayers and then to the library to study for the next day at school. But it was chiefly on Sunday evenings that the Executive Mansion became a pulpit of the model home. Hymn books were distributed; the Vice-President's hostess went to the piano, and favorite hymns were sung. On these occasions William A. Wheeler, who was attached to the Hayes family, used to sing his favorite folk songs.

The Hayeses were simple, kindly folk, and Washington's slum world must have hurt Lucy's motherly heart, as it would Edith Kermit Roosevelt's and Ellen Axson Wilson's. Thomas Pendell, the doorkeeper at the White House, says that he was often called upstairs to be told: "Mr. Pendell, here is some money and here is a note. Take this and find out where they

live and give it to them." On one occasion on coming out of
the house of one of the clerks, whose little son had died, he
was embarrassed to meet Mrs. Hayes in the White House carriage and flattered to be invited to ride home, though too
abashed to accept. It was something to remember, however. On
Thanksgiving Day all the secretaries and clerks of the White
House were invited there with their families to consume the
flock of turkeys which always crammed the pantry shelves. At
Christmas there were presents for everybody, gifts addressed
by Lucy Hayes herself and sometimes selected by her. The
children crouched in corners, staring at pink-ribboned Fanny
Hayes or sleek-haired Scott Hayes as they stood first on one
foot and then on the other until they could dance about scat-
tering bounty.

To stifle the sighs of the more worldly and the pleasure-
loving, the gas jets glimmered gallantly on occasions. Naturally there was the usual succession of sumptuous state dinners
and of the glittering, ostentatious receptions which are the
necessary trappings of every term. One mammoth banquet towered above all the ghosts of White House feasts in the thirty-
six years of Mr. Pendell's experience. To appease the twenty-
five hundred people who crowded into the mansion, the state
dining room was filled with a flock of small tables. Another,
smaller dinner cost four thousand dollars, lavish for those days.

One of Lucy's habits was to ornament the house with bevies
of young girls, who were entertained so sufficiently that one
sixteen-year-old guest went back to Cincinnati declaring she
would never be satisfied with anyone less than a man destined
to be President of the United States. She was Helen Herron
Taft. The task of squiring, beauing and taking sight-seeing fell
upon young Webb Hayes, who was burdened with as many as
eight girls at a time. It has been recorded that at one desperate
moment he hurled an enormous dictionary on the floor above

the Red Room to speed a tarrying gentleman caller. To entertain her house guests Mrs. Hayes once gave an elaborate luncheon for fifty young daughters of prominent Washingtonians.

However, it was by her quiet informal evening gatherings that Lucy made her social regime unique; little groups of tourists and townspeople were delighted to find the merry first lady and her young guests in the parlors at night, not to mention the President himself when he was not engrossed with tedious business.

In giving dinners the Hayeses did their duty: a grand repast for the Grants, another for the board of trustees of the Peabody Fund, another for the inaugural banquet of the Garfields. There was such a pressure for invitations that it was a feat for anyone, even with the son of the President requesting it, to be placed at a state dinner. Just before the annual Supreme Court dinner a messenger came with an announcement that a guest was ill and could not come. Rutherford Hayes, Junior, getting a hasty permission from his mother, galloped off in a White House carriage to the house of a friend. "Taking three steps at a time, I told her to put on her hat and jump in. But a young lady attending her first White House dinner does not want to go with her toilet incomplete. She made record time, however, and added the finishing touches as we raced for the White House, fastening her shoes on the way." Our American Cinderella had no idea of losing her slipper.

In parties that were their own, not the product of etiquette books and state tradition, the Hayeses rejoiced. There was, for instance, that sentimental orgy of the seventies, the silver wedding. It was planned with all the zeal for detail, all the fond devotion, of that day of pressed rose leaves, of cluttered curio cases and scented valentines. Since the festal day fell on Sunday the real celebration was postponed until Monday. The Hayeses' first notion was to duplicate the original gathering, but political obligations and a natural hospitality expanded the list of guests to include cabinet members and their wives, several old Kenyon and Cincinnati friends, the literary club and comrades of the Twenty-third regiment. The invitations were written by one of the clerks, but went out addressed, autographed, and inscribed, "I hope you will come," by the chief executive himself. They did come: the Mitchells, the Herrons, and many more. Even Dr. L. D. McCabe, who had performed the original ceremony a quarter of a century before, was present, for the ceremony itself was to be duplicated. The white-flowered satin that had sheathed the slim bride of the fifties generously conceded a few more inches out of its well-stocked seams as Lucy Hayes walked into the Blue Room to be married all over again. By her side stood Laura Mitchell, her husband's favorite niece, holding her hand as Laura had done as a little girl at the wedding. The duplicate assembly wept a little because death had made it incomplete, or because life had made it imperfect—bald, wrinkled, thickened. The sentimentality of the seventies was insatiable. Later the wedding of a niece, Emily Platt, was the talk of Washington. There was lavish decorating for this occasion—a mammoth bell of thousands of white roses, floral medallions of the initials of the bride and groom, imported plants. That October Hayes joyfully played host to his old literary club from Cincinnati. Yet the Hayes regime tolerated no dances, balls, lawn parties, or card parties. Not even Victoria and her consort surpassed Rutherford Hayes and Lucy Hayes in presenting an example for the nation to follow.

Not far from the White House there used to be little Foundry Methodist Church, which arrested the progress of the executive family on the way to a bigger one and so was honored by their patronage, their attendance, their generosity. That might have rewarded its builder, one Foxall, who had promised the Almighty a church on that spot if He would ward off the British troops from his foundry. Since that time the Colorado Building has replaced it, but in its day it was a sturdy little chapel built by direct contract with a Higher Power and so bearing with equanimity the honor of housing a temporal one.

Lucy Hayes's position upon a moral pedestal excited fashionable ridicule and political anxiety as well as applause. Presidential abstinence was not practiced before or after the Hayes term until prohibition became the law of the land. Wine had never been served on the Hayes table. Hayes himself drank little before he came to the White House, less when he came there, and not at all when he saw that the publicity given this deviation from form had moral influence as well as political force. His stand on this matter was both sincere and courageous. In fact, the Hayeses resented advice on the matter. When a minister's wife called on Lucy Hayes not long after she came to the mansion and begged her not to have liquor served during her residence her temper rose. "Madam," she said, "it is my husband, not myself, who is President. I think a man who is capable of filling so important a position as I believe my husband to be is quite competent of establishing such rules as will occur in his house without calling on members of other households."

The temperance stand created a furore of political gossip. The cabinet whimpered about international complications in case the diplomats should take the absence of liquor at state functions as an affront. It happened that at the first great banquet, which was given in honor of the Grand Duke Alexis Alexandrovitch and the Grand Duke Constantine, Secretary of State Evarts, who had often expressed his distress at the reign of dryness, saw to it that their imperial highnesses were enticed to praise America by food, drink and flattery. The worldly brilliance of this affair, however, bruised the sensitive Wesleyan conscience of Lucy Webb Hayes. She resolved that it should never be repeated.

There was an occasion when the diplomats thought that some clever chêf must be hoodwinking the President. When oranges, stuffed with a frozen punch smacking of rum, appeared in the middle of a dinner, the diplomats winked at each other, asked for more, and told it all over town. "The President," babbled one journalist, "appeared to be wholly ignorant of anything to cause unusual satisfaction." Hayes claimed later that the joke was on his guests. "My orders," he wrote in his diary on January 10, 1887, "were to flavor the punch rather strongly with the same flavor that is found in Jamaica rum. This took! There was not a drop of spirits in it."

There were crudities about the executive mansion in those days. Telephones were in the stage of infantile uselessness, typewriters not yet invented. Congress was too sullen during two years of the Hayes administration to make appropriations for the upkeep of the place, and repairs were sadly needed after the ravages of sight-seers. The morning after every public reception men went around with baskets of crystal pendants to replace those taken from the chandeliers. The Hayeses could barely keep up appearances. They had to resort to reversing the ends of curtains and covering worn spots in the carpet with furniture to make the place pass muster as an executive mansion.

In addition to the inadequate arangement and spacing of rooms, the capacity of the place was strained by Mrs. Hayes's expansive hospitality. Rutherford Hayes, Junior, said: "In the old days I considered myself fortunate to sleep on the soft side of a billiard table. Cots in the hall, couches in the reception room, billiard tables, and even bath tubs had to serve as beds. Even Father had virtually no privacy. I have seen him retire to the bathroom, lock the door and prepare some important state paper."

Perhaps the British diplomats formed a quaint impression of American manners, for Lady Thornton was put in an embarrassing situation. She had asked to leave the White House early by a side doorway. But the White House was not obligingly open on all sides, and one of the sons of the house had to pilot the jeweled, bepowdered personage through a labyrinth of coal bins and junk rooms to a black exit that made the clean air outside look pale.

Office work then was tedious because all writing had to be done in long hand. Modern efficiency and system had not yet accelerated business. Hayes, however, had a stenographer, being the only President during the last half of the century to have a stenographer present in his private office during conferences. By having every word taken down in shorthand he protected himself against calumny. He had had considerable difficulty in selecting a secretary, for the importance and influence of the position were then underestimated. General Force considered it beneath his age and dignity, nor did William Henry Smith think it worth accepting. The errant honor fell upon Hayes's friend, W. K. Rogers, a gentle, impractical, scholarly soul, a dignified gentleman who fumbled a bit in public affairs. Fortunately when he talked to newspaper correspondents on public matters, Webb Hayes was there as confidential secretary. The latter was a serious young man of tact and good sense who was always on hand at cabinet meetings with just the papers that might be required. The cabinet meetings themselves were convivial club-like gatherings at which speech and jests flowed freely, not clotted by acrimonious disputes. They were pleasant, earnest, and fairly efficient.

Some criticism was aroused when Hayes appointed a negro journalist as marshal of the District of Columbia. This Fred-

erick Douglass had had a checkered career, having escaped from
his master in Maryland in 1838, given lectures on slavery all
over England, organized colored troops for the war, and married a white woman. As he could not fill the marshal's duties
at the White House, Webb Hayes presented all guests to his
father while Colonel Casey of the Corps of Engineers introduced them to his mother.

Hayes, ever methodical, was addicted to the scrapbook habit.
He had one of his clerks go through the daily papers, clipping
out and classifying the news and pasting the various clippings
according to subjects so that matters could be brought before
the executive in the most concise and orderly form. He also
kept a little notebook which he intended to be a sort of quieting
drug for office-seekers. Charles Foster told a correspondent of
the Chicago *Times-Herald* that when he had trouble in interesting the President in a certain person, Hayes would take out
his little book, saying, "Oh, well, Charlie, we will fix that in a
day or so." Finally Foster told him that he owed definite and
exacting obligations to some would-be consular agent. "Why,
certainly, Charlie. Yes, yes, to be sure." But as he delved for
the book Foster snatched it from him. "Hold on there, General. I'll be switched if that man's name goes in that jackass
book!" Hayes, who was ever of obliging temper, laughed and
yielded the appointment. When letters were sent to the President a short epitome of each was attached, so that he had merely
to scan these digests before indicating responses to his secretary.

When the four years had run their course, Hayes thought
that they had perhaps had enough of it, although they had enjoyed the journeys around the country and the brilliant entertainments in their honor. Lucy Webb Hayes had been heralded
by a Democratic paper in Washington even before her arrival
as "The second Dolly Madison." "You are getting on even
faster than I am," Hayes wrote to her. When he asked her how

it felt to be the central figure of such a fairy scene as the Academy of Arts reception, "Humble!" she replied. "I always feel humble on such occasions. I enjoy them very much but am humbled by them." But all sincere tributes gratified her. They gave her soul a serenity, she said, like the consciousness of being well-dressed. To be sure, not all had been praise. But the Hayeses had weathered the suspicions of American citizens, the insults of Congress, the ridicule of society and had somehow managed to render a sober, satisfactory service to the country. For their social independence, for their virtues of private life, for their forbearance of slander and ridicule, they were respected by the majority in the nation. The worst that could be said about their tenure of the White House was that it had been dull. When they left Washington they had fairly won the affection of a great part of the people.

PLEASED by the remark of old Alexander H. Stephens of Georgia that he had never seen an Administration "go out so well spoken of," Hayes and his family took their Baltimore & Ohio train back to Ohio. The White House had poured out vanfuls of scrapbooks, documents, clothing, and furniture, and had been left empty and varnished for President-elect Garfield. Once more the capital city had spent Inauguration Day staring, cheering the newcomer, shrieking good-bye to the departing leader, making holiday of its great quadrennial occasion.

In going home Hayes was escorted by Troop A, of Cleveland. But the homeward trip, though unharrassed like the anxious journey to Washington in 1877, was interrupted by a cruel accident. A crash of trains delayed Hayes for twenty-four hours, killed several passengers, and injured some of the official military escort. Fortunately Fate, which had shielded him from assassination if not slander and abuse, guarded Hayes from any harm. Proud Fremont waited in its dooryards. From his front porch the homecoming statesman looked into the faces of the politician's best friends, his loyal neighbors.

He was home again! Spiegel Grove flung its long, bending roadway to them. Its sheltering hedges shut out the curious peering of many eyes, its verdant lines of trees hushed the questions of a gossipping world; the Hayes family no longer had to live under constant inspection. Did they console themselves for the loss of luxury and adulation by breathing the windswept air, so unlike the heavy atmosphere of the White

House? Later when Grover Cleveland left the mansion, Hayes wrote with keen appreciation of the perils of the Presidency: "For them it is no doubt well to leave the high place now. Those who are in such a place cannot escape the unfortunate influence on habits, disposition, and character. In that envied position of power and distinction they are deferred to, flattered, and supported under all circumstances, whether right or wrong, or wise or foolish, by shrewd and designing men and women who surround them. Human nature can't stand this too long. . . . A long life in the hothouse atmosphere of the high station would leave an impress which would color unfavorably all of their later years."

The Hayes family wished so to live that people would not suspect them of any longing for past glories. "We wish . . . to keep out of the public observation long enough to show that we have no hankering after the pleasures we have left." But they naturally desired to live in somewhat greater dignity than before. The house at Spiegel Grove had been enlarged to nearly double its old dimensions, and greatly improved inside. The hall, which had been bounded on the left by two rooms of moderate size, was dressed up in white walnut panelling and led now on the right into new rooms of ample proportions. It is today much as it was in 1881. Shadows of the East Room still lurk in the dim corners of the immense brown-and-gold drawing-room. For refuge back of it there is a long narrow library filled with impressive historical sets and decorated with pictures of the Presidents of the United States. At the rear of the hall there is a state dining-room; the imitation is unmistakable. Upstairs is a labyrinth of guest rooms—twenty altogether. One room on the second floor was promptly filled so full of curios and souvenirs that the family dubbed it the "Smithsonian." Over this domain the middle-aged colored Eliza ruled with a rod of iron, while Jack Ryan tended the

PRESIDENT AND MRS. HAYES AND WILLIAM HENRY SMITH
On the Piazza at Spiegel Grove, 1889

garden and Jeff Patterson, a coachman, looked after the five horses.

Indeed, Spiegel Grove, a sprawling, spacious brick house set in a park of twenty-five acres, was for the times a pretentious dwelling. It had a miniature ravine and two tiny lakes. The broad acres were garnished with trees stately enough to be named after Presidents. Here was a tree which became Grover Cleveland, and there one which was long after to be named William Howard Taft—"about my size," chuckled the heaviest of Presidents.

Across the wide piazza, eighty feet long, Hayes took his constitutional on every inclement day, thirty-three round courses making a mile. He was careful of his health, and allowed the public to know it. For a correspondent of the Cincinnati *Commercial* he sketched the rigid routine which he had set for himself: "I rise with the sun both winter and summer and seldom use the gas to dress by. This makes me get up very early in the long days of the year, but in the winter I sometimes lie abed as late as seven o'clock, though I usually get out by six, dress and come down to my library and work from that time until breakfast. I do all my disagreeable work before breakfast, and I solve my most knotty problems at that time. . . . I walk at least six miles a day and often more."

The New York *Sun* prattled about the chickens at Spiegel Grove, and falsely reported that Hayes gave all his time to chicken farming. On the contrary, he gave most of it to his correspondence and to reading, to which he set apart several hours a day. He had purchased the six thousand volumes of Americana collected by the Cincinnati publisher, Robert Clarke, and carefully explored the biographies, histories, and travels. In general literature his favorite prose authors were Emerson, Hawthorne, Scott, Lincoln, and Howells; his favorite poets were Byron, Browning, and Edwin Arnold. Not endowed with the political, agricultural, or journalistic tastes of various other ex-Presidents, Hayes took his pleasure in his own library. The main objects of reading, he wrote, were "mental improvement—for information—to keep the faculties alert and alive." He pursued studies in education and philanthropic fields. Much of the time when he had newly returned was spent in selecting books for the Birchard Library of the town. Then he went over his scrapbooks, a hobby of the Hayes family. Lucy had a veritable anthology of toasts such as George W. Cable's tribute to her: "That woman's hand that puts away the cup, Is fair as Joan's with the sword lifted up."

Hayes had an enormous correspondence to keep up; telling him of mountain-born namesakes who might never be able to write the name but who were confessedly receptive of presents, telling him what a good President he had been, what a bad President he had been, how needy the correspondents were, and a thousand other things.

He was soon shaken out of his privacy to take up his share of local duties, the Odd Fellows' Lodge and a Grand Army Post drawing him regularly to meetings. Having once emerged from his retirement, he became the natural prize of chairmen of memorial committees and similar bodies. He fitted exquisitely into special public entertainments, into ceremonial occasions and memorial gatherings. Here was an ex-President, a veteran of impressive speech—for what more could any public ask? Hayes busied himself raising funds for public purposes, and serving as head of a committee to erect and dedicate the soldiers' monument in Lake View Cemetery in Cleveland.

It befitted Hayes to become a prominent figure at occasions of national mourning. Garfield was snatched from the scene— a reminder of the dangers of the Presidential office. Hayes was stunned at the ruthlessness of the blows that felled Lincoln and this latest Ohio President. How luckily he, who had entered office under such perilous circumstances, had escaped! Solemnly he rode in the cortege of his fellow-veteran and successor. Ulysses S. Grant, immortal as a general, failure as a President, passed. That August day in 1885, Hayes rode with ex-President Arthur, who in a five-hour procession "proved an excellent companion for such a drive." They rode to the rhythm of clapping hands punctuated occasionally by the calling of "Hayes!" "Arthur!" The Ohio delegation let loose as much cheering for their beloved Hayes as, under the lugubrious suspense of the occasion, they dared. A little lapse of time—it was Arthur himself who died. Hayes rode in the carriage with Cleveland. He had wondered why he was not a pallbearer until General Sherman explained that Cleveland had regarded himself and Hayes as mourners, a little apart from the pallbearers in dignity. The knell again—this time for General Sherman. Hayes went to New York and accompanied the body to St. Louis for the final rites. Before long he was to mourn with President Harrison for the latter's wife. His age, his contemporaries, were passing.

Hayes was soon dragged into the movement of organized charity which was then beginning to rise throughout the country. He had natural talents and taste for philanthropy, and he had long cultivated them. He was not wealthy, because much of his property consisted of unproductive real estate, and the pretentious life he was obliged to lead drained his means. The demands of various good causes upon his purse made him die in debt. He never refused a worthy plea, and was hurt when, after giving $250 to the fund for the Garfield monument, a rumor ran through the press that he had declined on the score of poverty.

While he was governor he had concerned himself with humane and scientific methods of dealing with men imprisoned for crime. He had presided at the first National Prison Congress in 1870, a momentous event in American penology. Now he was made president of the National Prison Association, throwing himself heartily into the work done by Dr. E. C. Wines before his death.

His chief interest, to which he gave constant attention in these later years, was education. Why should the nation not stir itself to the task of developing its common-school system? Did not universal suffrage presuppose universal education? He believed that manual training should supplant a portion of Latin, Greek, science, and history, since most pupils would probably serve the nation with their hands rather than with their heads. It seemed to him a shame that there was not a single manual training high school in the country and very little equipment in the best of the standard high schools. When he was President he had been placed upon the board of the Peabody Educational Fund, a position which he so enjoyed that he never missed a meeting. The sessions of the body in New York were such pleasant affairs that Lucy or Fanny usually accompanied him, attending the grand dinner which closed the gathering. This office, together with his connection with the Slater Fund, of which he was president from its establishment in 1882 until the end of his life, offered Hayes one of the most interesting and useful experiences of his later career. He was now also one of the prominent laymen of the Methodist Church, to which he gave a great deal of time and money. He believed in organized religion without being himself at all deeply religious.

The active management of both the Slater Fund and the Peabody moneys was in the hands of the Rev. J. L. M. Curry, with whom Hayes in 1891 went on a lecturing tour in the South. The two men spoke together in Montgomery, Columbus, Jackson, and Memphis. Hayes was still interested in the Southern problem, which he had done so much to help solve, and grateful for the South's unfeigned regard. When he was in Atlanta he wrote: "All descriptions of people publicly and to me personally said that the South owed a debt to me greater than to any man since Washington." His speech at the Montgomery Exposition was widely published. He showed his regard for the negro by presiding over the early conference on the race question at Lake Mohonk.

He believed in temperance, but with a touch of humor. When he rose to speak one day ruddy with poison ivy, he twinkled: "When your eyes met mine a suspicion arose in your minds which I assure you is without foundation. I have not forsaken my temperance principles and practise. Appearances, I admit, are against me. But in truth it is not whiskey but poison ivy which did it."

Hayes was introduced at the State Fair in Ohio as "a citizen who stands higher in the hearts of the people than any other man living." Such praise he called "agreeable." He enjoyed the acclaim that his journeys elicited, and even revelled in reminiscences of his administration. He enumerated his services to the government; he did not forget his renunciation of a second term. Washington and Jackson and others had scoffed at a second term, but had not failed to accept it when offered, while "you," said his friend and old law-partner, W. K. Rogers, "have the distinction of being the only President who, believing in the one-term principle, were true to your convictions." Rogers forgot Polk. But Hayes praised his predecessors in office. All of the Presidents from Washington to Jackson were "free of the least taint of personal corruption. All were honest men. All were in the best sense gentlemen."

It was natural for him to relish his portion of glorification. Even on the night of Harrison's election in 1888 he could steal a little of the glory of the Republican victor. He was in Cincinnati, at the office of the *Commercial Gazette*. "A mass outside anxious but hopeful, waiting for definite results. It became noised outside among the multitude that I was inside. Calls began. They grew more frequent. The notion, I suspect, prevailed that I hesitated to show myself until a certainty was reached. At any rate, when I appeared finally at the window my appearance was hailed with a shout from the 'sea of upturned faces' that was indeed the shout of victory. I never before saw or heard anything like it." When General Sherman wrote to him to come east for the unveiling of the Washington Monument, he at first refused, but later succumbed. "Seeing the prominent place in the program given to ex-Presidents, and in view of my active interest in the monument, and thinking what is due the Father of his Country, I am not sure but I ought to come." He went, received the honors that were his due.

Yet an element of bitterness mingled with these pleasures—the old element. He was the only inmate of the White House whose title was clouded, and he was forever snatching at fresh nettles of suspicion. The aging gentleman of Spiegel Grove declaimed wrathfully against attacks that the vigorous President of Washington days had borne serenely. If only those States concerning which there was no dispute had been counted, and the others omitted, his title would have been clear. Why would people not take the verdict of the Electoral Commission in 1877 or of the election in 1880? If the Democrats were still such champions of Tilden, why had they not matched him against Garfield? Had not the Republicans connected with that disputed election repelled slander after the manner of honest men—Sherman, Evarts, Garfield? Yet many of the newspapers had assailed him, some of the people whom he had served still eyed him suspiciously; he guessed that he might be dismissed in condensed high school histories in one paragraph as the President of the tainted title. Chance incidents often stung him

cruelly. We find him writing to a Texas friend in 1882, seeking
to find comfort in the attacks:

I am pursued personally by the organs of two factions—each
a minority faction—in the opposing parties. The ultra supporters of Tilden for next President, in order to keep alive the
"fraud issue" for his benefit, let no chance for calumny go un-
improved. But the better brethren of the Democratic party
have no hand in this. They follow Hancock, Bayard, Pendle-
ton, McDonald, Lamar, Stephens, Hampton, Gordon, Gibson,
Bailey, Colquitt, etc. In my own party the organs of the ultra
Stalwarts—Butler, Conkling, etc., etc.,—are, if possible, still
more bitter. The death of Garfield turns their batteries on me.
The blows which he would receive, if living, I now get. But it
does not injure me or my Administration. A mere nothing—a
King Log—a dead level, never attracts so much attention.
Hence the satisfaction I find in this stream of obloquy. It means
that their political system—the spoils system and boss system
united into one—has been sorely wounded. "But something too
much of this."

He refrained from making any public defence of his official
acts. He wrote with satisfaction in his diary that if there were
any two men in the country whose hatred was a certificate of
good character and statesmanship, they were Ben Butler and
Conkling. And little by little the slanders were worn out and
ceased to pass current.

Hayes was even more proud of having been a soldier than of
having been President. "I am more gratified by friendly references to my war record than by any other flattery." Of course,
he apologized for this vanity: "I know that my place was a very
humble one—a place utterly unknown in history. But I also
am glad to know that I was one of the good colonels." It did
not disturb him greatly that Sherman told people that his war
record had been negligible, because he knew that he had done
his best and served in his place. In parades it was his practise to

walk in the ranks. He objected to waving the bloody shirt, to keeping alive the bitterness of the war. "The truth is," he wrote when disgusted by some G. A. R. demagoguery, "the men of the South believed in their theory of the Constitution; there was plausibility—perhaps more than plausibility—in the States Rights' doctrine under the terms, and in the history, of the Constitution. Lee and Jackson . . . fought for their convictions, for their country as they had been educated to regard it."

His battle days had been glorious, glamorous days. His intimates endured the tale of South Mountain, of Cedar Creek, of Fisher's Hill. He had never missed a meeting of the Loyal Legion or of his Grand Army post. He liked to recall that he had never sought military promition. "My aversion to office seeking," he reflected, "was intensified by the consideration that to get a place beyond my capacity might lead to disaster or failure which would involve the lives of the men under me." He made the cares of the soldiers his own, burdening himself with the support of their grievances against the government. As congressman he had been kept busy pursuing pensions for veteran friends; now he used the weight of his position for the same purpose. While it seemed to Cleveland and others that the pension system was a prostitution of patriotism, in the name of which camp followers and three-day veterans gorged on the government, Hayes thought that the opposing attitude was cheeseparing.

Ohio had barely welcomed him from Washington before the Loyal Legion, with headquarters in Cincinnati, made him commander. Before long the national organization, taking its cue from the State, made him commander-in-chief, succeeding General Sheridan. He wrote his wife: "This is on the whole the pleasantest of the honors which have come to me since Washington, and has some advantages over that."

Hayes did not cease to concern himself with large political

RUTHERFORD B. HAYES, 1892
At the age of seventy; the last photograph

questions; in fact, he was a shrewd and careful observer of contemporary affairs. The social life of the Arthur administration disgusted him, and he wrote of it in frank terms. "Nothing like it ever before in the Executive Mansion—liquor, snobbery, and worse. Outbreaks of ill temper caused by drink no doubt were odd enough sometimes." Cleveland he had the discernment to admire warmly. "I no doubt like him better than the majority of those who elected him," he wrote. "He is sound on the currency, the tariff, and the reform of the civil service." He was sufficiently acquainted with Harrison to deplore his lack of tact and amiability, and jotted down a story about a friend who, about to introduce some ladies and gentlemen to Harrison, warned them: "Don't think he means to insult you; it is his way!" He suspected Blaine of "insincerity and lack of honesty;" he knew well how to estimate McKinley, for whom he had a feeling of positive affection, and Tom Reed.

It was his belief, while President and later, that it would be a wise course to effect an amicable union with Canada. There should be "no artificial stimulants" of annexation, but if the Dominion could be acquired, so much the better for both countries. He advocated a single Presidential term of six years established by constitutional amendment. The agitation in behalf of women's suffrage did not meet his approval. "My point on the subject," he commented in his diary, "is that the proper discharge of the functions of maternity is inconsistent with the like discharge of the duties (the political duties) of citizenship." It is worth noting that while he believed in temperance and even teetotalism, he did not believe in harsh prohibitory legislation, refusing in 1883 to vote for a prohibition amendment to the Ohio Constitution. Such an amendment, he predicted, would be worse than a dead letter. He issued a grave warning also against the tendency of the Methodist church to identify itself with the Prohibition party, wishing it to keep entirely out of politics. He gave to questions of wealth and poverty, and the influence of money upon government, a notably liberal attention. We find him writing in his diary in 1890:

Began to read Dudley Warner's fine new novel, "A Little Journey in the World." Sensible, sound, and charming. Curiously enough, it adds another to the list of "Nihilistic" novels —to the "Hazard of New Fortunes," by Howells, "A Yankee at King Arthur's Court," by Mark Twain, etc., etc. Of course I mean no disparagement by the word "Nihilistic." I use it to mean all opinions tending to show the wrong and evils of the money-piling tendency of our country, which is changing laws, government, and morals, and giving all power to the rich, and bringing in pauperism and its attendant crimes and wickedness like a flood. Lincoln was for a government of the people. The new tendency is "a government of the rich, by the rich, and for the rich." The man who sees this and is opposed to it I call a "Nihilist."

And again he told a friend that he often lay awake nights worrying over the growing arrogance of plutocracy, especially in its new forms of trusts or other monopolies. He said in conversation:

"Monopoly is offensive; it destroys individual enterprise; it antagonizes the principle of personal liberty which is the very cornerstone of republican government; it is a menace to the people. . . . It would be well if the power of supervision exercised by this government over the national banks were extended to other things. The Interstate Commerce law, one of the crudest ever passed, is yet one of the most beneficent in its results. The government should say to dangerous combinations, 'Thus far and no farther!' The Dartmouth College decision you and I have always regarded as an anchor that fixed things permanently in this country. I guess that it was a mistake, and that it gave to capital a power that should rest only with the people."

These years following the Presidency were an idyllic period for Mrs. Hayes. Spiegel Grove, blanched with biting blasts of snow, stung with ice storms; Spiegel Grove, splashed with the gold of forsythia, daffodils, crocusses; Spiegel Grove, sprinkled with pale pink roses, perfumed with buried violets and lilies of the valley—so the seasons passed. With flowers, books, friends, church, family, Mrs. Hayes should have felt entirely content; and doubtless but for her failing health she was. But grief entered when the scythe of death grazed the rippling grass of this idyllic world. The first grandchild and namesake went, and it seemed strange that the old were left. Hayes, with his warm sense of family ties, was pained by this shearing of his line. He anxiously watched his daughter-in-law in the poignant days of her loss, and confided to his diary: "Mary is to me the perfection of womanhood. Takes the place of my sister Fanny—the dear, dear memory of early life."

Then, with startling suddenness, came the death of Mrs. Hayes. She had gathered the grace of her garden to comfort Mary. Hayes was on his way to Columbus to attend to business of the State University, and she did not delay him to mail the flowers. "It makes no difference," she said; "I can send them by express at noon." But he never again saw her in health, for before he returned the blow had fallen. Some days before in church, finding that she was in danger of falling, she had a premonition of the stroke that followed. Fears that she might be paralyzed or lose her mind, as her brother had done, assailed her. If she were paralyzed or worse, she begged, would not her husband take her to Philadelphia and hide her in an asylum to the end, so that her friends might remember her as radiant and lovely?

Sitting in the afternoon after Hayes's departure plying her needles, she watched the young people striking balls on the tennis court, and listened to the harder tapping of carpenters making Spiegel Grave still larger. Suddenly the needle grew heavy. She was unconscious, and some one put her to bed; the children looked in hushed horror. Hayes came back, dazed and dull-eyed. In a few days it was all over. He leaned on his daughter Fanny's arm, letting the morning sunlight drench his soul and lighten the agony.

There came a flood of telegrams. She had been a national figure, and kings and clowns, priests and people, sent their assurance that they sorrowed. There came people. She had been a good wife, neighbor, and mother. The funeral brought a concourse of ten thousand. The Twenty-third Regiment, which had always idolized her, was the escort, and its band played softly the hymns she loved. There had been no popular grief like it, Hayes was sure, since the death of Lincoln. As for his own heart, that was too old to heal. "I think of her," he wrote, "as the Golden Rule incarnate."

Striving to control himself, he grasped for what was left of living. He took a melancholy pleasure in answering anecdotal letters and in preaching the new gospel of what Lucy had meant to his world—he believed to all the world. What a great life he had given Lucy: That trip of theirs to Quebec by the St. Lawrence and Niagara, trips to New York and other cities; seeing the review of the Grand Army in '65, going to Petersburg and Richmond under a special permit of Grant; congressional winters in Washington, sitting up nights to see the bills soar over the vetoes of Andrew Johnson; the sudden fierce footlights flashed on the campaign of '76 and burning mercilessly through four years at the White House after the strain and doubt of the disputed election; the pouring of herself into causes—home missions, jails, poorhouses, asylums, reunions, the suffering sentiment of family and neighborhood life. The cup had been full and running over!

"The stream of abuse has gone by. The reaction is coming.

Lucy was more hurt by calumny than I ever was. She cared no more for praise—perhaps less than I do but slander gave her more pain." And "Mrs. Hayes was personally known and loved by more people than any other woman in the world."

When he went to hotels he used to unpack several pictures of her and place them on the bureau. His daughter Fanny became his companion. She went with him to Bermuda, where the British officers bestowed countless attentions on them; she went with him to New York to attend the meetings of the Peabody and Slater trustees and to be guest of honor in the incessant stream of parades and their accompanying festivities. There were still reunions. There was the Grand Army banquet in Washington in September, 1892. To New York to trustee meetings; to Indianapolis to mourn for Mrs. Harrison; to Chicago to help dedicate the World Fair buildings; to Baltimore to a prison congress to protest against the sweeping of the felons and defectives of foreign countries upon our shores; to Cleveland to preside over a banquet of Kenyon alumni; to Brattleboro, Vermont, to learn more about his ancestors. It amused him to find at the Hayes Inn, a place kept by his Puritan ancestors in old times, that games and drink had been indulged in until the setting of the sun on the Sabbath, at which time the place was closed, even on the fourth of July, 1807. What a charming old world, that! The old nostalgia for it came back to him. There was rumor that he meditated matrimony again. "It is not generally known," gossiped the New York *World*, "that at the time of his death General Hayes was engaged to be married to his cousin Mary Anne Hayes Bigelow of Brattleboro, Vermont. The engagement was announced privately last year in Brattleboro. The marriage was put off on account of the death of Mrs. Bigelow's eldest son, Russell, a young lawyer. . . . Mrs. Bigelow is the widow of Wm. A. Bigelow, one of the wealthiest men in Vermont."

If it were so, it was not because Hayes had forgotten Lucy but because he missed her. The family burden of deafness was shutting him in; as a deaf old man he was growing suspicious of unintelligible whispers. His hair and beard were blanched now, his step had slackened, his speech became slow, his figure thickened, his complexion flushed, and a sudden illness impaired his memory. After talking a minute or two, the topic of conversation eluded him. The recent past seemed out of reach of recollection. What was it that the newspaper correspondent was asking him about the activities of the Slater Fund trustees? He lowered his head, passed his hand over his forehead as if to brush the cobwebs away, his expression became pathetic, his voice disconsolate. "I will give you an account of what was done as well as I can remember, but my memory is not as good as it was." For a minute the subject flashed on his mind and he smiled and grasped for it like a child after a bubble. He talked happily. Then, like one of the dreams of his past, it eluded him and he blushed that a reporter should know his discomfiture.

The memories of younger days came oftener now: Lucy, with her black eyes, camp fires spitting gold flames from their deep coals, parades with crowds straining to stare at his famous features, glittering chandeliers at the White House, bands lustily streaming sound, people patiently waiting to shake his hand. All the bustle and glitter of forty stirring years of American life must often have risen to his mind.

He had gone to Columbus to attend a meeting of the board of trustees of the State University. On Thursday afternoon, after having done his duty in calling on relatives, he took the train for Cleveland. In the smoking car he sank into the comfortable company of men. Talk flowed by with the passing landscape. As usual, he had an audience, and it led him to ignore the draught, which caused a cold that brought the end.

He spent Friday looking after the affairs of Western Re-

FUNERAL PROCESSION OF PRESIDENT HAYES

serve University and visited the University School. That afternoon, as he and Webb left Mrs. L. C. Austin's to start to Fremont, he was taken ill at the Cleveland Station; angina pectoris
had set in. Webb brought him a little brandy and had him placed
as comfortably as possible in the drawing-room of the car because he refused to return to Mrs. Austin's. "I had rather die
at Spiegel Grove," he said, "than to live anywhere else." When
they arrived at Fremont at seven o'clock, Doctor Hilbish, one
of the old family physicians who were the salt of the age and
the profession, met them and took the patient home to bed. The
doctor did not know that the case was fatal; the patient did.
The weary system was too listless to respond to treatment.

Hayes remembered how he had driven in a sleigh with
Ruthford around Lucy's grave the previous week and how "My
feeling was one of longing to be lying quietly in a grave by
her side." "I know that I am going where Lucy is," he told the
doctor. And so his life tide drifted out in little ebbs of pleasant talk. It was January 18, 1893. He slipped quietly enough
from the world, but the world, which expects spectacles of all
her great men, made one now of his death. There must be a
magnificent state funeral against the snowy background of
Spiegel Grove in January; the chilly crust would give way easily
to clasp him to rest in his own ground. In a moment of exas-
peration in raising money for other men's monuments, he had
had his own built.

The great of the land were expected and many of them
came. The Toledo Battery, the Sixteenth Regiment of Ohio;
Governor McKinley riding with the guards; President Cleveland coming all the way from New Jersey. "He was coming to
see me," Cleveland told his wife, "but he is dead now and I
will go to him." It was a courteous act. Officers of the marines
would be in mourning for a month, the West Point corps of cadets for six months, some soldiers for six months. Congress

passed resolutions; the President sent four representatives; the Ohio legislature and the Sons of Veterans came *en masse*.

It was a brilliant spectacle: blue uniforms, gold tassels, puffing horses, fur coats, gleaming carriages, and a winter's wealth of hothouse bounty moving on the white snow of Spiegel Grove. It was a grand finale, the sweeping mass of tone and color of a splendidly produced play upon which the quick curtain of dusk dropped too soon.

HAYES is important as being the first modern President. Behind him lay the gulf of the slavery struggle and the Civil War. He lived in that period rather than belonged to it. His outlook was toward the future. Hayes never really became interested in the slavery issue, which awakened the emotions and stirred the passions of so many thousands of men. His moral enthusiasm was rather evoked by such reforms as prohibition, of which he was the first protagonist of national note. He was the forerunner by many years of Bryan and his grape juice; prohibition as a presidential issue would have appealed to him.

He was not of his period because, although he was a Union soldier and a Republican from Ohio, he had no hatred of the South in a time when South-baiting was the surest road to popularity with the generation that had passed through the Civil War. Spiritually, Hayes belonged to the new generation that was just coming on in the year of the Centennial and was looking ahead to the business expansion of the United States rather than backward to sectional feuds; when he died in 1893 he was living in the epoch to which he belonged. He foreshadowed civil-service reform and the triumph of the gold standard. Above all things he was filled with zeal for the prosperity and welfare of the United States as a whole. Although he was elected as a Republican and only by such means as have never before or since been used to seat a President, he was actually more of a Democrat than a Republican—more in sympathy with the aims of Tilden, his rival, than with those of his associates. He was a lonely figure in the Presidency, but there was a certain grandeur in the way in which he stood for what he thought was best in spite of the pressure of politicians and of the clamor of the mob calling for cheap-money panaceas. He paved the way for Grover Cleveland and for a reorganization of the government on honest foundations. After the hate and heat of the Civil War and the wholesale corruption of the Reconstruction, he came as a healer and as a guide to a better future.

Allen, Walter. Governor Chamberlain's administration in South Carolina. New York. 1888. Valuable for conditions in South Carolina.

Alexander, De Alva Stanwood. Political history of New York. vol. 3. New York. 1909. Valuable but biased in favor of the Republican party.

Andrews, E. Benjamin. The history of the last quarter-century in the United States. 2 vols. New York. 1896. Valuable general work.

Andrews, E. Benjamin. The United States in our own time. New York. 1903.

Badeau, Adam. Grant in peace. Hartford, Conn. 1887. A very partizan account.

Bigelow, John. The life of Samuel J. Tilden. 2 vols. New York. 1895. An important old-fashioned biography that favors its subject.

Blaine, James G. Twenty years of congress. 2 vols. Norwich, Conn. 1884. Blaine's own account of important happenings.

Boutwell, George S. Reminiscences of sixty years in public affairs. New York. 1902. A dull account by one of the principal actors of the period.

Bowers, Claude. The tragic era. New York. 1929. One of the most engrossing books on American history and by far the best treatment of the reconstruction period in general. Leans a great deal to the Democratic party.

Brevard, Caroline Mays. A history of Florida. Deland, Fla. 1924. Useful.

Burgess, John W. The administration of President Hayes.

New York. 1916. A disappointing series of lectures by a noted historian.

Burton, Theodore E. John Sherman. (American statesmen series). Boston. 1906. A good book but very dry.

Cary, Edward. George William Curtis. (American men of letters series). Boston. 1894. Useful but leaves much to be desired.

Chamberlain, D. H. Reconstruction in South Carolina. Atlantic Monthly, vol. 39. Valuable.

Congressional Record, 1866–80.

Conkling, Alfred R. The life and letters of Roscoe Conkling. New York. 1889. Of no value.

Conwell, Russell H. Life, speeches and public services of James A. Garfield. Portland, Me. 1881.

Conwell, Russel H. Life of Rutherford B. Hayes. 1876. Gives some interesting details.

Cook, Theodore P. Life and public services of Samuel J. Tilden. New York. 1876.

Cortissoz, Royal. The life of Whitelaw Reid. 2 vols. New York. 1821. A formal biography that leaves much to be desired.

Crook, William H. Through five administrations. New York. 1910. The main source of information for White House life.

Davis, Elmer. History of the New York Times. Useful but a partizan defense of the *Times*.

Davis, William Watson. The Civil War and Reconstruction in Florida. New York. 1913. (Columbia University studies in Political Science). The most important work on the election of 1876 since it demonstrates that Tilden carried Florida.

Detroit Post and Tribune. Zachariah Chandler. Detroit. 1880. A mere eulogy.

Depew, Chauncey. My memories of eighty years. New York. 1922. Gives some valuable details.

Dunning, W. A. Reconstruction political and economic. New York. 1907. A scholarly and shrewd account.

Foulke, William Dudley. Life of Oliver P. Morton. 2 vols. Indianapolis. 1899. The usual eulogistic biography, of no critical value.

Fortier, Alcée. A history of Louisiana. vol. 4. New York. 1904. One of the best histories of the Lower South.

Goode, John. The Electoral Commission of 1877. (Va. State Bar Asso. Reports). Richmond, Va. 1903. A good outline.

Gresham, Matilda. Life of Walter Quintin Gresham. 2 vols. Chicago. 1919. Contributes some useful details.

Hamilton, Gail. Biography of James G. Blaine. Norwich, 1895. Valuable but partizan.

Hancock, Mrs. W. S. Reminiscences of Winfield Scott Hancock. New York. 1877.

Haworth, Paul L. The United States in our times. New York. 1920. Useful.

Haworth, Paul L. The Hayes-Tilden election. Indianapolis. 1927. The most comprehensive book on the election of 1876. A very well worked out treatise and generally fair in tone, an effort to get at the truth. The author is somewhat handicapped by his lack of knowledge of Southern affairs.

Hayes Papers, Fremont, O. This collection contains all the Hayes letters of note, more than 50,000 in number. The collection was extensively used by Williams in his biography, but many important letters were overlooked. An invaluable source.

Hoar, George F. Autobiography of Seventy Years. 2 vols. New York. 1903. Interesting and valuable but not altogether reliable.

Holcombe, J. W. and Skinner, H. M. Life and public services of Thomas A. Hendricks. Indianapolis. 1886. Old-fashioned biography.

Howard, O. I. Life of Rutherford B. Hayes. Ohio archaeological publications, No. 4.

Howells, William Dean. Life in letters of William Dean

Howells, edited by Mildred Howells. Two volumes. Garden City. 1928. A charming picture of Ohio, with some interesting references to Hayes.

Kerr, Winfield S. John Sherman. 2 vols. Boston. 1908.

Laughlin, J. L. The history of bimetallism.

Lowell, James Russell. Letters. New York. 1894.

McCulloch, Hugh. Men and measures of half a century. New York. 1888.

Nation, The. 1876–81. One of the most valuable sources for the history of the times, since it was one of the least prejudiced publications dealing with politics.

Nevins, Allan. The Emergence of Modern America, 1865–1878. New York. 1928. Social and economic history of the Reconstruction period.

New York Times, 1876–79. A most valuable source but an intensely partizan and unscrupulous newspaper.

Oberholtzer, E. P. Jay Cooke, financier of the civil war. 2 vols. Phila. 1907. Valuable.

Oberholtzer, E. P. A history of the United States since the Civil War. 3 vols. New York. 1917–1926. The most detailed general history of the period 1865–1878.

Pearce, Haywood J. Benjamin H. Hill. Chicago. 1928.

Porcher, F. A. Last chapter of reconstruction in South Carolina. Southern Historical Society Papers, vols. 12–13. Very important.

Rogers, Joseph M. How Hayes became President. *McClure's Magazine,* vol. 23.

Schurz, Carl. Reminiscences. 3 vols. New York. 1909. Valuable.

Seitz, Don C. Horace Greeley. Indianapolis. 1926. Interesting.

Seitz, Don C. The dreadful decade. Indianapolis. 1926. An interesting, highly colored account of the years preceding and including the election of 1876.

Sherman, John. Recollections of forty years. 2 vols. Chicago. 1895. Dull but important as giving Sherman's viewpoint on affairs.

Shores, Venila L. The Hayes-Conkling controversy. (Smith College studies in history). Northampton, Mass. 1919. An important treatise on an interesting phase of Hayes's career.

Simkins, F. B. The Tillman movement in South Carolina. Durham, N. C. 1926.

Smith, Theodore Clarke. The life and letters of James Abram Garfield, 2 vols. New Haven. 1925. Valuable but old-fashioned and non-critical.

Spencer, Edward. Life of Thomas F. Bayard. New York. 1880.

Stanwood, Edward. James Gillespie Blaine. (American statesmen series). Boston, 1905. One of the driest of a dry series but of value.

Stryker, Lloyd Paul. Andrew Johnson. New York. 1929. A most dramatic account of a great crisis. Valuable and engrossing.

Williams, Charles Richard. The life of Rutherford Birchard Hayes. 2 vols. Boston. 1914. The "official" life of Hayes, begun by William Henry Smith and finished by Williams. It is very valuable as printing many of the letters in the Hayes collection, but it is utterly non-critical and unscientific. Hayes is pictured as right in every incident of a long life.

Williams, Charles Richard. Diary and letters of Rutherford Birchard Hayes. 5 vols. Columbus, O. 1922–26. The most important source for the life of Hayes. The autobiography is especially valuable, as it covers many years. A number of important letters are included, but certain letters have been omitted for prudential reasons probably.

Wells, Edward L. Hampton and reconstruction. Columbus, S. C. 1907.

INDEX

Abbott, J. S., 211

Adams, Charles Francis, 93, 94, 114, 120; supports Tilden for presidency, 147

Adams, John Quincy, 17

Alexis Alexandrovitch, Grand Duke, 320

Allen, William, 98, 100, 103

Allison, William B., as silver leader in Senate, 293

Americana collection acquired, 327

Anderson's Ferry, 70

Andrews, Eiphalet, 314

Antoine, proclaimed lieutenant-governor of Louisiana, 252

Appointive power in President, 277

Arthur, Chester A., 335; as collector of customs, 268, 269, 272; resignation requested, 273; removed from office, 275; charges against, 276

Augur, General, 249; directed to withdraw troops from South Carolina, 251

Austin, Mrs. L. C., 341

Babcock, General, 258; implicated in Whiskey Ring, 112

"Bargain, The," 218-27

Barlow, Francis C., 192

Bayard, T. F., 211, 274, 277; quoted, 293

"Beast" Butler. See Butler, Benjamin F.

Beck, James B., in Senate, 245

Beckley, Alfred, 64

Beecher, Henry Ward, true to principles, 302

Belknap, Secretary of War, impeachment proceedings, 112

Bibliography, 345-49

Bigelow, Mary Anne Hayes, reported engagement, 339

Bimetallism. See Currency problem

Bingham, John A., Congressional oligarchy, 239

Birchard, Sardis, 3; as head of family, 1, 2, 5; influence over Hayes, 17, 20, 78; Texas trip, 23; financial help to Hayes, 29, 33; politics, 34; Hayes, affection for, 50; Hayes's speech sent to, 85; deeds Spiegel Grove to nephew: death: character, 97

Birchard Library, 97, 328

Black Friday, 285

Blackburn, J. C. S., 216; quoted, 230

Blacklist invented, 300

Blaine, James G., 335; letter to Hayes, 102; charges against, 113; candidate for presidency, 115, 121, 127-30; corruption charges, 117; Mulligan letters, 118, 120, 130; illness, 119; bloody-shirt oratory, 128, 143; balloting at convention, 133; defeat, 134, 135; magnanimity, 136; cheated out of New York vote, 231; quoted on Hayes election, 232; seeking presidential nomination, 240; Congressional oligarchy led by, 241; grievance against Hayes, 244; attempt to prevent confirmation of cabinet, 245; opposition to Hayes, 282, 283; stand on silver, 293; as Republican nominee in 1880, 305, 306, 307, 308

Bland, Richard P., as leader of silver forces, 293, 294, 296; quoted, 294

Bland-Allison Act, 293, 297; amendment, 294; veto: message, quoted, 295; passed over veto: superseded, 296

Bloody-shirt politics, 86, 117, 128, 141, 143, 144, 149, 151

351